The Anthropology of Security

Anthropology, Culture and Society

Series Editors:
Professor Vered Amit, Concordia University
and
Professor Christina Garsten, Stockholm University

Recent titles:

The Anthropology of Security

Perspectives from the Frontline of Policing,
Counter-terrorism and Border Control

Edited by Mark Maguire,
Catarina Frois and Nils Zurawski

PlutoPress
www.plutobooks.com

First published 2014 by Pluto Press
345 Archway Road, London N6 5AA

www.plutobooks.com

Copyright © Mark Maguire, Catarina Frois and Nils Zurawski 2014

The right of the contributors to be identified as the authors of this work
has been asserted by them in accordance with the Copyright, Designs and
Patents Act 1988.

British Library Cataloguing in Publication Data
A catalogue record for this book is available from the British Library

ISBN   978 0 7453 3458 5   Hardback
ISBN   978 0 7453 3457 8   Paperback
ISBN   978 1 7837 1162 8   PDF eBook
ISBN   978 1 7837 1164 2   Kindle eBook
ISBN   978 1 7837 1163 5   EPUB eBook

Library of Congress Cataloging in Publication Data applied for

10   9   8   7   6   5   4   3   2   1

Typeset by Stanford DTP Services, Northampton, England
Text design by Melanie Patrick
Simultaneously printed digitally by CPI Antony Rowe, Chippenham, UK
and Edwards Bros in the United States of America

Contents

Afterword

Figures

Acknowledgements

This volume emerged from various encounters and conversations between the editors at conferences and meetings held by other disciplines. As anthropologists, we recognised that we had much in common and much to say, but we also recognised that anthropology was not at that stage speaking to the theme of security with enough depth or in sufficiently coherent ways. In 2012, with the generous support of the Irish Research Council (IRC) we held a one-day workshop in Ireland, 'Securing Europe'. Thereafter, we convened a panel at the 2012 meetings of the European Association for Social Anthropologists (EASA) in Nanterre, Paris. Many people encouraged the development of this volume – too many to mention – all of whom remain connected to the emerging Anthropology of Security Network. We gratefully acknowledge the generosity of our funders, the support and advice of our colleagues, and the forgiveness of our families.

Series Preface

Anthropology is a discipline based upon in-depth ethnographic works that deal with wider theoretical issues in the context of particular, local conditions – to paraphrase an important volume from the series: *large issues* explored in *small places*. This series has a particular mission: to publish work that moves away from an old-style descriptive ethnography that is strongly area-studies oriented, and offer genuine theoretical arguments that are of interest to a much wider readership, but which are nevertheless located and grounded in solid ethnographic research. If anthropology is to argue itself a place in the contemporary intellectual world, then it must surely be through such research.

We start from the question: 'What can this ethnographic material tell us about the bigger theoretical issues that concern the social sciences?' rather than 'What can these theoretical ideas tell us about the ethnographic context?' Put this way round, such work becomes *about* large issues, *set in* a (relatively) small place, rather than detailed description of a small place for its own sake. As Clifford Geertz once said, 'Anthropologists don't study villages; they study *in* villages.'

By place, we mean not only geographical locale, but also other types of 'place' – within political, economic, religious or other social systems. We therefore publish work based on ethnography within political and religious movements, occupational or class groups, among youth, development agencies, and nationalist movements; but also work that is more thematically based – on kinship, landscape, the state, violence, corruption, the self. The series publishes four kinds of volume: ethnographic monographs; comparative texts; edited collections; and shorter, polemical essays.

We publish work from all traditions of anthropology, and all parts of the world, which combines theoretical debate with empirical evidence to demonstrate anthropology's unique position in contemporary scholarship and the contemporary world.

Professor Vered Amit
Professor Christina Garsten

Introduction
The Anthropology of Security: Prospects, Retrospects and Aims

Mark Maguire, Catarina Frois and Nils Zurawski

Prospects

Security demands anthropological attention. The concept of security saturates contemporary politics, policy and media. It circulates globally in images of threats and conflicts, chaos and order. In its name, governments expend precious public resources on surveillance, identification, futuristic technologies, weapons and wars. Security is a matter of life and death in the world's conflict zones, but it can also prove deadly in other contexts. There is endless talk of 'smart borders' today, but from Tijuana to Spanish Ceuta old-fashioned fences are occasionally festooned with fragments of human clothing. Beyond fantastical threats and high-tech deployments, then, one often finds monotonous forms of security that separate, exclude and 'wither bodies slowly' (Farmer 2004: 309). Therefore, depending on the breadth of one's definition, security may refer to everything from war to structural violence, and from cutting-edge technology to barbed wire fences. Today, security is everywhere. Today, the concept of security is fashionable yet elusive, elastic yet operational.

Anthropology offers critical perspectives on the great emphasis placed on security in the contemporary moment. The politics of security and insecurity, policies, policing, border control and counter-terrorism cannot and should not be understood as 'natural' responses to quasi-natural phenomena. Instead, one must understand security as always emergent within specific material, historical and socio-economic conditions. In this volume, we explore various forms of security; our perspectives and sidelong glances are based on anthropological fieldwork and are attentive to unofficial articulations of security. It is noteworthy that in recent years a significant literature has emerged on 'human security', a United Nations-inspired effort to humanise strategic and development studies by focusing on 'freedom from want and freedom from fear' (UNDP 1994: passim; see also Eriksen et al. 2010). Conceptual vagueness still plagues this research area, but discussions of human security have played an important role by calling attention to the many and sometimes contradictory forms that existential and material security may take.[1] In this volume, anthropological projects show not only alternative and unofficial versions of security but also dis-ease within contemporary (in)securitisation processes, even within the security apparatuses themselves. And, as many countries in Europe and internationally face crises in social security, we hear growing calls for answers to the question: what is security?

The temptation, of course, is to rush to define security using false empiricism, as if security grows naturally and one can elicit its essential qualities with the correct formulation of words. Instead, the contributions in this volume track the expansion of security in the contemporary moment, critically evaluating its culturally sensitive forms and articulations, and eliciting the experiences it produces. Rather than seeing security growing naturally, we see the discourses and practices through which it becomes naturalised in various ethnographic contexts (see also Masco 2010a). Indeed, it is obvious that definitions of security have been expanding, since well before the events of 11 September 2001, to encompass areas such as crime, migration, rights, mundane forms of government and various (redefined) ideas of social disorder. Dutch national policy now refers to the security of *vital interests* ranging from the economic to the ecological; Russian policy connects external military security to internal 'public safety', articulated in terms of education, health care and welfare (see Sweijs 2012: 14–63). In the realm of contemporary policy, then, older definitions fail to account for expanding processes of (in)securitisation that encompass the protection of vital interests and critical infrastructures in an interconnected world of complex threats emanating from a risk-filled near but deep future (see Collier and Lakoff 2008). Narrow definitions therefore risk missing the important point that, for many people in Europe and around the world, it is security itself that creates insecurity (see Fassin in this volume). And, just as definitions seem to offer only false solidity, public debates about security seem ill-suited to the expansive world of (in) securitisation, grasping, to paraphrase Friedrich Nietzsche, at the smoke of an evaporated reality.

Today, public debates are often characterised by fallacious discussions about the proportionate 'balance' that must be struck between security and liberty, freedom, privacy, ethics or fundamental rights, as if each were a distinct property. Security can no longer be regarded as the preserve of national security, nation-states and their performative balancing acts, if indeed it ever could be.[2] The diverse security landscape is filled with state, non-state and international agencies, universities, think tanks, arms manufacturers, various private contractors, 'user-experiences' and the experiences of victims. This landscape is traversed by new techno-science, forms of expert knowledge and imaginaries. Venturesome anthropologists use 'security-scapes' (Gusterson 2004: 166; Albro et al. 2012: 11) to help frame and explain multiple and diffuse security locations that often refuse conventional notions of 'locality' (Feldman 2011, and in this volume). But while anthropologists wrestle with conceptual matters and sharpen research tools, security experts and policy-makers show increasing exasperation. A recent security report on the *Conceptual Foundations of Security* grumbled:

> Conceptualising security is more than merely a semantic issue that can safely be left to scholars to quibble about. It has real-life (and often costly) implications for the capability portfolios our governments and societies pursue in creating security – and consequently also for the R&D efforts they stimulate towards that goal.... What we view as a dimension and what as a source of security drastically affects the nature of our *calculus*. (Sweijs 2012: 4, emphasis added)

European security industries now have a combined turnover of approximately €96 billion and are supported by vast research and development activities (Tajani 2013: 4). The outputs of these industries – often in the form of techno-scientific 'solutions' in search of problems to solve – are sold within a truly global market. For example, biometric identification systems, born of European colonialism and efforts to know and thereby govern populations in the heartlands of empire, now enable reconfigurations of governance globally, from banking transactions in Latin American and universal identification in India to efforts to control the European Union's (EU) internal and expanding external borders (see Rao 2013; Maguire 2009). And, techno-scientific interventions and governmental calculations are situated within broad security imaginaries.

Take for example the vision of the EU's near future in a respected foresight report:

> By 2050 it is estimated that Lagos will have a population of 25 million. In 'mega-slums' communities grow up outside the societies upon whose fringes they exist. The infrastructure of the host cities cannot cope with the additional quantities of people who then construct their own societies, their own rule of law and their own employments which rely on illicit and non-state activities based on a 'Darwinian survival of the fittest' culture. This culture in its turn is based around and is 'governed' by armed gangs which interact with each other. For Europe ... the risk is in importing problems (principally crime) from the 'mega cities' of Latin America, Africa, and Asia. (Langton 2009: 59)

Here we have a dark vision of threats emanating from life itself. Here we also have *potential* dangers transformed by a calculus of risks and precautions that demands reconfigurations of the military, the police, and international and domestic security. Threats are now blended in an 'in-security continuum' (Bigo 2009: 585) that encompasses transnational terrorism, crime, migration and even diseases.

One of the core aims of this volume is to further develop a 'critical anthropology of security' (Goldstein 2010) with historically informed anthropological perspectives on the politics of insecurity, the key areas of policy and policing and, of course, experiences of security in different domains. Following Daniel Goldstein (2010), we aim to explore security by going beyond conventional approaches that focus on states, official institutions and authorised speakers. Our work is an effort to shake common-sense and taken-for-granted notions of security, showing them to be contingent, contested and always cultural, even within security apparatuses. We begin questioning the conceptualisation of security today by first drawing out some of the perspectives available in the history of anthropology.

Retrospects

What is security? Surely this question may be answered by referencing a straightforward history of security? But this is not so. As Frédéric Gros shows in *Le Principe sécurité* (2012), security has a diverse past. In ancient

Roman thought, *securitas* denoted the characteristic unconcern and deliberateness of a virtuous man. Later, Christian millenarianism promised an era of peace and security before Judgement Day. Later still, we find an entirely different version of security in the work of Thomas Hobbes (1994 [1668]) and other contract theorists. They developed a powerful juridical-philosophical myth in which the 'state of nature' – a war of everyone against everyone – was escaped from when the multitude united for security in a commonwealth, *civitas* or state: a mortal god or great *Leviathan*. With its public laws and institutions, Hobbes's state banishes war beyond its borders, and one only hears the rumble of battle in the 'legitimate' use of force to safeguard property and promote freedom. Hobbes elides the history and politics of actual states, especially those formed by conquest, in favour of a seductive story about sovereign legitimacy.

The juridical-philosophical tradition remains powerful even to this day. For example, Martin Van Creveld's *Transformation of War* (1991) – regarded as a prophetic masterpiece by military types – begins by presuming Hobbesian states before heralding the coming age of security. In the dawning era, he tells us, every man, woman and child alive should expect 'to have their identity checked and their persons searched at every turn' (1991: 223), because:

> the burden of defending society against the threat of low-intensity conflict will be transferred to the booming security business; and indeed the time may come when the organisations that comprise that business will, like the *condottieri* of old, take over the state. (1991: 207)

The inevitability flows from teleological history. But why is the juridical-philosophical tradition so enduring? What might we learn from the history of comparative anthropological engagements with security?

Anthropology is a broad discipline and anthropologists of various stripes have long engaged with security. David G. Horn (2003) describes how criminal anthropologists played central roles in the 'co-production' of the nineteenth- and early twentieth-century criminal body and criminological expertise. Moreover, eugenicist Francis Galton situated himself under an anthropological umbrella when establishing modern biometric security (see Galton 1892). His contributions are noteworthy: Galton understood security as essential but only meaningful in terms of what it facilitates (see Maguire 2009). A similar concept of security manifests itself throughout the early history of socio-cultural anthropology – a *doxic* and deeply political relation to the world.

Nineteenth- and early twentieth-century anthropology is replete with studies that take safety, certainty and security to be integral to ritual life, magic, totemism and kinship (see Crawfurd 1863; Roth 1887; Tufton 1894; Tylor 1899; Warner 1930). Typically, however, those studies gesture at security rather than explain it.[3] This, to borrow from Fernand Braudel, is because 'the search for security over the ages' is a 'non-eventful' story of 'events not yet considered as such' (quoted in Ricoeur 1980: 56). How could one write about something essential but only recognisable by its absence or by what it facilitates? The response, in early anthropology, was a rendering of security as a natural requirement expressed culturally, a perpetual need and driving force. According to Leslie White, the human 'struggle for survival assumes the cultural form', thus, 'existence is a never-ending attempt to make of culture a more effective instrument with which to provide security of life and survival of the species' (White 1943: 338–339). Here the concept of security acquires content *as* culture. In Hobbes's *Leviathan* (1994 [1668]) people escape the state of nature by uniting contractually for security, whereas in work of materialist Leslie White culture is the security required for natural life itself to survive and flourish.

Morten Axel Pedersen and Martin Holbraad (2013) excavate a broadly similar concept of security in British social anthropology. Bronislaw Malinowski's psychological functionalism elevated ethnographic work on Melanesian safety magic to propose a universal need in individuals for certainty and safety that is addressed by institutions and societies. The theory is reductive and carries the Hobbes-like assumption that societal stability *requires* coercive authority (see Malinowski 1939: 947–949; cf. Gregg and Williams 1948).[4] Malinowski's preoccupations with stability and security manifested themselves as practical governmental expertise in his valedictory essays:

> The ethnographer … has the right and duty to formulate his conclusions in a manner in which they can be seriously considered by those who frame [colonial] policies and those who carry them out. He also has a duty to speak as the Natives' advocate. But he can go no further.… The discovery of long-run tendencies; the capacity of foreseeing and forecasting the future in the light of full knowledge of all the factors involved; competent advice on specific questions – these are the tasks

of the contact-ethnographer as a practical expert. (Malinowski 1945: 161–162 passim)

E.E. Evans-Pritchard once remarked:

It may be held that it is laudable for an anthropologist to investigate practical problems ... but if he does so he must realise that he is no longer acting within the anthropological field but in the non-scientific field of administration. (1946: 93)

However, the *mise-en-scène* of social anthropology shows few anthropologists willing to make such distinctions and many subscribing to a powerful if allusive concept of security imbricated with applied expertise.[5]

Later, the structural-functionalism of A.R. Radcliffe-Brown eschewed Malinowski's focus on individuals. 'We are conditioned', Radcliffe-Brown explained, 'by the community in which we live.' 'And it is largely by the sharing of hopes and fears, by ... common concern in events or eventualities, that human beings are linked together in temporary or permanent associations' (1952: 149). Pedersen and Holbraad (2013) note the obvious substitution: individuals and their magical rites to conquer uncertainty are far too uncertain; it is society itself that provides the wellspring of (in)security. Thus structural-functionalism also transposes a version of Hobbes's juridical-philosophical myth into the core of so-called 'primitive' societies – essentially organic collectives that require security (variously named) to develop societies and maintain equilibriums.

There is a long-standing body of research on the connections between imperialism and European anthropology (see Asad 1973). There is also a growing literature on the links between US anthropology and the military during the two world wars and the Cold War (see Price 2008). Franz Boas adopted a strong position during the First World War and was censured by the American Anthropology Association for denouncing colleagues who used their professional status to disguise espionage activities (see Boas 1919). Second World War service had profound effects on the scholarly contributions of many leading figures in the discipline such as Gregory Bateson. But strong connections were established between social science research and the national-security complex. Boas's students in the so-called 'culture and personality school' are illustrative. Ruth Benedict's concern with how culture controls and shapes the psychological dimensions of human life lent itself to practical expertise during the Second World War (see Benedict 1946). Simultaneously, Alexander and Dorothea Leighton (1942) investigated sources of fear and security among the Native American Blackfoot, with the former going on to help manage a Japanese internment camp and publish *The Governing of Men* (1945), a well-regarded volume on effective administration and security. Moreover, Benedict supervised early anthropological research on safety and security among the Blackfoot undertaken by psychologist Abraham Maslow. She disagreed with his conclusions, but this project was central to the development of his famous 'hierarchy of needs', a foundational notion in modern Security Studies (see Maslow 1954; Smith and Brooks 2013).

During the period from the 1950s, marked by the disintegration of European colonies and the Cold War, anthropology attuned itself more to matters such as cultural change, and war and peace (see Barth 1959). Several culture and personality scholars focused specifically on security (see Gillin 1951; Field 1960), and a strong ethnographic literature emerged on prisons and other secure institutions (see Sykes 1958). However, security yet again manifested itself as a theme within applied studies. Anthropologists studied security as part of the controversial Vicos and Camelot projects (see Fried 1962), and the Vietnam War saw numerous applied ethnographic projects (e.g. Donoghue 1963; Hickey 1964). That said; this period was one during which uses of anthropology as governmental expertise were questioned and concerns were raised in the discipline about power and anthropological knowledge (see Jorgensen 1971). An inchoate cluster of anthropological studies of security soon emerged on themes such as environmental catastrophes, risks, hazards, insecurity and war (Orr 1979; Turton et al., 1974; Enloe 1980; Nader 1986).

During the decades from the 1980s to the present day there has been a noticeable if tentative security 'turn' in anthropology. During those decades, it seems, security ceased to be a 'non-eventful' story, and important efforts were made to open dialogues between anthropology and critical International Relations (see Weldes et al. 1999). Cultural anthropologists became especially attentive to issues relating to the US military and defence industries and the relationships between anthropological knowledge and security (see Gusterson 1996; Lutz 2001; Price 2008). As Cold War national security transformed into the post-Cold War counter-terrorism apparatus, cultural anthropologists tracked this shift in the heart of contemporary security apparatuses (see Masco 2006, 2010b). Anthropologists have already made important contributions to understandings of security from the perspectives generated in diverse ethnographic research, from studies of urban fears in São Paulo (Caldeira 2001) to the provision of security to citizens in Bolivia (Goldstein 2004), and from the enforcement of order in Paris (Fassin 2013) to the roll-out of mass biometric identification in India (Rao 2013). Moreover, important and related bodies of scholarship are emerging in the anthropology of violence and war (see Whitehead and Finnström 2013) and in 'the anthropology of the contemporary' (see Collier and Lakoff 2008; Caduff 2010; Stavrianakis et al. 2011). The latter body of scholarship is especially important because it challenges and extends anthropological concept work and research practices.

As Daniel Goldstein (2010) notes, anthropologists have been slow to engage with powerful bodies of thought in International Relations, Security Studies or even Surveillance Studies. In part, this arises because of a discomfort with anthropological work done in 'security-scapes' with explicit military or security goals (see McFate 2005). In part, we venture, this is also the case because of a discomfort with prevailing research practices and conceptual work. Increasingly, for example, Security Studies, once the preserve of hard-headed positivism, is expanding to co-opt ethnographic 'methodology' (see Salter and Mutlu 2013). But for anthropologists ethnography denotes far more than case studies or 'user experience' research. A critical anthropology of security has far more potential, as already shown in exciting research that uses anthropological techniques to explore secrecy, critical infrastructure protection and 'vital systems', bio-threats, and professional security expertise. There are also conceptual differences to be explored. Frequently, the technological fetishism evident in security policy and discourse is transposed uncritically in Security Studies, and 'security' is granted excessive power as a consequence.

Each of these areas – International Relations, Security Studies and even Surveillance Studies – makes use of Foucauldian insights. Michel Foucault's venturesome discussions (see 1991, 2007: 5–22, 42–45, 64–65) are a starting point for those interested in the relationships between calculative modes of governing through probability, statistical regulation and *dispositifs* of security (see Ewald 2002); others explore security and freedom of mobility (Bauman 2000). Some commentators even argue that security is central in much of Foucault's oeuvre (Dillon and Lobo-Guerrero 2008). But it must be remembered that his tantalising discussions of security were ultimately abandoned in favour of research on governmentality and biopolitics. Caution is needed then; and even in Surveillance

Studies, which leans so heavily on panopticism, there are warnings about substituting unanchored critical theory for research on contemporary life (see Lyon 2009: 107). Like his similarly fashionable concept of biopower, there is a danger that Foucault's work may be used to 'describe everything but analyse nothing' (Rabinow and Rose 2006: 199).

As anthropology turns more and more to contemporary security as an 'eventful' object of analysis that nonetheless requires detailed consideration of often quotidian and 'uneventful' experiences, we must draw carefully from existing bodies of scholarship and refine the conceptual tools and research practices that anthropology will bring. Rather than being guided by all-powerful and abstract 'theory' or ethnography rendered as 'methodology', our goal here is to further develop a critical anthropology of security that attends to experiences of insecurity across a number of interconnected domains: the politics of security, policy and policing, and the everyday lives of people who experience security at the thin end of the wedge. Our modest ambition is to see security and insecurity from differing vantage points and thereby de-familiarise it; and to critically explore the styles of reasoning, calculations and operations in very powerful domains. We aim to provide truly critical evaluations of policing and policy-making, to show up the fissures in security-scapes, and to open space for future projects.

Aims

Anthropologists have long noted the elasticity and occasional vacuous uses of the concept of security but they are by no means alone in doing so. Contemporary Security Studies recognises that security is an 'essentially contested concept' (Schwell in this volume). The Copenhagen School, for example, emphasises the process of securitisation, whereby threats and dangers posed to the survival of 'our way of life' (Goldstein 2010: 492) are performed, socially constructed – and are understandable via speech-act theory. This approach has the virtue of casting light on 'the state of exception' lodged at the heart of many democratic nation-states' sovereign power, but it is not so clear that speech-act theories cast light on non-Western contexts (see Buzan et al. 1998; Agamben 2005; cf. Stritzel 2007). It seems likely, indeed, that by focusing on the securitisation performed mainly by authorised persons and institutions the so-called Copenhagen School replay what Michel Foucault once termed 'the overvaluation of the problem of the state' (2007: 109; see also Abrams 1988 [1977]) – an assertion of power that fails to attend to configurations of sovereignty, discipline and governmental management that have population as their target and apparatuses of security as their 'essential mechanism' (Foucault 2007: 107–108).

In this volume, Marion Demossier and Catarina Frois both discuss the politics of security in ways that confound any handy configuration of nation-state security and the (in)securitisation of target populations. Borrowing from Gregory Feldman's (2005) approach to performativity, Demossier focuses on the French 'essential crisis' over the Roma. Rather than lending phantom objectivity to Nicolas Sarkozy's government, Demossier takes as her starting point Sarkozy's securitising 'Grenoble speech', but from there situates the nation-state in a contested political landscape of international rights and conventions, European politics and municipal machinations. Around the time of the 'Grenoble speech' the diversity of people categorised as 'Roma' were constructed as an alien, rootless and threatening intrusion. Demossier shows the effects in terms of excluding legislation, accelerated deportations and horrific living conditions, but she is also careful to use those data to reflect back on the performative nation-state asserting its ontological existence, often in defiance of France imagined as home of the Rights of Man.

Frois provides us with another complex ethnographic portrait of (in) securitisation, focusing on the roll-out of public CCTV video-surveillance in Portugal. CCTV is now one of the preferred solutions to crime and social order problems globally. The UK, with 20 per cent of the world's surveillance cameras, is of course one of the most striking examples. The trend recently provoked columnist Brendan O'Neill to accuse the UK government of becoming, 'the Willy Wonka of social control, churning out increasingly creepy, bizarre and fantastic methods for policing the populace' (2010: no pagination).[6] But these are global trends. The New York Police Department recently teamed with Microsoft to launch Domain Awareness System (DAS) to convert their 3000 old-fashioned CCTVs into real-time public safety data sources to be read by artificial intelligence analytics. A critical anthropology of security must attend to these global trends without being seduced by the evident technological fetishism.

Frois describes a two-stage process (2005–2010 and 2010 onwards) of public video-surveillance implementation in Portugal. The first stage was characterised by a distinct lack of inter-institutional cooperation and a strong stance by many public bodies. What were these CCTV solutions attempting to solve? After all, Portugal does not have unusual crime or public order problems; there is no strong evidence that CCTVs prevent crimes; and Portuguese history led to a favouring of policing in the form of close ties with local communities called 'proximity policing'. However, since 2010, as Frois shows, in the teeth of a severe economic recession, 'emergency' and 'exception' are now routinely invoked. The requirement for public video-surveillance, to borrow from Pierre Bourdieu, seems to have come without saying; it now goes without saying; and, despite the lack of evidence supporting its efficacy, in Portugal it refuses to go away.

Meditations on the politics of security inevitably call our attention to policy, because security so often manifests itself in seemingly neutral and common-sense ways. Of course 'neutral' statements refer to a reality, and anthropologists have been particularly keen observers of how reality comes in many forms. In this volume, Gregory Feldman extends his work on the migration apparatus (2012) by questioning the 'local' for policy workers and technocrats working on the EU's border-'neighbourhood' with North Africa. For those in the migration apparatus the local is often a place of alienation and instrumentalisation rather than mutuality and agency. But Feldman goes well beyond descriptions of the isolation felt within an apparatus capable of standardising discourse among a great diversity of people. Drawing on Foucault's meditations on the *coup d'état* and the philosophical insights of Hannah Arendt, Feldman shows us that the alienation and instrumentalisation of policy technocrats results in an incapacity on their part to constitute the 'local' and interact with one another on their own terms. Instead, they work within apparatuses capable of bureaucratised state violence. As 'migration management', EU agencies such as FRONTEX, and numerous technology-laden border-control operations move to the forefront, Feldman's insights into the violence of the apparatus present a challenge that a critical anthropology of security must take seriously.[7]

Alexandra Schwell draws from Gregory Feldman and other scholars working on the anthropology of policy (see Wedel et al. 2005) to explore how the Viennese police transposed the enlargement of the EU and removal of border controls with neighbouring countries in the form of so-called 'compensatory measures'. The Viennese police engage in theatrical operations and clamp down on a variety of 'illegals', but the always-present suspicion of profiling spreads out these actions under a disturbing banner – according to one officer, 'Nobody should feel safe!'[8] Schwell tracks the 'governmentality of unease' (Bigo 2009) from politics to policing, attending especially to the normalisation of insecurity in the everyday lives of the targets of compensatory measures. At first glance, so-called compensatory measures seem temporary and excessive, but Schwell shows them to be routinised and excessive. A high-ranking official casts the situation plainly – the new measures will 'stand in their own right'. The compensatory measures Schwell tracks allude to a disturbing state of exception in urban policing.

Urban policing is an enormous site of transformation in the contemporary moment. Sally Howell and Andrew Shryock (2003) describe the rise of 'inner city Orientalism', an analysis that could easily be extended to encompass the urban more broadly, especially trends towards gatedness and private security. Anthropologists have done much to show the complex imbrication of security and perceptions of urban danger across a variety of regions. Setha Low (2003), in particular, has called attention to the explosion of gated residential and commercial properties in the United States of America – as of 2002 one in eight Americans lived in a 'secure' and 'exclusive' gated neighbourhood. That number is still growing, though gatedness is no guarantee of either exclusivity or security. Indeed, in some neighbourhoods, gatedness may denote a fake checkpoint manned by a cardboard-cut-out guard to reduce insurance premiums. Moreover, the uneven tilting of residential patterns in many parts of the world towards gatedness converges with the privatisation of security provision. The year 2012 was a historic moment in UK policing: the private security company G4S was contracted to build and staff many functions within a police station by the Lincolnshire Police Authority. The Police Authority claimed that the move would result in 'the leanest police force in Britain', capable of delivering 'services' at an even lower 'cost per head of population' (see Plimmer and Warrell 2012: 4). The disturbing portents in Lincolnshire foretell a vision of the future already available elsewhere. Jean and John Comaroff's accounts of law and order in the South African post-colony include the example of the burgeoning private security industry. One well-known firm in Cape Town called Baywatch operates profitably in areas perceived to have inadequate police cover. Indeed, Jean Comaroff (2010) tells us that the local police share this view, and some stations now have panic buttons to alert Baywatch should they need support.

It is Giorgio Agamben's version of 'the state of exception' and his reassessment of Carl Schmitt that serves as the starting point for Didier Fassin's ethnographic essay on the enforcement of order in Paris. Fassin locates a 'petty' state of exception in the intensive and often brutal policing of the urban poor, denoting specific locations and times in which there is a partial suspension of 'normal' legal practices in policing Paris. Fassin's work examines the actually existing transformations to the way order is enforced in particular neighbourhoods. From the vantage point of an engaged public ethnography, Fassin allows us to see the spectacular operations mounted by the police in the presence of media audiences. But he is careful to emphasise the routine interactions police officers have with residents in poor urban neighbourhoods coded as 'jungles'. Like Frois in her analysis of Portugal, Fassin notes that serious crime is not a major issue, thus policing becomes reactive and intrusive in a petty state of exception. The 'stop and search' of youths may often be a response to boredom, but it is rarely directed towards 'white', middle-class university kids. The enforcement of order, then, is the enforcement of a social (dis)order that separates policing from the communities it was once believed to serve. In Parisian neighbourhoods a social contract is being hammered out as officers police communities 'by numbers' and residents are often brutalised.

Maguire's analysis of the counter-terrorist apparatus in airports reveals a shadowy world in which different styles of policing are contested. His fieldwork is partially occluded – locations and persons are not identified. Nonetheless, he proposes to explore the skilled vision of counter-terrorism officers who borrow transnational models to detect so-called 'abnormal behaviour'. In this corner of the security apparatus we find the valorisation of intuitions and professional skills, and efforts by officers to briefly 'empathise' with suspects as a pre-condition of detection. But this is also the realm of techno-scientific solutions that aim to use high-tech computing to screen the emotional states of passengers. Maguire situates skilled vision and techno-science together, and aims to locate fissures in the prevailing styles of reasoning and quality of evidence.

Many anthropologists have come to study security because of previous work on international migration and racialisation. Contemporary security seems, to borrow from Jonathan Xavier Inda (2006), to be particularly targeting immigrants. The everyday lives of many migrants throughout the world are affected by fear of deportation, and a significant minority are already warehoused in asylum and deportation regimes. In her chapter, Ines Hasselberg describes the deportation of foreign-national offenders from the UK. Hasselberg sees deportation as a point in a process that includes the 'construction' of foreign-national offenders as a threat to UK security and the progressive intrusion of deportability into their everyday lives. Again, the question of evidence is raised: do foreign-national offenders actually present a great risk? Echoing Didier Fassin's analysis of 'policing by numbers' in Paris, Hasselberg indicates the existence of a migration system infected by 'management by numbers'. And the effects of deportability are significant: one research participant describes being denied access to any life worth living, reduced by migration management to nothing more than a 'cockroach'. Again, we are reminded of Gregory Feldman's incisive analysis of the violence at the core of routine, technocratic administration and policy.

Contributions in this volume cover many domains. The process of deportation of foreign-national offenders from the UK at first glance seems far away from the grey zones of illegality described by Jutta Lauth Bacas on the Greek-Turkish border. On closer inspection, of course, we are looking at different nodes in the emerging EU security apparatus. Jutta Lauth Bacas' discussion of securitisation within the reception process for 'uninvited' foreigners after their clandestine arrival in Greece is chilling. At some points the sea crossing between Greece and Turkey is no more than 5–10 nautical miles. Tourists travel from one side to the other. However, when clandestine migrants cross to Greece they encounter an area of 'freedom, justice and security' composed of amorphous security agencies like FRONTEX and processing centres that are little more than camps made of tarpaulins that have 'gaps' in the food supply. In one way or another, the contributors share a concern to track 'grey' zones, discretionary measures and powers, and states of exception. Giorgio Agamben's work (2005) hovers in the background but is not imported wholesale as a diagram that explains everything everywhere. If Agamben is correct in saying that the refugee camp is the paradigm of our modernity, however, then Jutta Lauth Bacas shows us a horrific vision of modernity on the Greek-Turkish border.

The contributions in this volume mark efforts to extend knowledge of contemporary security politics, policy, policing and the experiences of some of those most sharply affected. This introductory essay and the contributions in this volume mark the continued development of a critical anthropology of security. The ethnographic focus is on Europe, mindful of the global qualities of (in)securitisation, but also mindful of the expansive historical and contemporary imaginaries of European security. We note the widening of the concept of security but see this in the context of 'official' conceptualisations in states, non-state and international agencies, universities, think tanks, and various techno-scientific assemblages and 'expert' persons that together comprise the 'security-scape' (Albro et al. 2012). A critical anthropology of security, then, involves moving beyond narrow visions of the state – the cold monster of Friedrich Nietzsche's imagination – towards understandings of:

> [T]he multiple ways in which security is configured and deployed – not only by states and authorised speakers but by communities, groups, and individuals ... [because] a perspective on security as made and understood by actors and groups outside of the state and its official institutions helps to broaden our perspective on what security means, how it is produced, what it includes, and what it excludes in the ordinary and exceptional struggles of daily life. It brings to light the manifold ways in which global discourses are adopted, manipulated, transformed, and deployed in quotidian interactions and events, revealing the full range of security as lived social experience in a variety of contexts. (Goldstein 2010: 492–493)

At stake in a critical anthropology of security, then, are matters of political economy and its imbricated discourses and practices, the changing relations between citizens and states, fears and global (dis)orders. But the possibilities of a critical anthropology of security exceed the disciplinary sympathy with ethnographically representing subaltern, 'grassroots' or ordinary experiences of security 'from below'. Conceptual work and research practices are challenged in any ethnography of (in)securitisation (see Albro et al. 2012). Even if one holds to a conception of the local as a jurisdiction intruded upon, resisting or accommodating security, anthropologically one is often forced to reformulate notions of space, scale or responsible ethics in confrontation with security apparatuses.

This volume brings together contributions to the development of a critical anthropology of security that share in an effort to understand experiences of security, spatially, epistemologically and in terms of power relations. While the chapters on the politics of security, migration, policing or counter-terrorism in this volume place different emphases, depending on the topic or geographic location, each shares in an effort to understand how security is deployed and lived, conceived and perceived. To borrow from Joseph P. Masco:

> what is novel about a 'critical anthropology of security' today is less the explicit focus on how the concept of security is deployed than it is on

attending to the implicit ideological and political structures that shape its means and naturalise its forms, including within the discipline of anthropology. (2010a: 509)

As an emergent critical anthropology of security grows it will need to give further consideration to important concepts, from vital interests and critical infrastructures to fear and abandonment, and from risks and precautions to threatening futures. The growing critical anthropology of security will also need to attend to disciplinary research practices, including the localities and ethical considerations they engage with and often call into being. This volume represents some of the early efforts in these directions.

Notes

1. Here we are pushing for recognition of particular formations of security. To speak of the powerful position held by security policy, politics and techno-science in the contemporary moment is to make reference to particular formations of security, for example the trend towards border security and wall building (see Brown 2010). Understanding the dimensions of these various formations of security is an important anthropological challenge. In terms of wall building, for example, one may draw inspiration for a cultural analysis from Franz Kafka's 'The Great Wall of China' (1988 [1931]). Kafka describes the involvement of multiple, isolated communities in the construction of a monument to strangers – barbarians who might one day descend 'like locusts'. Its effectiveness was questionable – it was rumoured to be riddled with gaps. But the act of building the wall solidified those involved into 'a ring of brothers, a current of blood no longer confined within the narrow circulation of one body'. Kafka ends the story with the terrible vision that to expose the Great Wall as a cultural project 'would mean undermining not only our consciences, but, what is far worse, our feet' (1988 [1931]: 65–83 passim). What Kafka captures so eloquently – and what many Strategic Studies scholars have noted since – is that security might easily denote peace, cooperation or mutual understandings between communities. However, certain formations of security such as border walls acquire phantom objectivity, mask the possibilities for peace making, cooperation or mutual understandings between communities, and actually contribute to insecurity (see also Sterling 2009).
2. Milton Lipson, a former US Secret Service agent and security expert, goes so far as to argue, 'Private security originated in that clouded time when man began to domesticate animals and graze his herds' (1988: 12).

3. An exception is F.E. Williams's (1930) ethnography of Orokaiva 'security circles' that stretch from outsiders to immediate kin (cf. Lawrence 1984).

4. Malinowski also presaged contemporary debates about balancing 'the interests of the state' against 'the elementary rights and interests of the individual' (1939: 964 passim), conceptual work that segues into later anthropological advice on the military dimensions of African pacification (1945: 88–90).

5. Burton Benedict was one of the few to recognise such sharp distinctions. He shares this anecdote:

> I once attended a seminar in London for district officers. One officer … became impatient with what seemed to him the endless meanderings of the anthropologists in attempting to understand the societies they were studying. 'What would you do,' he said, 'if you came out on your veranda to find hundreds of natives with torches and spears running towards you?' After a short silence, one anthropologist said, 'Run like hell.' (1967: 584)

6. O'Neill also called attention to some less well-known interventions, such as 'weaponised' classical music and Mosquito alarms. Across the UK, according to his report, local councils and transport companies are deterring loitering youths by blasting Beethoven's Pastoral Symphony through loudspeakers. Mosquito alarms, on the other hand, are widely used devices that are deployed to prevent loitering by emitting a high frequency sound set to be audible only to young people.

7. FRONTEX is the European Agency for the Management of Operational Cooperation at the External Borders of the Member States of the European Union.

8. Here, again, we encounter matters of 'security theatre', the performative and symbolic dimensions of security and its meaningful content (for a thorough treatment see Svenonius 2011).

References

Abrams, P. (1988 [1977]) 'Notes on the difficulty of studying the state', *Journal of Historical Sociology*, Vol. 1, No. 1, pp. 58–89.

Agamben, G. (2005) *State of Exception* (Chicago: University of Chicago Press).

Albro, R., Marcus, G.E., McNamara, L.A. and Schoch-Spana, M. (eds) (2012) *Anthropologists in the Securityscape: Ethics, Practice, and Professional Identity* (Walnut Creek, CA: Left Coast Press).

Asad, T. (ed.) (1973) *Anthropology and the Colonial Encounter* (London: Ithaca Press).

Barth, F. (1959) *Political Leadership among Swat Pathans* (London: Athlone Press).

Bauman, Z. (2000) *Globalization: The Human Consequences* (London: Polity Press).

Benedict, B. (1967) 'The significance of applied anthropology for anthropological theory', *Man*, n.s., Vol. 2, No. 4, pp. 584–592.

Benedict, R. (1946) *The Chrysanthemum and the Sword* (New York: First Mariner Books).

Bigo, D. (2009) 'Immigration controls and free movement in Europe', *International Review of the Red Cross*, Vol. 91, No. 875, pp. 579–591.

Boas, F. (1919) 'Scientists as spies', *The Nation*, Vol. 109, p. 797.

Brown, W. (2010) *Walled States, Waning Sovereignty* (New York: Zone Books).

Buzan, B., Waever, O. and de Wilde, J. (1998) *Security: A New Framework for Analysis* (Boulder, CO: Rienner).

Caduff, C. (2010) 'Public prophylaxis: pandemic influenza, pharmaceutical prevention, and participatory governance', *BioSocieties*, Vol. 5, No. 2, pp. 199–218.

Caldeira, T.P.R. (2001) *City of Walls: Crime, Segregation, and Citizenship in São Paulo* (Berkeley: University of California Press).

Collier, S.J. and Lakoff, A. (2008) 'Distributed preparedness: the spatial logic of domestic security in the United States', *Environment and Planning D: Society and Space*, Vol. 26, No. 1, pp. 7–28.

Comaroff, J. (2010) 'Theory from the South: why Europe is evolving towards Africa', paper presented at the 2010 NUI Maynooth Anthropology Seminar Series, 21 October, Ireland.

Crawfurd, J. (1863) 'On the relation of the domesticated animals to civilization', *Transactions of the Ethnological Society of London*, Vol. 2, pp. 387–468.

Dillon, M. and Lobo-Guerrero L. (2008) 'Biopolitics of security in the 21st century', *Review of International Studies*, Vol. 34, pp. 265–292.

Donoghue, J.D. (1963) *My Thuan: A Mekong Delta Village in South Vietnam* (Washington, DC: Agency for International Development).

Enloe, C.H. (1980) *Police, Military, and Ethnicity: Foundations of State Power* (New Brunswick, NJ: Transaction Publishers).

Eriksen, T.H, Bal, E. and Salemink, O. (2010) *A World of Insecurity: Anthropological Perspectives on Human Security* (London: Pluto Press).

Evans-Pritchard, E.E. (1946) 'Applied anthropology', *Africa*, Vol. 6, pp. 92–98.

Ewald, F. (2002) 'The return of Descartes's malicious demon: an outline of a philosophy of precaution', in Barker, T. and Simon, J. (eds) *Embracing Risk: The Changing Culture of Insurance and Responsibility*, pp. 273–301 (Chicago: University of Chicago Press).

Farmer, P. (2004) 'An anthropology of structural violence', *Current Anthropology*, Vol. 45, No. 3, pp. 305–325.

Fassin, D. (2013) *Enforcing Order: An Ethnography of Urban Policing* (London: Polity Press).

Feldman, G. (2005) 'Essential crisis: a performative approach to migrants, minorities and the European nation-state', *Anthropological Quarterly*, Vol. 78, No. 1, pp. 213–246.

—— (2011) 'If ethnography is more than participant-observation, then relations are more than connections: the case for non-local ethnography in a world of apparatuses', *Anthropological Theory*, Vol. 11, No. 4, pp. 375–395.

—— (2012) *The Migration Apparatus: Security, Labour and Policymaking in the European Union* (Stanford, CA: Stanford University Press).

Field, M.J. (1960) *Search for Security: An Ethno-psychiatric study of Rural Ghana* (London: Faber & Faber).

Foucault, M. (1991) *Discipline and Punish: The Birth of the Prison* (London: Penguin).

—— (2007) *Security, Territory, Population* (London: Palgrave Macmillan).

Fried, J. (1962) 'Social organization and personal security in a Peruvian Hacienda Indian Community: Vicos', *American Anthropologist*, n.s., Vol. 64, No. 4, pp. 771–780.

Galton, F. (1892) *Finger Prints* (London: Macmillan).

Gillin, J. (1951) *The Culture of Security in San Carlos: A Study of a Guatemalan Community of Indians and Ladinos* (New Orleans: Middle American Research Institute, Tulane University of Louisiana).

Goldstein, D. (2004) *The Spectacular City: Violence and Performance in Urban Bolivia* (Durham, NC: Duke University Press).

—— (2010) 'Toward a critical anthropology of security', *Current Anthropology*, Vol. 51, No. 4, pp. 487–517.

Gregg, D. and Williams, E. (1948) 'The dismal science of functionalism', *American Anthropologist*, Vol. 50, No. 4, pp. 594–611.

Gros, F. (2012) *Le Principe sécurité* (Paris: Gallimard).

Gusterson, H. (1996) *Nuclear Rites: Weapons Laboratory at the End of the Cold War* (Berkeley: University of California Press).

—— (2004) *People of the Bomb: Portraits of America's Nuclear Complex* (Minneapolis: University of Minnesota Press).

Hickey, G.C. (1964) *Village in Vietnam* (New Haven, CT: Yale University Press).

Hobbes, T. (1994 [1668]) *Leviathan: With Selected Variants from the Latin Edition of 1668* (London: Hackett Publishing Co.).

Horn, D.G. (2003) *The Criminal Body: Lombroso and the Anatomy of Deviance* (London: Routledge).

Howell, S. and Shryock, A. (2003) 'Cracking down on diaspora: Arab Detroit and America's war on terror', *Anthropological Quarterly*, Vol. 76, No. 3, pp. 443–462.

Inda, J.X. (2006) *Targeting Immigrants: Government, Technology and Ethics* (Malden, MA: Blackwell).

Jorgensen, J.G. (1971) 'On ethics and anthropology', *Current Anthropology*, Vol. 12, No. 3, pp. 321–334.

Kafka, F. (1988 [1931]) *Metamorphosis and Other Stories* (London: Penguin).

Langton, C. (2009) 'Demographics and security in Europe', in Giegerich, B. and Comolli, V. (eds) *FORESEC D4.5: Report on European Security*, pp. 53–63. www.foresec.eu/wp3_docs/FORESEC_Deliverable_D_4_5.pdf (accessed 28 September 2013).

Lawrence, P. (1984) *The Garia* (Manchester: Manchester University Press).

Leighton, A.H. (1945) *The Governing of Men* (Princeton, NJ: Princeton University Press).

Leighton, A.H. and Leighton, D.C. (1942) 'Some types of uneasiness and fear in a Navaho Indian community', *American Anthropologist*, n.s., Vol. 44, No. 2, pp. 194–209.

Lipson, M. (1988) 'Private security: a retrospective', *Annals of the American Academy of Political and Social Science*, Vol. 498, pp. 11–22.

Low, S. (2003) *Behind the Gates: Life, Security, and the Pursuit of Happiness in Fortress America* (New York: Routledge).

Lutz, C. (2001) *Homefront: The Military City and the American Twentieth Century* (Boston, MA: Beacon).

Lyon, D. (2009) *Identifying Citizens: ID Cards as Surveillance* (Oxford: Polity Press).

Maguire, M. (2009) 'The birth of biometric security', *Anthropology Today*, Vol. 25, No. 2, pp. 9–14.

Malinowski, B. (1939). 'The group and the individual in functional analysis', *American Journal of Sociology*, Vol. 44, No. 6, pp. 938–964.

—— (1945) *The Dynamics of Cultural Change: An Inquiry into Race Relations in Africa*, Kaberry, P. (ed.) (New Haven, CT: Yale University Press).

Masco, J.P. (2006) *The Nuclear Borderlands: The Manhattan Project in Post-Cold War New Mexico* (Princeton, NJ: Princeton University Press).

—— (2010a) 'Comment on "Toward a critical anthropology of security" by Daniel Goldstein', *Current Anthropology*, Vol. 51, No. 4, pp. 509–510.

—— (2010b) 'Sensitive but unclassified: secrecy and the counter-terrorist state', *Public Culture*, Vol. 22, No. 3, pp. 433–463.

Maslow, A. (1954) *Motivation and Personality* (New York: Harper).

McFate, M. (2005) 'The military utility of understanding adversary culture', *Joint Force Quarterly*, Vol. 38, pp. 42–48.

Nader, L. (1986) 'The drift to war', in Foster, M.L. and Rubinstein, R. (eds) *Peace and War: Cross-cultural Perspectives*, pp. 185–193 (New York: Transaction Publishers).

O'Neill, B. (2010) 'Britain deploys Mozart to police its people', *Pittsburgh Post-Gazette*, 18 April. www.brendanoneill.co.uk/post/530694516/britain-deploys-mozart-to-police-its-people (accessed 1 July 2013).

Orr, D.W. (1979) 'Catastrophe and social order', *Human Ecology*, Vol. 7, No. 1, pp. 41–52.

Pedersen, M.A. and Holbraad, M. (eds) (2013) *Times of Security: Ethnographies of Fear, Protest and the Future* (London: Routledge).

Plimmer, G. and Warrell, H. (2012) 'Cuts prompt police to use more contractors', *Financial Times*, 7 March, p. 4.

Price, D. (2008) *Anthropological Intelligence: The Deployment and Neglect of American Anthropology in the Second World War* (Durham, NC: Duke University Press).

Rabinow, P. and Rose, N. (2006) 'Biopower today', *BioSocieties*, Vol. 1, pp. 195–217.

Radcliffe-Brown, A.R. (1952) *Structure and Function in Primitive Society: Essays and Addresses* (Glencoe, IL: The Free Press).

Rao, U. (2013) 'Biometric marginality', *Economic & Political Weekly*, Vol. 47, No. 13, pp. 71–77.

Ricoeur, P. (1980) *The Contribution of French Historiography to the Theory of History* (New York: Oxford University Press).

Roth, H.L. (1887) 'On the origin of agriculture', *Journal of the Anthropological Institute of Great Britain and Ireland*, Vol. 16, pp. 102–136.

Salter, M.B. and Mutlu, C.E. (eds) (2013) *Research Methods in Critical Security Studies: An Introduction* (London: Routledge).

Smith, C. and Brooks, D.J. (2013) *Security Science: The Theory and Practice of Security* (Oxford: Elsevier).

Stavrianakis, A., Fearnley, L., Bennett, G. and Rabinow, P. (2011) *Safety, Security, Preparedness: An Orientation to Biosecurity Today* (Berkeley, CA: Berkeley Human Practices Lab).

Sterling, B.L. (2009) *Do Good Fences Make Good Neighbours? What History Teaches US about Strategic Barriers and International Security* (Washington, DC: Georgetown University Press).

Stritzel, H. (2007) 'Towards a theory of securitization: Copenhagen and beyond', *European Journal of International Relations*, Vol. 13, pp. 357–383.

Svenonius, O. (2011) Sensitising Urban Transport Security: Surveillance and Policing in Berlin, Stockholm and Warsaw (unpublished PhD dissertation, University of Stockholm).

Sweijs, T. (as part of The Hague Centre for Strategic Studies) (2012) *Conceptual Foundations of Security.* WP1.1 deliverable report for European Security Trends and Threats in Society FP7-SEC-2011-1 (Collaborative Project). www.ettis-project.eu (accessed 22 July 2013).

Sykes, G.M. (1958) *The Society of Captives: A Study of a Maximum Security Prison* (Princeton, NJ: Princeton University Press).

Tajani, A. (2013) 'A new deal for European defence', Communication from the Commission to the European Parliament, the Council, the European Economic and social Committee and the Committee of the Regions, COM. (2013), 542 final.

Tufton, O. (1894) 'Migration and the food quest: a study in the peopling of America', *American Anthropologist*, Vol. 7, No. 3, pp. 275–292.

Turton, D., Woodhead, L. and Hendrie, K. (1974) *The Mursi: A Film* (London: BBC Disappearing World Series).

Tylor, E.B. (1899) 'Remarks on totemism, with especial reference to some modern theories respecting it', *Journal of the Anthropological Institute of Great Britain and Ireland*, Vol. 28, No. 1/2, pp. 138–148.

UNDP – United Nations Development Programme (1994) *Human Development Report 1994* (New York: Oxford University Press).

Van Creveld, M. (1991) *The Transformation of War* (New York: The Free Press).

Warner, W.L. (1930) 'Morphology and functions of the Australian Murngin type of kinship', *American Anthropologist*, Vol. 32, No. 2, pp. 207–256.

Wedel, J.R., Shore, C., Feldman, G. and Lathrop, S. (2005) 'Toward an anthropology of public policy', *Annals of the American Academy of Political and Social Science*, Vol. 600, pp. 30–51.

Weldes, J., Laffey, M., Gusterson, H. and Duvall, R. (eds) (1999) *Cultures of Insecurity: States, Communities and the Production of Danger* (Minneapolis: University of Minnesota Press).

White, L.A. (1943) 'The energy and evolution of culture', *American Anthropologist*, Vol. 45, No. 3, pp. 335–356.

Whitehead, N.L. and Finnström, S. (eds) (2013) *Virtual War and Magical Death* (Durham, NC: Duke University Press).

Williams, F.E. (1930) *Orokaiva Society* (Oxford: Clarendon Press).

1

Sarkozy and Roma: Performing Securitisation[1]

Marion Demossier

'Hey, Hey, Sarkozy, why don't you like the gypsies?' chanted the Romanian rock group Vama on YouTube in autumn, 2010.[2] The anthem was inspired by the waves of Roma deportations orchestrated by the French government earlier that year. Against the background of a no-man's-land, the band performed its interpretation of the 'essential crisis' being played out by Sarkozy. At first glance, it seems like an imaginative denunciation of the French President's Roma integration policies. However, a close ethnographic reading reveals a series of subtle divisions within the meanings located at the heart of the crisis – meanings that this chapter will scrutinise. Mocking the state as personified by Sarkozy (*l'État, c'est moi!*) rather than the French nation, presenting Gypsies as a nation-state issue, and playing on national/European cultural markers of belonging, the song crystallises some key performative features of the nation during an 'essential crisis'. By 'crisis' I mean the construction of Roma as a security threat through media and journalistic narration. By constructing Roma as an internal security crisis through stylised and repetitive bodily acts of expulsions and through a language reaffirming their existence as an essential ontological actor, the French state performs through 'the reiterative power of discourse the phenomena that it regulates and constrains' (Butler 1993: 2). As a result, it creates its own existence in the context of wider economic, social and political configurations and at a time when its legitimacy is arguably waning. How the crisis has been framed, for whom, with what results and under what conditions are the key questions at the core of this chapter.

My anthropological investigation of the crisis relies on the study of texts, news reports, images, government documents, discourses, speeches and other forms of communication.[3] I include analyses of websites as cultural products and as avenues into cultural understandings about migration and nation in European contexts. The primacy of the visual and speech acts in securitisation processes suggests the need for analysis of performance and audience. This is why they are at the core of my analysis of the construction of the crisis.

An 'Essential Crisis'

The Roma crisis came to national prominence following the events of 16 July 2010 in Saint-Aignan (Loir et Cher département) when Luigi Duquenet, a French citizen, was killed by a gendarme while escaping from a road-block. The following weekend, the police station in Saint-Aignan, a bakery, several cars and traffic lights were damaged by approximately 40 *gens du voyage*.[4] Several other incidents occurred at the same location that weekend. Thereafter, President Sarkozy announced a crisis meeting on 'Roma and *gens du voyage*' to address the 'problem associated with some individuals belonging to the community'.[5] Sarkozy's speech on 30 July 2010 following agitation in the Villeneuve district near Grenoble – described by some commentators as the Grenoble speech – represents the first peak of the crisis. Emphasising authority, order and securitisation of immigration and crime, Sarkozy put the Roma issue on the national agenda by comparing the illegal camps of Roma and the *gens du voyage* as a '*zone de non droit*' (lawless enclave).[6] He pledged to dismantle camps that were not recognised legally, repeating a promise he made in October 2002 as the then Interior Minister.[7] A series of orchestrated and publicised expulsions followed in different parts of France, including Marseille, Lyon, Lille and the suburbs of Paris. Drastic measures were also announced, such as possible suspension of child benefits and loss of French citizenship (*Libération*, 31 July 2010). Eric Fassin (2010b) and Alexandra Nacu (2011) argue that the Roma crisis emerges from contemporary French nationalist fears of the foreign rather than from the Roma. Yet the construction of Roma is characterised by distinct and complex political and cultural processes of 'othering' that I wish to explore here.

Another crucial dimension of the crisis is the battle between France and the European Union (EU) over the treatment of Roma who are legally European citizens entitled to freedom of movement following the 2007 accession of Romania and Bulgaria. Indeed, Viviane Reading, EU Justice

Commissioner responsible for upholding these rights for EU citizens, fuelled a bitter row over the French deportation of Roma by comparing the policy to Nazi round-ups of Gypsies and Jews during the Second World War. The publication of a French ministerial circular openly targeting Roma as an ethnic group and subsequent public debates also illustrate the tensions between the EU and France over the implementation of European legislation.[8] These events also raise underlying questions about the nature of sovereignty and political trust as EU officials were misled during formal meetings with Eric Besson (French Interior Minister) and Pierre Lellouche (France's European Minister). Despite visible embarrassment, French politicians and European leaders brushed the Roma affair under the carpet.

What is striking about the crisis is that the press and social commentators interpreted it as a performative act: a process by which group identity is essentialised, reinforced and communicated. Following Gregory Feldman's (2005) approach to performativity, the crisis unfolded through repetitions (almost daily reference to the topic in French newspapers, especially during the summer), regular periods of expulsions, key speeches by the President and the Interior Minister, and practices of representation (pictures of expulsions in the press and the news), creating the reiterative power of discourse to produce the Roma crisis.[9] This construction of Roma has produced its own economic, cultural and political imaginary landscape through specific relational practices embedded in institutional arrangements that construct essentialised subjects – Roma, securitisation and the French nation – in reference to each other. For Feldman (2005), threats identified in global processes serve as foils against which the nation-state constitutes itself, enabling it to assert its own ontological existence. Here Roma are constructed as 'aliens', a cause of economic and societal instability, displaced bodies without territorial roots who are denied their national, European and even human rights. At the same time, Roma are presented as a threat to both French cultural essentialism and republicanism with their territorial forms of belonging and citizenship (*jus solis*). We must note, to borrow from Didier Fassin in this volume, that security itself creates insecurity. According to Paloma Gay y Blasco (2008: 299):

> The resilience and dominance of the image of the wandering Gypsy needs to be investigated and its effects closely examined, if only because today the majority of European Roma are not nomadic and because the

Roma populations of many European countries have been sedentary for several centuries.

By coupling Roma with second- or third-generation migrants and *gens du voyage*, they become part of a wider threat to the fragile nation. As Gupta and Ferguson (1997: 4) argue, the Hobbesian idea of culture as orderly and set against the ever-present threat of chaos and anomie is a powerful and prevailing idea in Western thought and politics. Yet here it takes a new form: Roma are presented as being without a national territory, in constant transit and belonging to a different kind of repertoire; their social construction is constantly on the move, which resonates with the main features of economic globalisation and grates against French national ideology. These, to borrow from the Introduction to this volume, are some of the emergent material, historical and socio-economic conditions for the (in)securitisation of Roma.

Performing Securitisation and Reformulating French Republicanism

Drawing from Feldman (2005) and critical theories of French republicanism, this chapter engages critically with the politics of subjec-tification – the processes by which individuals are constituted as social beings within complex configurations of meaning and political strategies. I argue that the Roma example is more complex than a binary opposition between the French state and Roma. Rather, the process of subjectification and categorisation is inscribed onto complex political, social, ideological and cultural contexts. I suggest a more nuanced analysis of how politics and the nation have responded to global forces and especially to EU expansion. This new context requires a subtle analysis of political rationalities, one that must attend to the republican framework, its ongoing contestation and its actual realities.

The last decade has seen a lively scholarly debate about Europe, the nation-state and immigration policies. A broad interdisciplinary literature has mushroomed and a more comparative European framework has been adopted. Anthropologists who traditionally focused on language and culture as lenses onto reconfigurations of the nation-state now argue that neo-nationalism results in a redefinition of internal and external boundaries. For example, Steiner (2000: 9) notes that language is a powerful tool for setting the political agenda, and in order to understand politics we must attend to the actions of political actors and to their rhetoric. Equally, Gullestad (2002) analyses transformations in Norway where equality is configured as 'imagined sameness' underpinning a growing ethnicisation of national identity via immigration debates. Socio-political closures and discrimination become rationalised ideologically in an otherwise economically globalised world. As Gullestad (2002: 176) argues:

> Cultural fundamentalism and the essentialism which goes hand in hand with it does reify culture, but it is, in reality, about relationships between cultures understood as bounded, internally homogenous, integrated and exclusive entities. As a result, forms of behaviour and meaning attached to the definition of the nation are thought to be inevitably threatened by foreigners who by definition have a different culture.

When these discursive and performative constructions circulate in the national imaginary, they are, in principle, debated, especially when transformed into visible policies. Yet, as powerful tropes of national reification they gather power in moments of confusion and chaos. As Feldman argues (2005: 218), by reconceptualising the relationship between the state and the immigrant minority as mutually constitutive the issue of whether or not the nation-state wanes in the face of globalisation becomes less relevant. The identification of nationals/non-nationals is essential to the state. Citizenship, minority rights and integration policy are fundamental to nation-state legitimacy and authority – an international cultural grammar of nationhood (Lofgren 1989). Much of the literature has focused on the construction of nation-state performances. In contrast, here I wish to explore the Roma crisis as a dynamic and complex site of engagement in which the securitisation agenda becomes 'fashionable' while being operational (see the Introduction to this volume).

According to Saskia Sassen (1996), nation-states try to rehabilitate their sovereignty by exercising power over immigrants and refugees. The Roma 'essential crisis' is a moment in which one sees the reification of the state against migrants. According to Jacobson (1996: 2–3), the state is becoming less of a sovereign agent in the face of an international and constitutional order based on human rights, yet this process is far from being straightforward and resistance is emerging from political actors and from the state. It therefore becomes clear why nations reify their citizenship discourse using it as a powerful instrument of social closure (Brubaker 1992).

Post-national and nation-state membership should not be regarded as mutually exclusive (Nordberg 2004: 721); rather the Roma crisis emerges from an entangled and counterintuitive mix of motives (Steiner 2000: 17).

The French republican model, emphasising universalist ideals of integration and aiming to transform migrants into full citizens, has been described by political scientists as the antithesis of the British model, which configures integration as a matter of allowing ethnicity to mediate societal relations and public order (Favell 1998: 34). This is no longer a tenable position. It is undeniable that European integration has transformed debates about immigration and the nation-state, institutional order and policy-making. Jennings (2000) traces three types of responses in French intellectual circles. First, the traditionalist view rejects multi-culturalism and reasserts the orthodox republican principles of the secular state. Second, modernising republicanism endorses elements of cultural pluralism while maintaining the validity of key republican concepts. Finally, multiculturalist republicanism calls for a pluralist civic identity and recognition of minority cultures' positive values.

Arguably, French public opinion partially reflects the radicalisation of a small, but electorally significant section of the population in relation to security and immigration. Sally Marthaler (2008: 393) argues that the sense of no longer feeling at home in France is experienced by a declining minority of voters. Sarkozy's strategy to win votes located on the extreme right wing of the political spectrum by using a discourse based upon security, migration and sovereignty has undoubtedly resonated with the broader electoral body. However, these ongoing debates are characterised by their confrontation with changing economic realities.

An increasing amount of legislation has been drafted in the area of immigration policy, especially since the immigration bills of 2003 and 2006 during Sarkozy's period as Minister of the Interior.[10] Most of the measures proposed in the 2006 bill met with the approval of a large majority of the public, especially on the right and the far right. However, public reactions to the Roma deportations are polarised, though the reliability of surveys presented in *Le Figaro*, *France Matin* and *Libération* is questionable. Sarkozy's election in 2007 witnessed a remapping of these intellectual debates on integration with new internal divisions emerging (see Fassin 2010a; Bleich 2008). The recent period is marked by what Jennings (2000: 597) foresaw as a 'reformulation of republicanism', though not as he expected. Sarkozy's government stood for the renewal of moral order, authority and orthodox republicanism, responding to extreme right voters. Sarkozy strategically reactivated a strong conception of civic space despite the apparent crumbling of traditional markers of French identity. Therefore, the Roma crisis became a stage upon which to perform republicanism and act out public anxieties. However, I also argue that we must attend to the EU level and to transformations of nation-states in the new international economic order.

Contextualising the Roma Crisis

The EU played a major role in constructing the Roma 'question' and defining Roma rights in a post-national context. According to the European Commission (2011: 1), rough estimates indicate that approximately 10–12 million Roma reside in Europe, mostly in EU Member States.[11] Roma comprise up to 10 per cent of the total populations in historical settlement societies such as Bulgaria, Slovakia, Romania and Hungary; in Western European countries such as Spain, Roma comprise approximately 2 per cent of the total population (these figures do not include Kosovo Roma categorised as asylum seekers). The majority of Roma are 'settled' and only a dwindling minority continue a travelling way of life (Wagner 2011: 5). Moreover, the term 'Roma' encompasses vast ethnic, historical, social, economic, linguistic and cultural differences.[12] Since the end of the Cold War, global attention to prejudice against Roma in Europe focused on violence and discrimination in Central and Eastern Europe (Atanasoski 2009). During the 1990s, Western governments reconfigured the potential security threat posed by Roma migrants as a human rights matter imbricated with EU policy towards accession countries (Sobotka 2007). It was only after the fall of communism that the EU formulated policy about Roma as a vulnerable ethnic minority, and even then their legal and political status only came under scrutiny in Central and Eastern Europe.

The recognition of Roma as an ethnic minority also raised issues of governance relating to the control of movement and the migration of peoples within the EU. Increasingly, Roma have become a target of Europeanisation. Huub van Baar (2011: 8) argues that the post-1989 Europeanisation of Roma representation marks a new phase in their history. The European Parliament, for instance, has called for their recognition as a 'European minority' and for their integration into Europe.[13] Both the EU and European institutions have simultaneously approached Roma in terms of European political and cultural integration (van Baar 2011: 3) through, for example, Holocaust remembrance and minority/majority cultural dialogue. This reflects their heritage as a diaspora and their importance for the process of European integration in Eastern Europe.

A review of policies towards Roma in Europe certainly reveals a strong security-oriented history (Guglielmo and Waters 2005: 765). Sovereign and disciplinary instruments, including security measures, have been variously mobilised to regulate the integration of Roma populations (van Baar 2011: 8). Each of the EU Member States has responded in its own way and the EU has failed to provide clear and decisive leadership on the issue.[14]

The first Eastern European Roma arrived in the Paris region in the early 1990s followed by more in the 2000s post-Schengen Agreement (from Romania in 2001 and Bulgaria in 2002), which allowed three-month tourist stays on condition that one could prove possession of a minimum amount of money (Nacu 2011: 136). In 2010, Macedonian and non-Kosovo Roma joined the migrants who found refuge in Germany, Italy and France. They fall into the category of asylum seekers and 3465 individual claims were filed. There are around 15,000 Eastern European Roma in France with 3000–4000 living in the Paris region.[15]

During this period, France attempted to expel Roma migrants and to block the migration of Romanian Roma. In 2004, as part of so-called 'control at distance' migration policies, Sarkozy, then Interior Minister, signed an agreement with Romania and Bulgaria for the return and reintegration of Roma migrants. The International Organisation for Migration (IOM) assists in voluntary return programmes, which migrants sometimes avail themselves of before returning to France. Social inequalities and ethnic discrimination have long been characteristic of the Roma situation in France (Nacu 2011: 137), with informal payments demanded at the border and continuous identity checks. Following the 2001 elections in France, law and order rhetoric took hold and was amplified by Sarkozy as minister and later as President. His tenure as President was marked by '*lepénisation des esprits*', and the sublimation of nationalist rhetoric.

Miriam Ticktin (2005: 350) argues convincingly that a security discourse emerged simultaneously with policing practices characterised by sovereign powers and a suspension of the law. These tendencies are shown during the Roma crisis. From 2007, with the accession of Romania and Bulgaria to the EU, citizens no longer needed visas in order to travel to France, but this did not mean that their status was legal. As Europeans, they have a right to travel and to reside for a limited period in France as well as in other EU Member States. However, since January 2007 they are theoretically entitled to work in France in 150 professions with labour shortages.[16] The painstaking bureaucracy involved in obtaining a work permit would deter any French citizen. Moreover, for Romanian and Bulgarian nationals, access to employment depends on having a residency permit. Long and costly, this procedure was imposed by the EU as part of transitory measures, which are contested by many voluntary and activist organisations and local elected officials. Many Roma living in camps were given the Obligation de Quitter le Territoire Français (OQFT; Order to Leave the French Territory) and this was followed by collective 'voluntary returns' by plane or bus organised by the IOM – meanwhile the police destroyed their camps.

Generally, Roma returned to France after a short stay in their home country (Nacu 2011: 138). After 2007, France devised a complex procedure of 'humanitarian' returns that include €300 grants and capture of biometric data in the Oscar25 database to prevent multiple applications and 'abuse' of financial assistance (Carrera and Faure Atger 2011: 5). Since the summer of 2010, a range of other decrees have consolidated the security status of Roma as described by articles L 121-4-1, L. 511-3-10 and finally L. 511.3.1 20, implemented on 18 June 2011. These three laws clarify the conditions under which a citizen from a Member State of the EU could be given an OQTF – basically, if he/she has not been granted a right of residence for up to three months and especially if he/she has become a 'liability' to the French state; if he/she has abused his/her rights and finally if he/she constitutes a threat to the fundamental order of the French nation. A year after Sarkozy's Grenoble speech, the policies put in place by the French government had led to increasing pressure on Roma in the form of deportations, the insalubriousness and overpopulation of camps, loss of personal belongings and official documents, loss of income, and health problems. Migrants' connections with mainstream society are numerous and outsiders visit camps frequently, though their status in France remains extremely marginalised (Nacu 2011: 141). One of the main NGOs (non-governmental organisations) involved in assisting Roma is Médecins du Monde, which regularly warns of the extreme poverty, deteriorating health conditions and increasing harassment of Roma by the police (e.g. Médecins du Monde 2004).

State, Regional and Party Politics

A great deal of (orchestrated) confusion and tension characterises the Roma crisis, illustrating the 'essentially contested' nature of security. The confusion resonates with French public discourse and among a population already prejudiced against Roma. French popular attitudes equate the Roma with Gypsies and, thus, a past they do not wish to relive. Because public memory is an important symbol of belonging in European societies, the lack of Member State endorsement of Roma Holocaust commemoration constitutes a refusal of national belonging (Gay y Blasco 2008: 300). The place they occupy in French political imaginations is therefore characterised by ambiguities, fears and invisibility. The debate over the Roma crisis has been constructed around a confused amalgam of populations who share little – Gypsies, *gens du voyage*, *gitans*, *Manouches* and migrants. This kind of confusion is also found in the discourse on securitisation, but this presents the opportunity to direct policies against different categories of French citizens such as *gens du voyage* as illustrated by President Sarkozy's speech to the Senate on 15 December 2003: 'Nomads, *gens du voyage*, Roma, never mind the denominations, what matters is that the local associations tell me that the situation has become unbearable' (*Libération*, 26 July 2010).

Sarkozy's rhetoric echoed in public discourse. In an article published on 26 July 2010, a group of intellectuals summarised the issues. There was a deliberate attempt to overgeneralise the conduct of *gens du voyage* by taking the Saint-Aignan events as symptomatic of a deeper social integration crisis; an attempt to explain the incident by denouncing the nomadic nature of the *gens du voyage*; and comparisons were drawn with (generally sedentary) Roma. Yet, what both groups do have in common is a dependency on the Besson Law, issued in July 2000 by the Jospin government, which obliged communes of more than 5000 inhabitants to provide a site for *gens du voyage*. This law was later relaxed and public funds were withdrawn, which halted the creation and maintenance of these sites by local authorities, thus increasing the pressure to house Roma in extant urban sites. Importantly, there are clear differences between the use of these sites by Roma and *gens du voyage*, which correspond to different spaces and specific concerns. *Gens du voyage* have a long history of semi-nomadism and they have to declare their itinerary in keeping with the law of 1969 on circulation, whereas Roma are not French citizens but European citizens from Eastern Europe who are entitled to freedom of movement, or Kosovars entitled to seek asylum. These groups do not speak the same language and do not share the same ethnic identity. To be *voyageurs* does not necessarily mean that you belong to an ethnic group. To be Roma does not, in turn, imply a specific lifestyle or a specific economic activity. According to Nacu (2011: 142):

> Struggles over the sociology of the Roma group are also a way of framing the Roma issue: for example municipalities who do not want to accept the Roma would tend to define them as 'nomads' whereas others who developed resettlement projects point to the fact that the Roma have been settled for centuries in eastern Europe and that they are simply migrants in search of a better life.

Coterminous with the semantic confusion, the French government further confused the debate by issuing data representing expulsions and voluntary repatriations as well as crimes committed by Roma. France Inter broadcast the number of evictions and evacuations on an almost daily basis. On 20 August 2010, for example, Brice Hortefeux and Luc Besson announced 51 camp closures, 86 evacuations from these camps and the return of 139 Roma to Romania and Bulgaria. However, the Minister of the Interior refused to identify the location of these camps or specify the numbers of individuals affected by repatriation. Various newspapers engaged with the controversy over the numbers involved, contributing to the performative and orchestrated construction of the 'essential crisis'. A few journalists did attempt to gain access to the local prefectures to check the exact numbers of expulsions, but their attempts sparked more public controversy. For example, out of 51 camp closures announced, *Le Monde* journalist, Marion Solety, was able to locate only 13 – her article challenged readers to consider government efficacy.

Similar confusion arises with Hortefeux's labelling of some Romanian migrants as '*la délinquance Roumaine*' – Romanian criminality. In September 2009, the Minister of the Interior claimed that Roma criminality had shot up by 259 per cent over a period of 18 months. These data are unverifiable and show only weak connections to informed sources and legal evidence. Nonetheless, numerous opinion polls indicate that much of the French population equates Roma with threats (Commission Nationale Consultative des Droits de l'Homme 2008).

Policies put in place by the French government have exacerbated the already fragile situation of Roma. NGOs such as Médecins du Monde regularly denounce the politics of expulsions, while Roma remain in a vulnerable position as the state, local and regional authorities pass responsibility from one to the other. Indeed, Nacu (2011: 3) argues that constant expulsions actually transform Roma into 'nomads'. A year after the beginning of the evacuations, Médecins du Monde warned against the potential for impoverishment and victimisation. Since 1 March 2011 Roma require an Aide Médicale d'Etat (AME) in order to access health care and other services, which must be obtained through the payment of €30 and a lengthy bureaucratic process. This has also contributed to a decline in health and there has been a simultaneous decline in access to education. According to Médecins du Monde, 77 per cent of Roma they asked about this have not applied for the AME.

Since 2007, regions such as Paris, Marseille and Lille have been targeted especially in this 'essential crisis'. Divisions have emerged within the political landscape, with fault lines opening along interpretations of the republican model. For example, while some towns are hostile to Roma others, such as Aubervilliers, Saint-Denis, Bagnolet, Saint-Ouen and Montreuil (the old communist red belt around Paris), have chosen to address the situation by experimenting with 'Roma integration villages'. Yet as Legros (2011: 3) has argued, the initiatives of the 'Roma villages' are the products of our time, instruments of regulation seeking to re-establish the authority of public officials over their respective territories and over a poorly defined population (with the promise of freeing land for urban development).

In Sucy-en-Brie, members of the local trade unions and churchgoers mobilised in support of Roma. Even within left-wing circles, attitudes towards Roma have uncovered old political cleavages and produced new positions about republican models. In Lille, Martine Aubry's socialist administration developed policies to facilitate the integration of Roma in the decade after 2000, but she changed her tune, organising the expulsion of a camp prior to Sarkozy's Grenoble speech. François Rebsamen, another socialist party heavyweight, Senator and Mayor of Dijon, declared bluntly: 'The PS (Parti Socialiste) is not the League for the Rights of Man.' *Le Monde* commented that Rebsamen's remark showed that the Parti Socialiste was not engaged in 'moral denunciation' of Sarkozy's policies, but rather in 'a critique of the inefficiency of current policies'. The Roma crisis is thus situated at the crossroads of different (trans)national interests, issues of territorial management by different actors, and urban marginalisation and economic exploitation. It is also characterised by asymmetrical power relations.

Liberty, Equality, Fraternity?

The Roma 'question' does not exist a priori, but is the result of complex social interactions that are formed and informed by 'discourses and practices of ordinary citizens, social organisations and the so-called "civil" type and politico-administrative institutions' (Legros 2011: 43). Such complexity is routinely neglected in discussions of the performative nature of 'essential crisis', because too often the audience is ignored. For example, during an anti-expulsion conference in the Parisian *banlieue*, attended by an impressive list of invited intellectuals, Étienne Balibar explored the strange *double jeu* (double game) that characterised the media spectacle:

> On the one hand, the implementation of the expulsions was done in a spectacular fashion in that it was highly mediatised and showed a strong police force in the face of purported social malaise of the gypsies' camps, whereas, on the other hand, these events were by no means transparent, for if they were to show everything, then there would have been public outrage and the political trick would not have worked.[17]

Yet this performative national reification is embedded in multiple levels of governance and is played out against the backdrop of a romantic vision of France as a bastion of human rights especially since the Second War World. France is often imagined as the '*pays des droits de l'homme*' (home of the Rights of Man), but it transposes the Geneva Convention narrowly. Miriam Ticktin (2005) notes the proliferation of a security discourse and corresponding policing practices in France, where the law is suspended and the police act as sovereign within, as Sarkozy put it, the '*zones de non droit*' (lawless enclaves). Moreover, the Schengen Agreement has challenged the territorial and controlling aspects fundamental to France's republican ideology. Further, Ticktin (2005: 351) argues that the 1994 creation of a Commission (Direction Centrale Contre l'Immigration et pour la Lutte contre l'Emploi des Clandestins [DICCILEC]) in the Ministry of Interior with enormous police power over entry, residence and employment is an example of the increasingly harsh immigration policies. And, today, humanitarianism and immigration control are two dimensions within the same moral economy.

The government, in keeping with the French republican tradition, has refused to recognise the minority status of ethnic groups such as Roma (see Amiraux and Simon 2006). In this line of thinking 'equality before the law' takes precedence over the logic of minorities. The terminological confusion that I describe during the Roma crisis has the effect of clouding the possibility of minority recognition. In reality, of course, the expulsions target Roma while other groups have been the target of harsh legislation. Few media articles focus on the status of Roma in migratory terms, as asylum seekers, economic migrants or EU citizens. Instead, (in) securitisation abounds and includes references to the threats posed by alleged criminal activities such as the trafficking of women and children, while camps are closed and expulsions continue.

Jane Freedman (2009) argues that attempts to limit asylum-based immigration, which have constructed asylum seekers as 'false refugees' threatening French society, have led to policies that result in exclusion. Roma are not discussed in terms of asylum or economic migration, but are presented as a threat and the legitimate target of French policies and the police. Roma are here legally, but end up being treated as illegals or 'aliens'. The first of Sarkozy's laws (2003) adopted a two-pronged approach offsetting more restrictive immigration control measures with provisions to improve integration. According to Sally Marthaler (2008: 387), the objectives were to restrict illegal immigration, fixing a target of 25,000 deportations in 2006, and to reduce the number of asylum seekers. The 2006 Sarkozy Law (2006-991, 24 July 2006) was more selective on immigration, and new workers had to sign a 'Reception and Integration Contract', committing them to learn French and respect French values (Marthaler 2008: 390). From 2004 to 2006, France was the leading destination for asylum seekers in Europe, with 61,600 first-time applications in 2004 (Freedman 2009: 345). In 2005, the Office of the UN High Commissioner for Human Rights noted that France received the greatest number of asylum applications in Europe and praised its anti-discrimination measures, but sharply criticised the failure of the integration system and the treatment of asylum seekers (see Emery 2010: 124). It is noteworthy that the total number of persons granted refugee status in France has fallen continuously in the last decade in real terms and as a percentage of asylum claims received (OFPRA 2008). Human Rights Watch criticised a recent bill, discussed by the Senate on 8 February 2011, which seemed to establish that legally resident Roma might be deported on the presumption that they would seek social assistance, as 'posing a real risk' and 'weakening the rights of migrants and asylum seekers'. A report drafted by the Commission Nationale Consultative des Droits de l'Homme, *Etudes et propositions sur la situation des Roms et des gens du voyage en France*, the text of which was adopted by the Plenary Assembly on 7 February 2008, argues that in order to characterise Roma identity the metaphor of a mosaic is a useful one: 'Each piece has its own profile which makes sense only as a whole' (Commission Nationale Consultative des Droits de l'Homme, 2008). This confusion is also evident elsewhere in the report.

The report underlines the growing complexity of the law applicable to both *gens du voyage* and Roma. There is a new legal emphasis on their lack of residency and mobility – both of which are exacerbated by the constant waves of expulsions. In terms of human rights, the laws have to conform to the *champ d'application* of EU citizenship and free movement by prohibiting discrimination on grounds of race, ethnic social origin or membership of a national minority (Article 21 of the EU Charter). Yet this needs to be read in parallel with the Council Directive on the Principle of Equal Treatment between Persons Irrespective of Racial and Ethnic Origin. Similarly, the prohibitions in the Oscar25 database used by the French police contradict Article 8 of the Charter (Carrera and Faure Atger 2010: 8). The Commission Nationale Consultative des Droits de l'Homme report mentioned above denounced the discriminatory practices put in place under Sarkozy's administration. Eight French NGOs, including CCFD, Climade, FAST, GIST, *Hors la rue*, LDH, MRAP and *Collectif Romeurope*, registered a legal complaint on 30 July 2010, which was not followed up by the EU. Despite some voices being raised in different fora, the Roma situation has worsened.

According to Carrera and Faure Atger (2011), the current set of monitoring and enforcement mechanisms to ensure that EU Member States comply with European law are not satisfactory in the context of the Roma crisis. Yet nothing has been done to confront France over its treatment of Roma. On 31 August 2011, a special carriage of the RATP, the French underground transport system, was used to deport Roma and several NGOs responded vehemently to this by organising a protest on 29 November 2011 on the Paris RATP line supported by local associations such as the Collectif Roms et Bulgares de Bobigny or the Comité de soutien aux Roms de Noisy-le-Sec. These very isolated and localised reactions reflect the lack of a strong, organised political movement behind Roma, which is symptomatic of their political invisibility at European and global levels, and their lack of power. It is widely acknowledged that most Roma are unaware of these transnational organising structures or the rhetoric of ethno-political entrepreneurs (McGarry 2008: 464). Today, only a few activists, a lawyer, a millionaire, the Catholic Church, and a handful of politicians and local authorities have added their voice to Médecins du Monde in support of Roma.

Conclusions

The performance of the Roma 'essential' crisis cannot be limited to the reification of the nation in the face of migratory challenges. The complex and intricate nature of the performance is a multifaceted story of national essentialism within a multi-level governance process. Several crises are enacted and, through their complex and dialectical effects, they acquire a symbolic content and persuasive efficiency. They work off extant political and cultural traditions and emergent norms at European and international levels. Yet it is their effects in society that amplify and reify the perceptions of individuals in relation to their nation-state and within the context of economic crisis.

It is undeniable that the Roma crisis had a strong resonance among the French population, showcasing France's sovereign power in the face of the EU: a double game has become a necessity to ensure that France is still taken seriously in the world. This is illustrated by the reaction of Minister Eric Besson following the adoption of the 9 September 2010 European Parliament Resolution: 'France regrets the caricatures (of the Roma) and the attempt to instrumentalise its action, which increases the risks of stigmatising this population' (Carrera and Faure Atger 2010: 15). Corresponding to the double language of the French government concerning the Roma crisis, the EU also developed a double language in the process of recognising discrimination against Roma (Dediu 2007). The configuration of double languages contributed to the reification of the French nation claiming sovereignty through the fact that it will not take any lessons from Brussels. The Roma 'essential' crisis therefore becomes embedded in a wide constellation of meanings, representations and discourses carefully orchestrated by the French government to facilitate its construction as a zero sum game in which Roma are constructed as a nomadic yet invisible group within the French nation. Since the election of President François Hollande in 2012 the daily news media have been more generous towards Roma, but their treatment by the new administration has not shown any signs of improvement. According to the recent report published by Philippe Goosens, intolerance and danger still characterise the Roma situation in France (see AEDH 2012).

Notes

1. Academics and others face difficulties in their choice of terminology which intersect with issues of representation, authorship and effect (Gay y Blasco 2008: 298). Here, I adopt the terminology used by the various actors because it is an intrinsic part of my analysis. However, terms such as 'Roma' or 'Gypsies' remain the subject of much debate.

2. The song was recorded with French composer and interpreter Ralflo. See: www.youtube.com/watch?v=3Q-sSavYNpA (accessed 6 June 2013).

3. Using Nexus search covering the period from 14 September 2009 to 14 September 2011 and three major national newspapers from different political orientations, Le Monde, Libération and Le Figaro, I collated more than 293 articles and analysed them using critical discourse analysis as well as a close reading of the images and titles describing the Roma crisis. The research has also integrated a number of other documentary sources, together with analysis of relevant literature on France. Alongside a qualitative analytic approach to the data, content analysis was used to obtain a systematic overview of press debates. An ethnography of the press material was conducted linking representations to texts and other visual materials.

4. Gens du voyage refers to an ill-defined administrative category of people under French law who are itinerant within France. The Law of Circulation was defined in 1969 to replace the 1912 one on 'nomads'. They are not fully fledged citizens as their lack of a permanent residence curtails the right to vote, for example. Gens du voyage is often taken to also denote Manouches, a term for Sinti and Cinti partly nomadic persons who are also referred to under the broad and controversial label 'Gypsies'. Moreover, Gypsies or Manouches are often referred to as Roma, though they tend to refuse this categorisation. Throughout the crisis, a great deal of confusion in the French terminology around gens du voyage, Roms and Manouches has been displayed by the various protagonists from the political class, and especially Sarkozy and his ministers. The confusion has contributed to the social construction of Roma as a security and economic threat in territorial, social and national terms.

5. See *Libération*, 31 July 2010. Around 400,000 *gens du voyage* are French nationals.

6. While Roma of Eastern European origin or from Kosovo have been portrayed as living in camps, the *gens du voyage*, Gypsies and *gitans*, as French citizens, have some rights in relation to access to sites. The Besson Law still obliges towns of more than 5000 inhabitants to provide a site for *gens du voyage*. Only a small proportion of towns have implemented this law.

7. For an overview of Roma as a public issue see: http://www.viepublique.fr/chronologie/chronosthematiques/romes-gens-du- (accessed 10 November 2011).

8. See: http: //ukhumaorightsblog.com/2010/09/16/france-expulsion-of-roma-the-eu-law-persp (accessed 15 February 2011). The circular IOC/K/lo16329/K (Ministère de l'Intérieur, de l'Outre-mer et des collectivités territoriales), dated 5 August 2010, aimed to 'return' Roma as a priority. See: http: //www.romeurope.org

9. Estimates suggest that around 8000 Roma have been returned to various countries of origin since 30 August 2010.

10. Marthaler (2008) and Freedman (2009) provide reviews of Sarkozy's immigration policies.

11. For more discussion about the relevance of surveys of qualitative nature on Romani communities see Rughinis (2010).

12. As Guglielmo and Waters (2005) argue, many Roma communities reject the notion that they share a single identity. Wagner (2011: 16) notes that most of his interviewees primarily identify themselves as members of their national communities and only then as Roma. According to the Organisation for Security and Co-operation in Europe (OSCE) the Roma diaspora comprises an extremely heterogeneous set of communities speaking 50–100 dialects as well as their national language (Kovats 2002).

13. For an excellent overview of the shift from rhetoric to actions in policy making about Roma see Guglielmo and Waters's (2005) analysis of European policy reports.

14. See Poole (2010) on Scotland and Nordberg (2004) on Finland. See also the recent special issue of the *Journal of Ethnic and Migration Studies* (see Sigona and Vermeersch 2012).

15. According to Médecins du Monde, see: www.lesechos.fr/22/07/2011/LesEchos/20979-18-ECH_le-nombre-de-roms-en-france-n-a-pas-baisse-depuis-un-an.htm (accessed 6 May 2013).

16. Accessible professions include the building industry, catering and hospitality sector, agriculture, mechanics and industries of processes. See Commission Nationale Consultative des Droits de l'Homme (2008: 24).

17. See: http://ladialectique.wordpress.com/2010/09/13/les-roms-et-qui-dautre-anti-expulsion-conference-in-the-parisian-banlieue-with-jacques-ranciere-etienne-balibar-luc-boltanski-and-others/ (accessed 6 June 2013).

References

AEDH (Association Européenne pour la défense des Droits de l'Homme) (2012) *Roma People in Europe in the 21st Century: Violence, Exclusion, Insecurity* (AEDH: Brussels).

Amiraux, V. and Simon, P. (2006) '"There are no minorities here": cultures of scholarship and public debate on immigrants and integration in France', *International Journal of Comparative Sociology*, Vol. 47, No. 3–4, pp. 191–215.

Atanasoski, N. (2009) 'Roma rights on the world wide web', *European Journal of Cultural Studies*, Vol. 12, No. 2, pp. 205–218.

Bleich, E. (2008) 'From republican citizens to "young ethnics" in the "other France"? Race and identity in France and the United-States', *French Politics*, Vol. 6, pp. 166–177.

Brubaker, R. (1992) *Citizenship and Nationhood in France and Germany* (Cambridge, MA: Harvard University Press).

Butler, J. (1993) *Bodies that Matter: On the Discursive Limits of 'Sex'* (London: Routledge).

Carrera, S. and Faure Atger, A. (2010) '*L'Affaire des Roms*: a challenge to the EU's area of freedom, security and justice'. www.ceps.be/ceps/download/3746 (accessed 29 June 2012).

Commission Nationale Consultative des Droits de l'Homme (2008) *Études et propositions sur la situation des Roms et des gens du voyage en France*. Texte adopté en séance plénière, 7 February 2008. www.cncdh.fr/sites/default/files/08.02.07_etude_sur_la_situation_des_roms_et_des_gens_du_voyage_en_france.pdf (accessed February 2014).

Dediu, M. (2007) 'The European Union: a promoter of Roma diplomacy', in Nicolae, V. and Slavik, H. (eds) *Roma Diplomacy*, pp. 113–130 (New York: Debate Press).

Emery, M. (2010) 'Europe, immigration and the Sarkozian concept of fraternité', *French Cultural Studies*, Vol. 2, No. 12, pp. 115–129.

European Commission (2011) Communication from the Commission to the European Parliament, the Council, the European Economic and Social Committee and the Committee of the Regions: An EU Framework for National Roma Integration Strategies up to 2020. COM (5.4.2011) 173 final. http://ec.europa.eu/justice/policies/discrimination/docs/com_2011_173_en.pdf (accessed 26 February 2014).

Fassin, D. (ed.) (2010a) *Les Nouvelles Frontières de la société Française* (Paris: La Découverte).

Fassin, E. (2010b) 'Pourquoi les Roms?' www.mediapart.fr/club/blog/eric-fassin/120910/pourquoi-les-roms (accessed February 2014).

Favell, A. (1998) *Philosophies on Integration: Immigration and the Idea of Citizenship in France and Britain* (Basingstoke: Macmillan).

Feldman, G. (2005) 'Essential crisis: a performative approach to migrants, minorities and the European nation-state', *Anthropological Quarterly*, Vol. 78, No. 1, pp. 213–246.

Freedman, J. (2009) 'Mobilising against detention and deportation: collective actions against the detention and deportation of "failed" asylum seekers in France', *French Politics*, Vol. 7, No. 3–4, pp. 613–626.

Gay y Blasco, P. (2008) 'Picturing "Gypsies"', *Third Text*, Vol. 22, No. 3, pp. 297–303.

Guglielmo, R. and Waters, T.-W. (2005) 'Migrating towards minority status: shifting European policy towards Roma', *Journal of Common Market Studies*, Vol. 43, No. 4, pp. 763–786.

Gullestad, M. (2002) 'Invisible fences: egalitarianism, nationalism, and racism', *Journal of the Royal Anthropological Institute*, Vol. 8, No. 1, pp. 45–63.

Gupta, A. and Ferguson, J. (1997) 'Culture, power, and place: ethnography at the end of an era', in Gupta, A. and Ferguson, J. (eds) *Culture, Power, Place: Explorations in Critical Anthropology*, pp. 1–29 (Durham, NC: Duke University Press).

Jacobson, D. (1996) *Rights across Borders: Immigration and the Decline of Citizenship*. Baltimore, MD: Johns Hopkins University Press.

Jennings, J. (2000) 'Citizenship, republicanism and multiculturalism in contemporary France', *British Journal of Political Sciences*, Vol. 30, pp. 575–587.

Kovats, M. (2002) 'The European Roma question', Working Paper No. 31 (London: Royal Institute of International Affairs).

Legros, D. (2011) 'Roma villages or the reinvention of *cités de transit*.' www.l.metropolitiques.eu/Roma-Villages-or-the-Reinvention.html (accessed 19 November 2011).

Lofgren, O. (1989) 'The nationalization of culture', *Ethnologia Europaea*, Vol. 19, pp. 2–3.

Marthaler, S. (2008) 'Nicolas Sarkozy and the politics of French immigration policy', *Journal of European Public Policy*, Vol. 15, No. 3, pp. 382–397.

McGarry, A. (2008) 'Ethnic group identity and the Roma social movement: transnational organising structures of representation', *Nationalities Papers*, Vol. 36, No. 3, pp. 449–470.

Médecins du Monde (2004) *Rapport Annuel de la Mission Roms* (Paris: Médecins du Monde).

Nacu, A. (2011) 'The politics of Roma migration: framing identity struggles among Romanian and Bulgarian Roma in the Paris region', *Journal of Ethnic and Migration Studies*, Vol. 37, No. 1, pp. 135–150.

Nordberg, C. (2004) 'Legitimising immigration control: Romani asylum seekers in the Finnish debate', *Journal of Ethnic and Migration Studies*, Vol. 30, No. 4, pp. 523–539.

OFPRA – Office Français de protection des réfugiés et apatrides (2008) *Rapport d'activité 2008* (Montreuil: Ofpra). www.ofpra.gouv.fr/documents/RA_2008_Ofpra.pdf.

Poole, L. (2010) 'National action plans for social inclusion and A8 migrants: the case of Roma in Scotland', *Critical Social Policy*, Vol. 30, pp. 245–266.

Rughinis, C. (2010) 'The forest behind the bar charts: bridging quantitative and qualitative research on Roma Tsigani in contemporary Romania', *Patterns of Prejudice*, Vol. 44, No. 4, pp. 337–367.

Sassen, S. (1996) *Losing Control? Sovereignty in an Age of Globalization* (New York: Columbia University Press).

Sigona, N. and Vermeersch, P. (eds) (2012) *The Roma in the EU: Policies, Frames and Everyday*, special issue of *Journal of Ethnic and Migration Studies*, Vol. 38, No. 8, pp. 1189–1331.

Sobotka, E. (2007) 'Human rights and Roma policy formation in the Czech Republic, Slovakia and Poland', in Stauber, R. and Vago, R. (eds) *The Roma, A Minority in Europe*, pp. 135–161 (Budapest: Central European University Press).

Steiner, N. (2000) *Arguing about Asylum: The Complexity of Refugee Debates in Europe*. (New York: Saint Martin's Press).

Ticktin, M. (2005) 'Policing and humanitarianism in France: immigration and the turn to law as state of exception', *Interventions: A Journal of Postcolonial Studies*, Vol. 7, No. 3, pp. 347–368.

van Baar, H. (2011) 'Cultural policy and the governmentalization of Holocaust remembrance in Europe: Romani memory between denial and recognition', *International Journal of Cultural Policy*, Vol. 17, No. 1, pp. 1–17.

Wagner, F.-P. (2011) 'Citizenship as Europeanization, Europeanization as citizenship: challenges, opportunities and realities of a European post-national political space and the question of the integration of European Roma, Sinti and Traveller communities', paper presented at UACES (University Association for Contemporary European Studies) Conference, 5–8 September, Cambridge.

2

Video-surveillance and the Political Use of Discretionary Power in the Name of Security and Defence

Catarina Frois

This chapter discusses the two-stage process of public video-surveillance implementation in Portugal that started in 2005. The initial phase, from 2005 to 2010, was characterised by a lack of institutional cooperation and coordination that resulted in few measurable outcomes and no real evidence of the effectiveness of video-surveillance for crime reduction. From 2011 onwards, however, the newly elected government's ideological penchant for securitarian policies gave renewed impetus to public video-surveillance and drove a search for ways to overcome the initial obstacles and weak results. Instead of re-evaluating the project of public video-surveillance and re-evaluating the process of implementation, from 2011 onwards the Portuguese government chose to 'solve' the various problems by introducing changes to the law that in effect granted the Minister of Internal Affairs absolute executive powers. What might we learn from anthropological perspectives on the changes that occurred in the domain of CCTV uses in open streets in Portugal since 2011? This chapter seeks to answer this broad question.

In this article I will show how the decisions guiding the video-surveillance project draw substantially from pre-existing ideological beliefs. The strength of these beliefs seems to overwhelm rational efforts to re-evaluate the goals of the video-surveillance project, or even to analyse the available data collected during the life-course of the project. Simply stated, questions over the actual need for video-surveillance or the appropriateness of CCTV in Portugal, a country with a low crime rate, were brushed off as if they were irrelevant, illustrating unequivocally the political and ideological processes of naturalising 'security' expressed in the introduction to this volume. The 'expert' opinions of the different police forces on the usefulness of CCTV as a crime-fighting tool were muted and financial concerns over the installation and operation of such systems were drowned out by the loud ideological proclamations about the need for public video-surveillance for public security. The dominant concern was to follow a pre-established political course, that is, to promote and create conditions for the dissemination of CCTV throughout the country. This political course of action brushed aside the protection of civil rights, in this instance represented by the Data Protection Authority – from the outset branded as an 'enemy' – and even institutional bodies such as the High Judicial Court. This chapter describes the course of the video-surveillance project in Portugal in an effort to trace the contours of public debates and explore the power of security discourse.

Politics From Below

On 14 November 2012, the CGTP (Confederação Geral de Trabalhadores Portugueses, General Confederation of Portuguese Workers) called a general strike in Lisbon, which resulted in a massive demonstration in front of the house of parliament. Thousands of protesters were met by several dozen intervention police agents at the steps of São Bento Palace. The police displayed considerable restraint; they endured for hours the provocations launched at them by the more rowdy elements within the crowd. But as night fell on the Portuguese capital and the main bulk of demonstrators gradually drifted away, a younger crowd of more restless protesters remained. The atmosphere soon changed: individuals with covered faces appeared; the relatively slow rhythm of the afternoon's occasional outbursts and provocations gained momentum and grew in intensity.

What had started as a civic demonstration of discontent with the government's management of the current crisis – namely, the course of an austerity policy which to most people's minds was to blame for turning a short-term financial crisis into a long-term political and social one – quickly escalated into a riot. The police issued several warnings that the crowd should disperse, but their warnings were either ignored by those engaged in acts of provocation and pure vandalism, drowned in the cacophony, or went unheard by those caught in the midst of the growing chaos. Police representatives would later justify their action by reminding journalists of these warnings. However, when the intervention police charged down the steps of the parliament building into the crowd most onlookers seemed genuinely surprised. As typically happens in these situations, it was too late at this point to distinguish common demonstrators from the *agent provocateurs*, and the usual scenes of senseless brutality ensued. The media dutifully provided Portuguese audiences at home with a hideous live spectacle – people scrambling desperately to get out of the way of police batons, in some cases falling over each other in search of shelter inside the nearby doorways or shops; others destroying city property to cover a retreat down adjacent streets. Injuries were sustained by both civilians and the police agents. A few protesters were arrested and taken away in police vans for identification, leaving behind them a scene of burning waste containers, shattered car windows and a state of 'temporary siege'.

When demonstrations of this magnitude are held in a country struggling amid conditions of deep economic and financial hardship, where the general feeling among the majority of the population is one of growing disheartenment and disbelief in the ruling classes – as it becomes increasingly clear that the insistence on a political programme of unrelenting austerity is failing to deliver on its promise of the much-needed reversal of the economic cycle – episodes like this one are not unprecedented or even surprising. However, and notwithstanding the actuality of what occurred, it must be pointed out that, in the Portuguese context, this is the exception rather than the rule, and confrontations such as those seen on 14 November 2012 are still a rare phenomenon.

In fact, more significant than the plight of the demonstrators or the contours of police action, that day's events revealed above all else the overall rejection of such acts of violence by the majority of those present. But something equally relevant transpired on this occasion, as the media gave shape to a disturbing piece of news over the following days. It was reported that Public Security Police officials had somehow managed to gain access to unedited media footage of the demonstration within hours of the event, or in other words, without previously securing the necessary legal warrant granted by a judge, and used it to identify individuals involved in the confrontations. This was certainly not the first time, nor would it probably be the last, that police forces followed this kind of procedure, legally or otherwise. This time, however, the public squabble involving institutional parties as to who should be ultimately made responsible for having authorised such material to be viewed and physically taken from the offices of RTP (Rádio Televisão Portuguesa) was probably the only reason why the case received considerable attention. As a result, the news director of RTP was alleged to have given this authorisation on his own recognisance and would eventually be fired. Many perceived this to be a straightforward example of scapegoating. The case slowly died out on this obscure note, leaving the most important questions unanswered: on whose command did police forces request, view and collect the images in question and, more importantly, on what grounds and for what purposes did they do so?

But the case did serve to bring an illegal police intervention to public knowledge, making Portuguese citizens aware that security forces in their country resort to recorded images as a means to identify and control people who participate in public demonstrations, an activity that is rightfully curtailed by the Portuguese Constitution, which grants protection to citizens' images and privacy. As a rule, security forces cannot film demonstrations – either with fixed or mobile cameras – except in cases where there are reasonable grounds to fear a real threat to public order and safety. In those cases, the Minister of Internal Affairs, advised by the Public Security Police's highest representative, must request the Data Protection Authority to expedite an 'urgent' permission, meaning that a decision must be delivered within 42 hours. On that day, however, despite the tense social atmosphere already alluded to, and even though the demonstration had been scheduled several days before, demonstrators were already on the streets when the request for an urgent authorisation arrived at the Data Protection Authority.

This episode raises issues connected with matters of security that deserve our reflection and analysis, especially considering that terms such as 'emergency' and 'exception' seem to have recently made their way into the common vocabulary of current political discourse in Portugal. First of all, we are led to examine the grounds on which public recordings of personal images are made legitimate, as well as the circumstances and limits of this practice. Regarding the use of surveillance cameras in public areas, in this chapter I will ask whether video-surveillance is being rightfully used as an instrument for the 'protection of persons and goods' or if its scope is being extended into a more generalised form of control? Moreover, to what extent are the Data Protection Authority's monitoring and regulatory powers (powers granted by the Constitution) being curtailed in favour of ministerial discretionary power? In short, we are forced to ask: once the principles of discretionary power, arbitrariness and absence of regulation come into force, are citizen rights not being effectively diminished?

Warning! CCTV (May Not Be) in Operation

Just as with other surveillance technologies, video-surveillance cameras have over the last decades become an important 'instrument' used by police forces in their fight against crime. It is practically a worldwide phenomenon, and we find these devices throughout public and semi-public spaces in most major cities (see Doyle et al. 2011; Norris 2012). It is generalised to such an extent that it renders helpless any objections raised in the academic community over the implications of its use. Objections have been formulated about the threats public video-surveillance poses to basic civil rights and freedoms, for example the right to privacy, free circulation, image rights and the right not to be surveyed (see Aas 2007; Haggerty and Samatas 2010; Lyon 2007). Objections have also been raised over the clear and objective failure of public video-surveillance systems as effective tools in preventing and dissuading people from undertaking criminal activity. The prevailing argument, however, is that the common good must override individual rights (see Bigo and Tsoukala 2008; Balzacq and Carrera 2006; Maguire 2012). The Portuguese case is no exception in this historical moment marked by the uncritical use of CCTV footage by security forces. Indeed, especially since 2005, there have been several attempts to spread video-surveillance to open areas, in what effectively corresponds more to an ideological stance than a 'solution' required to address an actual problem of security in this country. As I point out elsewhere (see Frois 2013), arguments claiming that CCTV cameras actually serve their purpose of deterring and preventing crime are mostly fallacious, intended to appease fears regarding real or imagined crime and insecurity (see also Smith 2012). The relevant question here is not so much whether people actually feel safer in environments where 'CCTV is in operation', or even if there is a real cause for the existence of fear or insecurity (Aas 2007: 61). Rather, the real issue is determining whether CCTV is in fact the most suitable tool to provide for public safety, especially considering that Portugal is a country where the feelings of fear and insecurity are more directly connected with the current economic and political conjuncture than with problems of criminality which, as will be shown, are relatively insignificant.

Therefore, the main issue is a broad one that far exceeds the fears elicited by and sustained by the global political and security discourse – fear of crime, and fear of terrorism, as Daniel Goldstein (2010) critically points out. Above all, one sees the danger that security and fear may result in the inversion of a basic principle of law in any state – the presumption of innocence. The maxim 'nothing to hide/nothing to fear' has become a kind of advertising banner for the discretionary and unsanctioned use of technological surveillance methods that seek to legitimise surveillance practices even without the knowledge of their targets, that is, of the citizens ostensibly being 'protected' from real or imagined threats.

The process of public video-surveillance implementation in Portugal carried out between 2005 and 2010, which I have termed the 'first stage' (Frois 2011, 2013), amounted to a government programme that sought to provide a technologically based solution to the existing problems in the area of public security. The programme turned out to be highly controversial and was characterised by constant tensions between its main players, that is, the police forces, the Ministry of Internal Affairs, local authorities and the Data Protection Authority. In Portugal, the use of public video-surveillance systems was only legally sanctioned in 2005, with Law 1/2005, which granted police forces the exclusive use of these devices, while decreeing that the financial cost of any such systems was not to be included in the ministry's budget, or financed by those same police forces, but instead should be carried by local authorities.

In very broad terms, the implementation of public video-surveillance in Portugal during the first years was characterised, on the one hand, by constant tensions among the different institutions with an active role in the matter and, on the other hand, by the strategy's overall negligible effect on crime reduction, especially since, as security forces' officials themselves confided, crime rates were already so low to start with. In the course of several interviews with a number of police officials and city councillors, it became increasingly clear to me that most projects had not been requested on their initiative and that they had often disagreed with the projects. During interviews with representatives of the Municipal Civil Protection and councillors of some city councils, I was given to understand that these systems were not even considered a priority in the areas in question, and that the recovery of derelict buildings or incentives to bring new residents to deserted urban areas presented far more effective strategies, as they did not imply the costs of installation of such surveillance systems. Furthermore, they assumed that this was a strictly political process intended to respond to pressures from local shop owners whose businesses were particularly targeted by burglars.

Throughout this first stage, any project requesting the installation of public video-surveillance would have had to go through the following procedures: police forces or the city council had to make a formal submission indicating the exact spaces where a device was deemed necessary – described by law as places 'where the reasonable risk of crime occurrence warrants such preventive measures'; this submission was carried over to the Ministry of Internal Affairs for preliminary approval, and then sent to the Data Protection Authority, which was responsible for the instruction and verification of the request's compliance with the conditions stipulated under Law 1/2005, namely regarding the principles of proportionality and suitability, as well as the adequacy of the motives invoked and the actual situation in terms of registered crime rates in the area.

Out of the ten submissions requesting authorisation to implement this kind of video-surveillance system made between 2005 and 2010, only five were granted approval by the Data Protection Authority, and even from these five, only two were effectively operating during this period (see Frois 2013). The reasons for these outcomes are varied, but they result mostly from the failure to establish in each case the proportionality and suitability of an electronic surveillance system in view of the reasons invoked for its implementation and the types of crime registered in those areas, thus not fulfilling the basic principles. Clearly assuming an antagonistic stance, the Data Protection Authority was particularly meticulous in its scrutiny of the reasons cited in the requests to support video-surveillance. Special care was taken to ensure the correct balance between the different civic rights (privacy, freedom of circulation and right to image versus security, public order, property, etc.). The Data Protection Authority even suggested alternative solutions to combat the feelings of insecurity allegedly claimed by the populations and often used as the main argument to support public video-surveillance. During these first years, the Data Protection Authority's rulings were handed down with binding power, which ultimately meant that its decision was final, and that even projects which had secured approval in previous instances were dependent on the Data Protection Authority for a definite authorisation.

From the Public Security Police's point of view, the possibility of using video-surveillance to a certain extent went against the grain of a strategy of deep internal restructuring carried out by this institution over the last couple of decades, and which was based on the concepts of 'proximity policing' and working closely with local communities (Durão 2010). This police force acknowledged the low levels of crime in Portugal, which is mostly composed either of petty theft and crimes of opportunity or crimes of passion. Therefore, the effectiveness of the Public Security Police's interventions largely depends upon their strong presence in neighbourhoods and on the streets. It is clear to the Public Security Police, then, that the use of surveillance cameras might in fact undermine proximity policing, given that it may lead to diverting essential human resources from the streets by relocating officers behind desks to carry out monitoring work. What was worse, it seemed, was that they were being subjected to a change of strategy without any regard whatsoever for their opinion on the matter.

But while the Data Protection Authority overtly assumed its opposition, and over the years its rulings accordingly became increasingly critical and discordant with the policy of surveying citizens in public spaces, this resistance was not so openly expressed by the police forces and local politicians who drafted the successive projects. Between 2005 and 2010 (especially in 2009 when there was a huge peak in projects submitted for evaluation) the negative rulings delivered by the Data Protection Authority caused a big stir in political and institutional spheres, turning this entity into a kind of scapegoat for the slow progress of the government initiative. In other words, this independent entity's obstruction of projects which the Ministry of Internal Affairs classified as 'urgent and necessary' produced an unsustainable political situation.

Following years of detailed ethnographic research, I came to the view that the case of Oporto was the most illustrative example of why early video-surveillance projects were such an utter failure. In 2007, this city was granted authorisation to go ahead with a project for the installation of 15 surveillance cameras in its downtown historical district. Initially, there appeared to be substantial data to support the need for this new system. Some of the area's specific features had already been identified as a cause of concern in terms of its policing: its typically medieval topography of irregular, narrow and poorly lit alleyways; the intense tourism and nightlife activity and resulting periods of high population density; the high levels of alcohol consumption, which were at the root of most incidents of disorderly conduct among the customers who visited its many nightclubs. Even though the project requesting video-surveillance installation had initially been drafted by the Commercial Association for the Oporto Historical District, and only later supported by the city council – which meant that the initiative resulted more from the pressure of business lobbies than from any previous study carried out by the Public Security Police assessing the need for this kind of device – it received partial authorisation to function only during the night-time hours (and not 24 hours a day as had been requested), and without sound recording, which had also been asked for.

Almost two years passed from the beginning of the difficult and slow process of obtaining authorisation to setting up the cameras in the designated spots and putting in place the necessary logistics to the time when the monitoring system was finally fully operational. It should be pointed out that due to unforeseen technical problems the cameras were installed and operational for one whole year before they actually began recording due to the financial costs of solving technical problems. This aspect raises a relevant point: considering that the project had been the initiative of the Commercial Association, they were ultimately financially responsible for the working and maintenance of the system, and not the city council. This much was confided to me by the representative of Public Security Police officers, who told me moreover that the low crime numbers in that area, including in the period before the cameras' installation, would never have justified the project on any other basis, and that almost identical crime numbers had been registered between the end of 2009 and the end of 2010, the period during which the cameras had operated. Despite their collaboration with the project, the Public Security Police did not consider it a priority, with the argument that there were other more pressing needs: more human resources or better technical and material equipment. Video-surveillance furthermore represented the disruption of a decade-long effort to build closer ties with the community whose goal was to invert the old authoritarian and repressive image of police forces (Frois 2013).

But the most revealing episode in this whole case occurred when the renewal for the temporary authorisation was filed at the beginning of 2011. This request asked for an extension of monitoring period to 24 hours a day (even though crime rates did not warrant it) with the argument that this district was no longer a centre of night-time activity, due to the opening of a new area of bars in another part of the city, and thus, according to the

Commercial Association's President, the idea was to 'make the most' of the system already in place. However, the Data Protection Authority's ruling vetoed the initiative on the grounds that the existing data did not support this request, and aside from this nothing had been done to evaluate the positive and negative impact of video-surveillance in the area. Faced with this decision, the Commercial Association's President concluded that it 'was useless to have the cameras working', since they cost its members over €3000 per month in electricity bills. Thus, a few months later, and finding no objection from either the police or the city council (or ultimately from the Ministry of Internal Affairs for that matter), the cameras were turned off and the system ceased to operate.

Yet, on another level, the fact that public video-surveillance in Portugal was not advancing at a fast pace – that is, implemented nationwide throughout Portuguese cities – was interpreted by the political opposition of the time as a reflection of government laxness and careless application of the law. The discourse of centre-right parties alluded to a serious problem of insecurity in the country, of a widespread feeling of lack of safety among the population, especially in the big urban centres of Lisbon and Oporto. They claimed that criminality threatened one of the founding pillars of democratic life – freedom. However, this political (in)securitisation was at odds with the statistical data provided both by the Annual Internal Security Reports and Eurostat, data that show that Portugal may be described as one of the safest countries in Europe with comparatively low crime rates. Regardless of the evidence, the opposition maintained that the rulings given by the Data Protection Authority should no longer have binding power in these matters, rather the Data Protection Authority should become merely a consulting organ, responsible for delivering an opinion, but never a final ruling on the subject.

When Institutional Mechanisms Fail, and Democracy is Brought Into Question

After this 'first stage', the results of which can be described unequivocally as disappointing for those advocating video-surveillance, the years 2011 and 2013 proved to be a period of great complexity and contestation. I would argue that during this period it was essential that an overall assessment of the process and a return to the original motives behind the idea of introducing public video-surveillance in Portugal be carried out.

Was this measure as 'urgent and necessary' as the Ministry of Internal Affairs claimed in requests? Did criminality in Portugal justify this kind of technological solution, and did the financial underpinning for its operation exist? And, on another level, what could be learnt from the Data Protection Authority's warnings regarding the balance between civil rights and security demands?

At this point we should bear in mind that in June 2011 there was a change of government due to the collapse of José Sócrates' executive in the face of imminent national bankruptcy. Eventually, the International Monetary Fund (IMF), European Commission and the European Central Bank were asked to intervene. A new government took office, headed by Pedro Passos Coelho, which was formed from a coalition between the CDS and PSD parties (both right-wing in orientation).[1] During their time in opposition these parties were emphatically in favour of enforcing and strengthening security measures, despite the lack of existing data in support of such a position. The empowerment of a government that was clearly in favour of video-surveillance, coupled with the pressures arising from the economic and social crisis, created some expectation as to the changes (if any) that might occur.

By the end of 2011, less than six months after taking up office, the new Minister of Internal Affairs, Miguel Macedo, proposed an amendment to Law 1/2205 that subtly but significantly modified its general goals to encompass prevention of terrorist acts (terrorist acts did occur during the transitional period immediately following 25 April 1974 but are rare in Portuguese history and have had few important effects). However, one fundamental change was made to Law 1/2205: the Data Protection Authority's binding authority was removed. From this point on, final decisions were in the hands of the Minister of Internal Affairs who could apply the law as he saw fit. Several public institutions declared themselves openly against this new formulation and the role ascribed to the Data Protection Authority. The Minister of Internal Affairs, for his part, considered the stances adopted by institutions such as the High Judicial Council and the Superior Council for the Public Prosecution as inflammatory, prejudiced, and generally as 'political declarations' against the government. We cannot ignore the contradiction between the ministry's simultaneous, uncompromising defence of 'stronger security' and growing 'concentration of power' and authority in the hands of police forces (arguing for the need to pursue crime fighting more effectively), and the Annual Internal Security Reports, which have consistently demonstrated that security is not a major concern of citizens – those same citizens who, allegedly, are victims of said criminality – as well as a significant decrease in crime rates.

Consider, for example, that the 2012 Annual Internal Security Report states:

> According to the data included in the 78th Eurobarometer Report [...] published on December 2012, the item crime/insecurity appears on average in 6th place in the list of European citizens' major concerns on a national basis, as an answer to the question, 'Which are the two most important problems that need solving?' On an individual basis this item occupies the 10th place (with a 6% value). (RASI 2012: 51)

And, in fact, the first places are occupied by concerns with unemployment (48 per cent) and the general economic situation (37 per cent) respectively. This report also states that 'since the year 2008, the data for this item clearly shows a decreasing trend' and that 'the value registered in 2012 is the lowest average of the decade, coming close to the values registered in 2006 and 2007' (RASI 2012: 52). It should be emphasised that volume crime in Portugal is characterised mostly by petty theft crimes, which also suffered a decline of approximately 20 per cent.

In other words, specifically regarding the uses of public video-surveillance, the Minister of Internal Affairs defended the elimination of all obstacles to the strengthening of security performance. This amounted to ignoring previous rulings from relevant institutional entities, which pointed out the constitutional breaches implied by some of these political measures. These opinions, all opposed to the withdrawal of Data Protection Authority's binding power of decision, came from institutions that supposedly act as guarantors of the constitutionality of the laws being passed and enforced. The tone was distinctly negative, exposing the discretionary nature of political power in this area.

The Portuguese Bar Association claimed, for instance, that 'the bill confirms its careless quality, encouraging security forces' excessive and indiscriminate reliance on public video-surveillance, thus neglecting the protection of civil rights, freedoms and guarantees in an unacceptable and unconstitutional fashion', and furthermore stated that taking those powers away from the Data Protection Authority is unconstitutional under national, and even European law. Similar opinions were delivered by the Prosecutor General's Office and the Data Protection Authority itself. Nevertheless, these arguments were interpreted by government as being 'politically motivated manifestoes', purely intended to thwart government action. The problem this raises in terms of evaluating the action of entities whose sole mission it is to regulate the democratic system, is the government's disregard for their opinions on its conduct as soon as they cease to support its action. Based on the crime numbers and their impact (or lack thereof) on the ability to perform the task of maintaining public order, we find that we are not facing any kind of serious or exceptional situation, but instead a reformulation of laws and procedures in compliance with a more authoritarian political understanding of the relationship between the state and its citizens.

This realisation is confirmed in spheres other than the area of security, in what clearly amounts to a general political orientation, which has repeatedly brought into question the balance between rights and freedoms that characterise modern democratic political systems. The public demonstration and ensuing episodes described in this chapter's opening lines, are simply the culmination of a sequence of political decisions, justified by economic and financial circumstances, which have gradually widened the gap between the 'demands of our creditors' (as politicians like to say) and the expectations of citizens faced with a situation of social crisis the likes of which had not been seen in this country since the days of the 1974 April revolution. In what Ugo Mattei describes as 'emergency-based predatory capitalism', the state of emergency is:

a thick ideological layer [which] constructs as in the interest of everybody what is in fact a project of domination. ... In this project, the law serves a double purpose as at the same time a coercive and an ideological apparatus of domination. (2010: 89)

The new government in power since June/July 2001 has been described by some political commentators as one of the most authoritarian that this country has seen, mainly because of its fixation on playing the 'good student' role in relation to its European counterparts and international institutions during the initial period of economic assistance. It has intransigently followed a course of action that, in little more than three years, has set the country back to levels of poverty and social instability that had not been seen since the last years of the dictatorship. While being characterised as politically neoliberal, the fact is that it displays features – namely in terms of the attitude of intransigence with which it has managed this crisis and communicated its decisions to the general public – that have led it to be perceived as an extremely repressive and interventionist force.

In 2011, the Troika, a team that included members of the IMF, European Central Bank and European Commission, in collaboration with the recently elected centre-right Portuguese government, had the task of putting the country's domestic affairs in order and bringing to an end uncontrolled public spending. An inversion of political rhetoric suddenly articulated a discourse (both internally and internationally) that described the Portuguese nation and its citizens as irresponsible, unproductive and essentially as having lived the last decades well above their real economic means. They had apparently bought fancy cars, taken vacations in exotic places, become used to inflated salaries that did not have any correspondence to the country's financial means or to their own productive power. The welfare system – one of the democratic revolution's most cherished triumphs – was now portrayed as overly protective, leading citizens to become easily dependent on benefits to the point where they would rather be on the dole than actually working.

Mainly since 2011, Portugal has been undergoing a major social and economic situation of 'crisis' the most serious consequence of which has been the implementation of an external financial assistance programme: the country has experienced increasing rates of unemployment, low family income, a significant immigrant population, tax growth, increased cost of living, and an overwhelming feeling of economic and social instability and of impending collapse, as well as an increasing population of older people that puts pressure on a range of social services and a declining national population. These traits have been reflected most significantly in the permanent and widespread feeling of uncertainty and fear for the future that has progressively taken hold, not only of citizens' minds, but even of the institutions that sustain the so-called social contract in this country (political opposition, major national syndicate forces and other corporate groups, etc.). As Daniel Goldstein writes in connection with the implementation in Latin America of neoliberal policies supported by the IMF: 'Democratically elected governments that are unable to reconcile the security demands of transnational corporations and lenders with citizens' demands for rights face a crisis of legitimacy, as citizens question the loyalties and priorities of national law and policymakers' (2012: 17).

One of the major arguments behind the rhetoric that has dominated political life in Portugal since the start of the international financial intervention, has been the claim for the existence of a 'state of emergency' in order to justify the adoption of 'exceptional measures' needed to solve the current national crisis. Although scholars are very familiar with this kind of vocabulary, and authors such as Giorgio Agamben (2005) have discussed the state of exception and its implications at length, in my opinion when the Prime Minister or the Minister of Internal Affairs claims that 'Portugal is currently living an exceptional situation in its history', these statements are intended more to justify the enforcement of political measures which can cause an unfavourable reaction, than to actually give an accurate description of the state of the country (Fassin and Pandolfi 2010).

Actually, the present government has frequently evinced a total disagreement with the other institutions that form the basis for this state's rule of law, most notably with the Constitutional Court. It starts to become exceedingly clear that behind these economic measures lies an ideology whose like had not been seen in Portugal since the end of the 40-year dictatorship with the April revolution of 1974. In a certain sense, Portugal is not merely restructuring and adjusting its financial system, it is also intent on structuring its public morality, with a discourse that betokens parsimony, humbleness, and anything that may dissociate Portugal from the stereotypes of a southern, sun-drenched country of idleness, living at the expense of the hard-working methodical northern European countries.[2] What we have been witnessing in countries that are currently being intervened in throughout Europe at this moment, especially in Europe's southern region, is that the measures being applied are having such dramatic effects that they are actually bringing into question whether the principles of the democratic model – based on civil rights and freedoms – are not being bent by an ideological right-wing orientation.

Conclusions

Europe is currently living an extraordinary moment of change, especially the EU Member States, and among them even more so the countries that are either under external financial intervention, such as Ireland, Portugal and Greece, or struggling with extraordinary economic challenges, such as Spain, Italy or Cyprus. One of the distinguishing marks of this financial and economic moment in Portugal is the implementation of political measures that threaten to reverse indicators of development and modernisation that, until recently, had been considered evidence of this country's successful European integration and, by extension, of the success of the whole European project.

After four decades of authoritarian rule, Portugal's swift recovery from a situation of economic, social and political stagnation in the decades following the democratic revolution during the mid 1970s, was considered exemplary. Setting up a social state that ensured, among other things, universal access to health and education, and a sustainable social security system, was perhaps the most important conquest of democracy. The results, reflected in some of the indicators typically used to measure levels of development, were astounding. The current economic crisis is questioning not only the evolution and consolidation of these indicators, but also the very foundations of the underlying premises, namely the need to ensure the proper functioning of institutional entities whose sole mission is precisely the regulation and supervision of the system itself. One of the issues that this chapter has sought to focus on, also expressed in the introduction to this volume, is precisely the elasticity of the concept of security, and how often, whether in the media, political and popular discourse (and even in the academy), the quest for security (Frois 2013) is ignorant of citizens' needs and may even run counter to the functioning of the democratic state that it is allegedly trying to save.

Acknowledgements

This research was supported by the Foundation for Science and Technology Starting Grant IF/00699/2012 and by PEst-OE/SADG/UI4038/2014.

Notes

1. That is, the Partido Social Democrata (Social Democratic Party, PSD) and Centro Democrático Social (Social Democratic Centre, CDS).
2. As Ferguson points out regarding the implementation of structural reform plans in Africa:

    Scientific capitalism seeks to present itself as a non-moral order, in which neutral, technical principles of efficiency and pragmatism give 'correct' answers to public policy. Yet a whole set of moral premises are implicit in these technicizing arguments. [...] There seems to be a puritan undertone of austerity as punishment for past irresponsibility: having lived high on the hog for so long, say the stern bankers and economists [...] it is time for Africans to pay for their sins. (2006: 80)

References

Aas, K.F. (2007) *Globalization and Crime* (London: Sage).

Agamben, G. (2005) *State of Exception* (Chicago: University of Chicago Press).

Balzacq, T. and Carrera, S. (2006) *Security versus Freedom? A Challenge for Europe's Future* (New York: Routledge).

Bigo, D. and Tsoukala, A. (eds) (2008) *Terror, Insecurity and Liberty: Illiberal Practices of Liberal Regimes after 9/11* (New York: Routledge).

Doyle, A., Lippert, R. and Lyon, D. (eds) (2011) *Eyes Everywhere: The Global Growth of Camera Surveillance* (New York: Routledge).

Durão, S. (2010) 'The social production of street patrol knowledge: studying Lisbon's police stations', in Cools, M., De Kimpe, S., Dornaels, A., Easton, M., Enhus, E., Ponsaers, P. et al. (eds) *Police, Policing, Policy and the City in Europe*, pp. 79–112 (The Hague: Eleven International Publishing).

Fassin, D. and Pandolfi, M. (eds) (2010) *Contemporary States of Emergency: The Politics of Military and Humanitarian Intervention* (New York: Zone Books).

Ferguson, J. (2006) *Global Shadows: Africa in the Neoliberal Order* (Durham, NC: Duke University Press).

Frois, C. (2011) 'Video surveillance in Portugal: political rhetoric at the centre of a technological project', *Social Analysis*, Vol. 55, No. 3, pp. 35–53.

—— (2013) *Peripheral Vision: Politics, Technology and Surveillance* (Oxford: Berghan).

Goldstein, D. (2010) 'Towards a critical anthropology of security', *Current Anthropology*, Vol. 51, No. 4, pp. 487–499.

—— (2012) *Outlawed: Between Security and Rights in a Bolivian City* (Durham, NC: Duke University Press).

Haggerty, K. and Samatas, M. (eds) (2010) *Surveillance and Democracy* (New York: Routledge).

Lyon, D. (2007) *Surveillance Studies: An Overview* (Cambridge: Polity Press).

Maguire, M. (2012) 'Biopower, racialization and new security technology', *Social Identities*, Vol. 18, No. 5, pp. 36–52.

Mattei, U. (2010) 'Emergency-based predatory capitalism: the rule of law, alternative dispute resolution and development', in Fassin, D. and Pandolfi, M. (eds) *Contemporary States of Emergency: The Politics of Military and Humanitarian Intervention*, pp. 89–106 (New York: Zone Books).

Norris, C. (2012) 'There's no success like failure and failure's no success at all: some critical reflections on the global growth of CCTV surveillance', in Doyle, A., Lippert, R. and Lyon, D. (eds) *Eyes Everywhere: The Global Growth of Camera Surveillance*, pp. 23–45 (New York: Routledge).

RASI (Relatório Anual de Segurança Interna) (2012) Gabinete do Secretário-Geral do Sistema de Segurança Interna, Lisbon.

Smith, G. (2012) 'What goes up, must come down: on the moribundity of camera networks in the UK', in Doyle, A., Lippert, R. and Lyon, D. (eds) *Eyes Everywhere: The Global Growth of Camera Surveillance*, pp. 46–66 (New York: Routledge).

3

Location, Isolation and Disempowerment: The Swift Proliferation of Security Discourse among Policy Professionals

Greg Feldman

While public attention focuses on dramatic border apprehensions of undocumented migrants, the vast majority of the work of migration management is far more mundane, occurring in countless offices, meeting rooms and conferences. Banal policy practices, routine calculations and administrative assessments must transpire before the sadly photogenic moment at the border becomes possible. Thus, to comprehend the extraordinary in the world of security policy (relative to migration, in this case), we must ask how such a diversity of people from so many different backgrounds come to share an understanding of 'security' as a particular kind of problem requiring a particular kind of solution.[1] This phenomenon gives an unexpected twist to the otherwise liberatory slogan 'unity in diversity'.

I arrived at this question after noticing references to emptiness, boredom, or powerlessness by biometric experts, border officials, and other policy players working on a harmonised European Union (EU) migration policy. One project leader working for a well-known international organisation sighed with futility: 'To be honest ... there are a couple of terms in the migration world that I don't understand: circular migration; migration and development; global approach to migration' (Feldman 2012: 164). She later added, 'I'm not sure I want to take part in this. It's a cynical business. We completely rely on what the donors [EU Member States] want' (2012: 114). Likewise, a European Commission official who drafted legislation for biometric standards on EU passports confessed that 'all of this is done for .001 per cent of travellers. For me, it's something like [firing] a cannon to [sic] a fly. It's not my decision' (2012: 148). Maria, who processes the paperwork of refugee applicants and detained irregular migrants, wistfully explained that at work 'they are just statistics. They are not real people.... I just get them on a piece of paper. Just files and files and files.... Is there more I can do, more than what I am doing?' (Feldman 2013: 136). Two junior researchers at the European Migration Policy Organisation (EMPO, pseudonym), both of whom held Master's degrees in anthropology, became unsatisfied with scanning migration studies journals for 'policy relevant' information to be used in consultancy reports commissioned by client states. Policy requires essentialisation, abstraction and objectification of its 'target population'. Anthropology's ethical coordinates rest on the opposite: particularity, actualisation and subjecthood. These young anthropologists resented contributing to projects that silence others. One began working in an NGO (non-governmental organisation) that provided migrant services and another decided it was time to get her PhD.

Prompted by these episodes of disenchantment, this chapter seeks the conditions that enable the rapid proliferation of state security discourse across policy locations and through a variety of policy officials. Central to this project is a re-examination of the 'local' in which the particularity of place is taken as a question rather than a given. This chapter reserves the definition of 'local' to spaces in which the actors inhabiting it can define the purpose of their association according to their own particular perspectives. The multiple policy-making locations I encountered – dispersed in space-time and composed of myriad actors – did not adequately meet this definition. Even when they cooperate, policy players work as isolated individuals advancing rationalised administrative agendas. These activities showcase their technical prowess, but rob them of the opportunity to negotiate policy agendas according to their own ethical judgements. Their feelings of disenchantment, described above, are effects of this isolation, which disempowers them by denying them the opportunity to constitute their policy locations on their own negotiated terms. This chapter, consequently, seeks to understand how the absence of particularised locations allows for the proliferation of security policies, which are strikingly similar in form despite the variety of places in which they are crafted and of people who participate in the task.

Lacking such a particular location, the spatial void is filled by the state's own security discourse aimed at maintaining social equilibrium and replete with rationalised policy formulations. This situation requires either the forfeiture of the policy actor's own perspective or that actor's internalisation of state security discourse. Therefore, while anthropology has well noted the spatial complications of pinpointing the local in a globalised world (Wolf 1982; Appadurai 1996; Gupta and Ferguson 1997a, 1997b; Feldman 2011), this chapter further problematises the 'local' on the basis of the extent to which people can jointly constitute the spaces they inhabit on their own terms. To the extent that they cannot, standardisation of form increases along with the isolation, alienation, and instrumentalisation of those physically present in a given space.

I approach this task by ethnographically examining the consolidation of migration policy discourse among officials participating in the Managed Mediterranean Migration Project (3MP) led by EMPO from 2006 to 2009. This exercise suggests how a wider policy milieu not only objectifies policy targets, which is not a new conclusion, but also instrumentalises policy officials, which introduces a new and perhaps controversial perspective to political anthropology. I will discuss the modes through which this consolidation is achieved (1) in their face-to-face meetings and (2) through the tools through which they communicate when they are dispersed. The chapter then discusses performativity theory and the often vaguely defined concept of 'agency' to show that the latter does not necessarily invite the conclusion that actors transform social relations simply because they instantiate those relations through their *in situ* acts. Finally, lacking particular locations in security policy circles, I draw on Michel Foucault's subtle understanding of the *coup d'état* and Hannah Arendt's perspective on violence, disempowerment and isolation to outline how violence conducted in the name of state security objectifies the policy target, instrumentalises the policy official and facilitates the proliferation of security discourse. The point of this chapter is not to claim that people are mere automatons with no capacity for originality, agency or creativity. It is, however, to accept that technocratic society makes it very difficult to deploy those capacities in such way that they reconfigure political relations. If such a deployment is to occur, then we must surely grasp how it is so easily precluded.

Empty Rituals: The Exchange of the Teddy Bear

The 3MP project consisted of 37 partners including European participating states (EPs), African participating states (APs), and international organisations (see Feldman 2012: 72–77). It held five meetings in different European cities during 2007 and 2008 to design common policy guidelines among countries tied into clandestine trans-Mediterranean migration routes. Each meeting focused on a particular aspect of clandestine migration: trafficking and smuggling; reception and detention; return and readmission; and border management. EMPO created a secretariat to manage the project composed of three young, highly educated and ambitious professionals, all of whom worked on short-term contracts. In charge was the Programme Manager, a rising migration policy star with postgraduate education in law and business crime who was assisted by a Programme Officer with a new Master's degree from the Diplomatic Academy of Vienna. A Project Officer handled all of 3MP's written documents, a task that surely enhanced her PhD dissertation on immigrant integration in Europe.

Preliminary meetings in 2006 were contentious. North African delegates accused their European counterparts of neocolonialism, and argued that the EU wants them to solve its own migration problem. Things began to stabilise when a Lebanese participant, a retired United Nations High Commissioner for Refugees (UNHCR) official, convinced the North African delegates that they had more to gain by cooperating with the process than contending it. From that point, meetings acquired a predictable, standardised, and tedious format. Typically, each was co-chaired by one EP and one AP delegate. The co-chairs routinely opened meetings by thanking the host country 'for making it possible to bring us together here in ... [insert city name]'. Delegates were identified by their country, not their name, with their national flag positioned securely by the right hand at their place at the large rectangular meeting table. Four translators, tucked away in booths in a corner of the room, provided simultaneous interpretation between Arabic, French, and English.

The meetings consisted of text-filled PowerPoint presentations from selected delegates about their own interior ministry's practices regarding the meeting's theme. On the detention of illegal migrants, a delegate would describe their country's holding facilities, the detainees' daily routines, and the legal framework governing their detainment. The subsequent discussion period drew questions of comparison from other delegates. Often, African delegates would explain how much they would like to improve their practices to meet European standards, but, alas, they lack the funding and so the 'migration problem' will remain. For example, one delegate explained that her country can only detain illegal migrants in a windowless storage facility underneath a bridge where lighting and air circulation are artificially maintained. An Algerian delegate noted that his country lacks migration detention centres and so must keep detained migrants in regular prisons: 'We need more solidarity from European countries. We are doing their job. We are trying to prevent migration into Europe. We should have the means to do so.'

The main point of disagreement among the delegates – whether or not they were European or African – hinged on whether migration is an economic problem or a security problem. It usually found expression when discussing the difficulty of determining whether an irregular migrant is an economic migrant or a genuine asylum seeker fleeing political persecution. Take for example the following exchange:

UNHCR: The vast majority of people who enter Europe irregularly do not apply for asylum. Secondly, more than half of asylum seekers in Europe are given some kind of protection. Any assumption that the majority of asylum seekers are not genuine is disproved by the statistics. Morocco: I do not agree. In Morocco 99 per cent are economic migrants.... We need international cooperation 'upstream and downstream'. This should be one of the recommendations of the dialogue.... I support what our colleague from Frontex said ... these trafficking networks are very well equipped. If we neutralise immigrant networks, then we neutralise also drugs and arms networks and these are likely the same thing.

After the Q&A, the co-chairs thank the delegates for their 'stimulating interventions'.

EMPO's Project Officer endures three gruelling days taking notes and preparing a draft summary of the meeting discussions. Much of this work occurred in the dead of night. I arrived one morning for breakfast at the meeting hotel at 6: 30a.m. only to find her exiting the dining room to catch two hours of sleep before things began. At the intense last session, the co-chairs proceed through her draft summary while delegates suggested alternatives to the text.

Morocco: Why do [you] call it an informal meeting? We know it's formal.
Belgium: We are not formal delegates of our countries and we cannot bind our countries to implement this or that measure.
Morocco: This term 'informal' poses a certain problem. We are working in a clear format between the two banks of the Mediterranean.
Algeria: I think that the informal character principle was agreed five years ago. These principles are not binding. So, I do not agree with my Moroccan colleague.
3MP: Probably a good compromise is to not mention either 'formal' or 'informal'.

To transcend the tedium, each meeting closed with the current host handing a brown teddy bear over to the next meeting's host. At the 2007 meeting in The Hague, the hosts – in this case the EU's Law Enforcement Agency (Europol), not the Dutch delegation – had dressed the bear in a blue Europol T-shirt. The Europol delegate, flashing a cute smile, explained to new delegates that ever since their first 2006 meeting in Beirut they have passed the teddy bear from one host to the next, 'like an Olympic torch', in order to build 'team spirit'. These remarks drew blank stares from some and awkward laughter from others. The next meeting's host broke the confused moment by announcing that she was 'looking forward to working with our partners in a few months' time'.

The following weeks find the secretariat finalising the meeting's conclusions, then returning them to the delegates to get their ministries' approval. The team also created a secure website to post questionnaires about the meetings' discussions to receive more feedback. The Project Officer laboriously assembles the varied input from participating states into a set of final recommendations, which are then translated into English, French and Arabic. While the policy guidelines are not legally binding, as the Moroccan delegate implied, the work of the 3MP still illustrates the condensation of a common migration policy discourse that prioritises the economy and security of national populations as the ultimate objective.

Monotony, Security and Locality

The meeting protocols ossify a social pattern: destablising views are marginalised, communicative standards get institutionalised and rituals take on, if not affective powers, then at least the hegemony of bourgeois manners. The face-to-face rituals – from greetings to the passing on of the teddy bear – establish what Annelise Riles (2000) calls an epistemological condition for policy knowledge, and a discourse through which migration can be described as a particular kind of problem. Discussions never move beyond economy and security, regardless of who is speaking. It takes a tremendous amount of preconditioning to standardise a discourse among such a wide variety of people.

Thus the meeting sites do not constitute 'local' events per se because the delegates are not in a position to speak as particular subjects. 'Local' implies the historical particularity of practices among the people who jointly constitute a locale on terms they negotiate among themselves (Feldman 2011: 378–382, 2012: 188–193, 2013: 139–140). It thus implies originality of perspective and control of the meaning of the practices they perform. These policy delegates lack such control because their input is beholden to their home bureaucracies, which, in turn, are beholden to the mass politics of their home countries. They may creatively do their jobs, but they are not present as particular speaking subjects, resulting in policy meetings that have a predictably impersonal and monotonous air about them. (This situation likely explains why policy officials so often begin interviews by asking the ethnographer if s/he 'would like to know what I think or what I have to say?')

Thus, the term 'ritual' was used ironically. A ritual is a repeatable ceremony through which the participants jointly confer and negotiate the meaning of a significant event that the ritual marks. Hence, the ritual does not constrain agency, but rather agency is actualised through the ritual itself. This actualisation of the participants qua particular individuals is what makes it a local, particular event. In contrast, the 'ritual' of circulating the teddy bear appeared like a weak effort to conceal the lack of Olympic team spirit rather than signify its presence. It yields a homogenising effect so often seen in bourgeois politesse that tends to bore those consumed by it more so than animate them as unique individuals. Of course, disempowered technocrats are not zombies lacking worldly impact. Their activities have tremendous consequences, and they creatively find the means to achieve their ends. However, these facts do not render them empowered as particular people if 'empowered' is understood as joint action undertaken by people that generates an original outcome based on their own assessments of the situation they confront.

The I-MAP and the Online Glossary

Such standardisation of policy meetings greatly conditions face-to-face communication by impeding the participants from defining the point of their association for themselves. The matter carries on through the tools through which they see and speak about migration while working in isolation. Policy discourse proliferates through many devices. I focus here on a visual and linguistic device. 3MP's most ambitious project was the creation of the I-MAP, a web-based interactive map containing detailed migration policy information of the 3MP states. EMPO developed the I-MAP and the Odysseus Academic Network verifies the information it contains. It is designed for analysts, law enforcement officers, border officials and decision-makers. The European Commission (EC) as well as the governments of Cyprus, Switzerland, France, Italy, the Netherlands, Malta and Sweden funded its production (Feldman 2012: 70).

The I-MAP's restricted version features such information as participating states' migration statistics, detention policies, migration-related laws, migration-related development programmes, border security policies, airport information, and regional and local migration-related information. The public version shows oceans in deep blue and continents in green with countries outlined in black. The navigation bar allows the viewer to move in the four cardinal directions and zoom in on cities and towns. Hover the mouse over Accra, for example, and a caption appears noting that the distance to the Canary Islands is 4000 km by sea and 3000 going mainly overland. Hover over the lines illuminating clandestine migration routes and the entire group of associated routes flashes in bright gold. Individual routes in the group are colour-coded according to major/ minor land routes, sea routes and air routes (Feldman 2012: 70). The Programme Manager explained to me that the I-MAP:

> provides you with the latest figures of apprehension, smuggling networks, etc. It can provide briefing notes. If countries use the I-MAP for policy positions, then this helps in creating agreements between countries. It will probably bring the positions of the countries much closer.... It's a tool at the service of states. (Feldman 2012: 69)

At the 3MP summit meeting in Rome, the Programme Manager gave a spirited presentation on the I-MAP, which, he mentioned, now had the financial support of 'end users' (that is several participating states).

He stressed the importance of information exchange as the basis for cooperation. Many delegates expressed considerable interest, particularly those living on the EU's southern external border. One delegate enthusiastically expressed that the I-MAP 'will provide a platform for bringing us together ... beyond the technological aspects'. Another delegate candidly expressed her country's interests in its applications for intelligence analysis.

A west European delegate asked how it could be used while avoiding a negative police-state image. The EMPO Director-General remarked defensively:

> [Our position] is absolutely clear. We are engaged in visualising the information for those who use this I-MAP. We want to be close to the user side. This is the way to make sure the information is useful.... It's for us absolutely clear that we should accommodate this need for visualisation. (Feldman 2012: 71–72)

The Director-General's remarks asserted the priority of utilitarianism: that is, as long as one is a 'user', then nothing else matters. As if to say, 'We can't be responsible for what the "users" do with it; we are only providing a tool for the service of the state.' To prioritise the ethical question 'why', as the west European delegate arguably asked, over the utilitarian question 'how' breaks the flow of information because it separates the asker from the ethical order of the policy that s/he is questioning. Moreover, to the extent that the asker reaches a new assessment of that order, s/he can no longer be relied upon to participate in the policy processes in the same way that others reasonably expect. The asker of the 'how' question need not separate from that order and would remain a reliable colleague as s/he would undergo no change of perspective. S/he only seeks a more efficient means of implementation or new areas of application. 'Why' places the policy in ethical contention, 'how' only seeks technical improvement.

So, how does the I-MAP assist in the proliferation of migration policy discourse? Rather than command from above, it *interacts* with people and conveniently integrates into their daily routines (Feldman 2011: 388–389). The I-MAP standardises a policy outlook – literally a policy vision – and draws people into its constant improvement. This happens not through external imposition, but rather through convenience: log on, click an icon and download the relevant information. Technicians easily upload information into it; academics double check accuracy; and web designers create a simplified cartoon-like visual interface.

Geographically disconnected officials easily relate to each other through a shared representation of the migration 'problem', a representation that will proliferate as more people log on. Tools like the I-MAP encourage atomised officials to literally see the world of migration through the same overall lens and with the same factoids. This standardisation requires little face-to-face contact because it is maintained online, thus mediating communication among isolated technocrats. The migrants and the nation-states through which they traverse are knowable, understandable and thus manageable, at least in conceptual terms. One 3MP participant jokingly referred to the I-MAP as the 'crystal ball' (Feldman 2011: 383).

The system is not seamless, of course, but it is clearly moving towards greater convergence. And the words of Mitch Kapor, technology guru and philanthropist, directly apply: 'As a society, we're leaving the landscape and moving onto the map, without paying much attention to the process or the destination' (cited in Der Derian 1998: 261). In other words, the map no longer guides someone to a location in the empirical world, but rather it denies that world by representing it to the policy-maker in his/her own language: no engagement with the empirical necessary. I add here Arendt's (1968: 470–471) second of three conditions necessary for ideological thinking: the emancipation of thought from the empirical world of the senses so that ideology replaces a locally constituted 'common sense'.

This type of self-referentiality that appears in mapping for policy purposes becomes even clearer when considering the linguistic media through which migration policy discourse proliferates. The best example with respect to migration management in the EU is the *Asylum and Migration Glossary: A Tool for Better Comparability* produced by the European Migration Network (EMN). The glossary provides common definitions of asylum and migration policy terms, which are then used to formulate policy queries and research for EU Member States (European Migration Network 2010: 5). It was designed (1) to reduce the variability of meaning in the migration and asylum lexicon among the different countries; and (2) to be instantly accessible from any location in the EU.

Of course, not all English or French terms have an exact analogue in other European languages, so the EMN focused on terms already present in EU-level policy. As explained in the glossary,

one consideration in the discussion and development of terms was for them to be of practical use at EU level, meaning that whilst the definition of the term might not reflect exactly that at the national level, nevertheless it was sufficient to give at least the same broad meaning. (cited in Feldman 2012: 66–67)

The appearance of the word 'development' reveals that the glossary does not merely organise current terminology across the EU. Rather, it actively shapes language by standardising terminology (and so narrowing its actual range of meanings). The adjective 'broad' to describe meaning is deceptive, as it effectively means 'practical' from the standpoint of EU cooperation. If national meanings are not practical (that is, if they are idiosyncratic) then they will likely fall out of usage. Or, terms must be invented in national languages to meet EU needs. The official representing Estonia's National Contact Point (NCP) explained that:

> Asylum terms were difficult because Estonia has very little experience in the asylum field, for example words like 'refugee in orbit', 'refugee in transit', 'asylum shopping.' … For 'asylum shopping', our language experts came up with a new Estonian equivalent *'varjupaigaostlemine'* [literally: shopping for asylum at a store]. (Feldman 2012: 67)

But, the question remains: where do the terms in the EMN glossary come from? In what lived reality do they have a historically particular basis? The glossary's online version provides hyperlinks to let the reader connect to the source of a term's definition. For example, 'resident document' comes from Council Regulation (EC) 343/2003 and 'Country of Transit' is also found in the International Organisation for Migration (IOM) *Glossary on Migration* (cited in Feldman 2012: 67). The IOM's glossary, in turn, found its definitions in nearly 60 other legal briefs, EU agreements, UN treaties and international agreements of other kinds. Thus, the entire range of migration policy vocabulary is sewn into a myriad of other legal and policy documents, which themselves draw on each other. Ultimately, these definitions were written from the standpoint of the nation-state, an entity that, as every critical theorist at least since Marx has pointed out, has no ontological basis – nothing springs forth out of it *sui generis* – but only functions as a social abstraction concealing a configuration of highly unequal power relations. If the diversity of migrants in Europe were invited to write the glossary's definitions, then it would surely look very different.

Edward Said (1979: 20) addresses the power of mundane practices of representation with his notion of 'strategic formation'. This refers to 'the way … groups of texts, types of texts, even textual genres, acquire mass, density, and referential power among themselves and thereafter culture at large'. In the world of defence/security intellectuals, Carole Cohn (1987: 390) describes the similar notion of 'technostrategic' language, which describes phraseology that (1) limits the number of people capable of speaking it; (2) maintains distance from the world it actually describes through the heavy use of metaphor; and (3) only attains meaningful coherence by referencing itself. François Ewald (1991: 154) notes that this 'rigorous principle of self-referentiality [... provides] no recourse to any kind of external reference point'. Therefore, a standpoint from which to critique it is difficult to find. And so, technostrategic languages attain their own agency without the need of particular speaking human subjects, because their viability is not premised on the subjecthood of any particular person. Bureaucracy become 'auto-authoritative', as Ilana Feldman (2008: 15) shows in a different, historical context.

This self-referentiality plays a crucial role in preconditioning state effects by taking us to what Uli Linke (2009) calls the 'limits of empathy'. We reach this limit, she explains, when bodies become mere signs in a hermetically sealed language; they become 'self-referential and auto-iconic: emptied of meaning, emptied of symbolic content, and devoid of emotions' (2009: 181). Empathy fails with the erasure of the speaking subject's power of narration because this erasure removes the subject from the living world of negotiable meaning. The body, then, can be brutalised or neglected with no ethical consequence (for the anthropology of violence see also Taussig 1987; Daniel 1996; Sluka 2000; Das et al. 2001; Hinton 2002; Scheper-Hughes and Bourgois 2004; Robben 2005).

Yet this omnipresent self-referentiality personally affects many technocrats who are paid to keep its wheels turning. Many feel instrumentalised and disenfranchised in relation to their work, as described at the beginning of this chapter. The argument that people (bureaucrats or anyone else) can become instrumentalised, and have their own subjecthood denied, does not easily resonate with current anthropological assessments because, for good reason, we are wary of the costs of denying agency to the people whom we study (cf. Hull 2012: 259–260). However, we have not endowed concepts like 'subjecthood' or 'agency' with much analytical precision. As the term is conventionally used, 'agency' seems to mean any activity an individual undertakes that is not historically, naturally or structurally predetermined. This tacit definition, however, does not positively explain what agency actually is. To answer this question, we have often relied on performativity theory. It explains that a field of power relations – often mystified through such objectified referents, for example, the state or gender – is only materialised in, and depends upon, the situated acts that themselves constitute those relations. It follows that these relations (1) are not a priori determinative of what people do; and (2) that people can potentially redefine those relations in more equitable ways since they only exist in the moments that people actualise them.[2]

Two caveats follow, however. First, people can only 'potentially' redefine social relations if they manage to overcome the hegemonies that oppress them and, second, people must act in concert, not just in isolation, to establish their sovereignty as subjects negotiating from their particular perspectives. Therefore, performativity does not necessarily invite the interpretation that actors qualitatively transform their field of social relations simply because their actions are not predetermined. Performativity can accommodate individual creativity and the reproduction of unequal relations at the same time. Apart from theoretical reasoning, the bureaucratised state violence that transpired throughout the twentieth century, and largely characterised it, should provide sufficient warning that the bureaucrat's instrumentalisation is much more the rule than the exception. We can add to this example the rapid corporatisation of the post-Cold War world, which has not been overcome despite the impressive examples of resistance to it.

The Permanent coup d'état and Instrumentalisation in the Violence of State Security

In his careful study of bureaucracy and poverty reduction programs in India, Akhil Gupta (2012: 16) writes that more theorisation of violence is necessary than Foucault develops in his concept of biopower. Gupta reasons that biopower does not sufficiently address either implicit violence, such as the suffering of India's very poor, or, drawing on Achille Mbembe, explicit violence such as war, resistance and counter-terrorism. Likewise, in asking how well-intended poverty reduction programmes in India still leave untold millions exposed to death, he notes that Foucault's biopower concept, and also Giorgio Agamben's (1998) *homo sacer* concept, do not account for bureaucrats who are highly committed to improving the welfare of these programmes' recipients. Gupta's reading of these theorists is that they assume the bureaucrats' indifference or antagonism towards their policy targets. In contrast, he seeks an explanation of how well-intended development programmes generate arbitrary effects, insofar as some people benefit but many other potential recipients remain neglected. If bureaucracy is based on rational practices, then all recipients should benefit equally (Gupta 2012: 24). Though bypassing the empirical of why rationalized policy practices fail to benefit all of their recipients, I will take up Gupta's important theoretical question of whether biopolitics accounts for violence. Arguing that it does account for it, but not explicitly, I necessarily address Foucault's understanding of the *coup d'état* and Arendt's understanding of violence, isolation and disempowerment. This task will likewise show how the proliferation of security discourse works by undermining the potential particularity of a policy location.

First, however, we should clarify that whether modern sovereign practices destroy life itself or encourage it, and whether state actors have good or bad intentions are secondary issues from a strictly biopolitical perspective. Either way, the goal of biopolitics is the maintenance of species life itself according to abstract, rationalised procedures, not the empowerment of people as speaking subjects, an effect point that includes both policy recipients or policy executors. This goal may involve the elimination or neglect of certain categorically defined segments of the population. As such, Agamben does not essentially argue that the concentration camp is the pre-ordained destination of thanatopolitics, but only a possible one. Thanatopolitics is primarily concerned with desubjectification, of which exterminating bodies is one particular method, to achieve its main objective of eliminating the individual as a political actor. Slavoj Žižek pithily expresses how easily the outcome can slip between the destruction and encouragement of life itself – between good and bad effects – when he suggests that 'the ultimate image of the treatment of the "local population" as *Homo sacer* is that of the American war plane flying above Afghanistan – one is never sure what it will drop, bombs or food parcels' (2002: 94).[3]

Given biopower's ambidexterity, we can make use of Foucault's understanding of the *coup d'état* to show how biopolitics encourages implicit and explicit violence as a matter of mundane policy practice. Foucault is logically compelled to address the *coup d'état* simply because it is a blatant act of state violence conducted in the name of security and apparently violates smoothly operating biopolitical administration (theoretically, at least). He takes it up in *Security, Territory, Population* (2007) and, interestingly, he portrays the *coup d'état* as a mundane state practice in which implicit violence would be equally common as explicit violence. Foucault explains that we conventionally understand *coup d'état* as the intrusion of military force into a chaotic, lawless situation. The *coup d'état* seems to appear with the failure of law and *raison d'état* (reason of the state). However, law itself is not the *raison d'état* because *raison d'état* commands the laws. *Raison d'état* refers to what is necessary to preserve the republic: the equilibrium between its territory, jurisdiction and the population. This goal is pursued on the authority of reason itself as the mode through which that equilibrium is understood and maintained, that is, the art of government. Divorced from empirical reality, pure reason renders *raison d'état* entirely self-referential because nothing about it 'refers to anything other than the state itself' (Foucault 2007: 257). Given all this, the *coup d'état* takes on a more nuanced meaning. It does not intrude from the outside, but rather it appears when law is suspended to re-establish equilibrium (Foucault 2007: 261), or during what Agamben (1998) would call a 'state of exception'. The *coup d'état* is the prerogative of the *raison d'état* to take direct measures so that the state may save itself. It is the self-manifestation of the state through violence and outside of the realm of law (Foucault 2007: 263). As the state is ever ready to assert itself, Foucault concludes that *raison d'état* involves a permanent *coup d'état* (2007: 339).

However, if the law is already obeyed and *raison d'état* is working normally, then why bother to speak of a permanent *coup d'état*? Foucault does not explicitly answer this question, but one can be uncovered in his reasoning. Throughout his argument, he uses the term 'police' as understood in early seventeenth-century France. Police refers to 'the internal regulation of' rather than exercise of the royal's judicial authority. 'Police' here resembles the contemporary English word 'policy', which differs qualitatively from 'law'. While law establishes the boundary between the permissible and the forbidden, *raison d'état* is achieved positively through direct intervention into the population planned according to ongoing assessments of its economic productivity and social order, that is, of its (dis)equilibrium (Foucault 2007: 339–340). Foucault calls the permanent *coup d'état* a world of indefinite regulation, of permanent, continually renewed and increasingly detailed regulation (2007: 339–340). This sounds much like policy and administration in biopolitical society. Similar to the *coup d'état*, policy operates outside the realm of specific legal commandments. It thus becomes the mouthpiece of the *coup d'état* as it identifies imbalances in the social body and rectifies them through policy interventions that are not illegal per se but clearly do not originate in positive law.

If Foucault explains the mundane presence of the *coup d'état* in biopolitics, then Arendt demonstrates how it instrumentalises the state official. This effect leads to the standardisation of location and facilitates the proliferation of security discourse. Again, it is the systemic removal of subjects' particular voices that precludes their mutual constitution of the local and creates a void to be filled by this permanent *coup d'état* during the state's pursuit of equilibrium. First, violence appears in the absence of power, which Arendt argues is inherent in the capacity of people acting in concert, that is whenever people can assemble themselves as a public (1970: 44, 52). Outside of a public realm, individuals are isolated and powerless against the apparatuses that condition their lives. Hence, the term 'bureaucracy' effectively means 'rule by nobody' even if some individuals have more authority than others. Relying on expert management rather than direct deliberation among equals, bureaucracy achieves the disempowerment of everybody through isolation, making it difficult for its victims to resist its implicit or explicit violence, and difficult for its individual perpetrators to challenge this violence.

Second, Arendt defines violence by its instrumental character – meaning it literally transpires through instruments that are dispassionately used for any given end. For the state's purposes, it is deployed to restore or maintain equilibrium between territory, jurisdiction and population. It mediates between isolated actors who would otherwise engage each other directly and so constitute a public space between them.[4] Arendt adds that those who oppose violence do not find particular persons wielding its instruments (1970: 53), but rather people whom bureaucracy instru-mentalises. Hence, they see themselves as superfluous (Arendt 1968: 459) and exchange freedom of thought for the straitjacket of ideological reason (1968: 474). This situation helps us to understand the disenchantment experienced by more reflective policy officials. Their work asks them to deploy their technical capabilities, which require no engagement with others as speaking subjects, rather than their ethical assessments of their policy work, which inherently requires such engagement.[5] They can ask 'how' to improve efficiency, but not 'why' are we doing what we are doing. This latter question removes them from policy's own technical-ethical order so they may question its foundations. In the absence of the question 'why', security discourse is free from obstruction and proliferates through the myriad of isolated officials attending only to its technical success.

Uncannily, violence and security policy share three things in common: specifically, they thrive in the absence of power, which means in the absence of locally constituted polities due to systemic isolation; they are instrumentalist and only instrumentalist (the technical question 'how' displaces the ethical question 'why'); and, they degrade both their recipients and their operators by removing their voices – the former become objects and the latter mere instruments (which are also objects). State violence does not destroy the body per se, but rather it silences the individual as a particular speaking subject, an effect that the executioner suffers as well. Importantly, the structure of this comparison remains the same whether or not the policy intends to destroy a population or nurture it to life. In either case, politics, if understood as the act of people jointly constituting their polity, is reduced to administration.

Conclusion

If we are to understand the ease with which security discourse integrates the work of many different policy officials working in many different nation-states, then our understanding of locality-cum-agency must be further developed. I have argued that the particularity that we attribute to place depends upon the particularity of perspective that the people who inhabit it can bring to its constitution. Lacking that particularity, locations take on a much more standardised feel and the individuals who inhabit those locales become consumed with the rationalised tasks of security policy-making above all else. This standardisation and rationalisation, divorced from the messy, empirical world, creates the conditions for state violence and enables the homogenising effects so familiar to security practices. Biopolitics functions by reducing policy recipients to objects to be preserved, destroyed or neglected according to what is necessary to maintain equilibrium. Necessarily, biopolitics is conveyed more effectively through policy than through law, which, in its most horrific appearance, might explain why the Nazi regime took care to first strip Jews of their citizenship so that they lacked legal recourse to their persecution and could be dealt with more freely as a matter of security policy. Such situations demand that the officials and experts executing such a policy ultimately act upon abstract logics rather their own ethical assessments. Lacking the latter, location does not take on the particular character born of the particular people inhabiting it. Hence, Agamben (1998: 175) can conclude that the correspondent to a location without order – the concentration camp – is an order without location – the state of exception.

Acknowledgements

Of course, my first thanks go to those in field who made my research possible, although they must remain anonymous. I also extend my gratitude to the editors' own input and the questions and comments received during a presentation given at the Utrecht University's Department of Anthropology in June 2013. Field research was supported by a Standard Research Grant from Canada's Social Sciences and Humanities Research Council (grant file 410-2006-0109).

Notes

1. Scholars in other disciplines have recently drawn on anthropological methods and concepts to study routine bureaucratic practices pertaining to border control and immigrant detainment though in pursuit of questions different from the present chapter. See Zaiotti (2011) in political science, Hall (2012) in international relations and Mountz (2010) in geography. For mundane bureaucratic practices in anthropology more generally see Herzfeld (1992), Shore and Wright (1997), Shore (2000) and Shore et al. (2011).

2. Butler (1999) pioneered performativity theory through her work on iterability and citabilty. She develops Foucault's work to help resolve the structure/agency debates of the 1970s and 1980s (see Morris 1995: 571–574). While she focuses on the construction of gender identity, the form of her argument influenced critical security studies in International Relations (Campbell 1998; Weber 1998) and the anthropology of the state (see Das 2007; Feldman 2005). Drawing on Derrida, Caduff (2012: 341–342), defines 'iterability' as the ability of the sign to break from its original context and acquire new signification in a new context. Signs are thus never fully anchored in any particular context. Iterability, I think, conveys a mechanism through which a security apparatus proliferates, and so exemplifies creativity among scientists rather than their empowerment as understood in this chapter. Again, to successfully argue that structure does not determine action is not to equate agency with the joint constitution of political community among speaking subjects. Performativity is capable of explaining both the *activity* of duty-bound bureaucrats and scientists creatively doing their jobs and the joint political *action* required to establish a new polity on terms they negotiate themselves. The former, however, is far more common than the latter.

3. Foucault's well-cited observation on the modern atomic situation more fully illustrated the point: 'to expose a whole population to death [… is] the underside of the power to guarantee an individual's continued existence' (1978: 137).

4. Similarly, Allen Feldman explains early in his book *Formations of Violence* (1991: 7–9) that violence requires the conversion of the subject into an object or a 'sign'– an inert medium of communication between an array of actors and so 'instrumentalises' the body.

5. Arendt draws this distinction between thinking and cognition most fully in the *Life of the Mind* (1978). The former requires ethical assessments based on one's experience with others in the empirical world, while cognition involves deductive reasoning from pre-given premises and so can ignore the empirical world. See Feldman (2013) for an application of Arendt's work on action, thinking, and appearance to anthropological research.

References

Agamben, G. (1998) *Homo Sacer: Sovereign Power and Bare Life* (Stanford, CA: Stanford University Press).

Appadurai, A. (1996) *Modernity at Large: Cultural Dimension of Globalization* (Minneapolis: University of Minnesota Press).

Arendt, H. (1968) *The Origins of Totalitarianism* (New York: Harcourt).

—— (1970) *On Violence* (New York: Harcourt, Brace, and World).

—— (1978) *The Life of the Mind* (New York: Harcourt).

Butler, J. (1999) *Gender Trouble: Feminism and the Subversion of Identity*, 2nd edn (New York: Routledge).

Caduff, C. (2012) 'The semiotics of security: infectious disease research and the biopolitics of informational bodies in the United States', *Cultural Anthropology*, Vol. 27, pp. 333–357.

Campbell, D. (1998) *Writing Security: United States Foreign Policy and the Politics of Identity*, 2nd edn (Minneapolis: University of Minnesota Press).

Cohn, C. (1987) 'Sex and death in the rational world of defense intellectuals', *Signs*, Vol. 12, No. 4, pp. 687–718.

Daniel, E.V. (1996) *Charred Lullabies: Chapters in an Anthropography of Violence* (Princeton, NJ: Princeton University Press).

Das, V. (2007) *Life and Words: Violence and the Descent into the Ordinary* (Berkeley: University of California Press).

Das, V., Kleinman, A., Lock, M. and Reynolds, P. (eds) (2001) *Remaking a World: Violence, Social Suffering, and Recovery* (Berkeley: University of California Press).

Der Derian, J. (1998) 'All but war is simulation', in O'Tuathail, G. and Dalby, S. (eds) *Rethinking Geopolitics*, pp. 261–273, (London: Routledge).

European Migration Network (2010) *Asylum and Migration Glossary: A Tool for Better Comparability*. Brussels: European Commission.

Ewald, F. (1991) 'Norms, discipline, and the law', in Prost, R. (ed.) *Law and the Order of Culture*, pp. 138–161 (Berkeley: University of California Press).

Feldman, A. (1991) *Formations of Violence: The Narrative of the Body and Political Terror in Northern Ireland* (Chicago: University of Chicago Press).

Feldman, G. (2005) 'Essential crises: a performative approach to migrants, minorities, and the European nation-state', *Anthropological Quarterly*, Vol. 78, No. 1, pp. 213–246.

—— (2011) 'If ethnography is more than participant-observation, then relations are more than connections: the case for nonlocal ethnography in a world of apparatuses', *Anthropological Theory*, Vol. 11, No. 4,pp. 375–395.

—— (2012) *The Migration Apparatus: Security, Labor, and Policymaking in the European Union* (Stanford, CA: Stanford University Press).

—— (2013) 'The specific intellectual's pivotal position: action, compassion and thinking in administrative society, an Arendtian view', *Social Anthropology*, Vol. 21, No. 2, pp. 135–154.

Feldman, I. (2008) *Governing Gaza: Bureaucracy, Authority and the Work of Rule* (Durham, NC: Duke University Press).

Foucault, M. (1978) *The History of Sexuality: An Introduction*, vol. I (New York: Random House).

—— (2007) *Security, Territory, Population: Lectures at the Collège de France, 1977–78*, Senellart, M. (ed.), Burchell, G. (trans.) (New York: Palgrave Macmillan).

Gupta, A. (2012) *Red Tape: Bureaucracy, Structural Violence, and Poverty in India* (Durham, NC: Duke University Press.).

Gupta, A. and Ferguson, J. (eds) (1997a) *Anthropological Locations: Boundaries and Grounds of a Field Science* (Berkeley: University of California Press).

—— (1997b) *Culture, Power, Place: Explorations in Critical Anthropology* (Durham, NC: Duke University Press).

Hall, A. (2012) *Border Watch: Cultures of Immigration, Detention and Control* (London: Pluto Press).

Herzfeld, M. (1992) *The Social Production of Indifference: Exploring the Symbolic Roots of Western Bureaucracy* (London: Berg).

Hinton, A. (2002) *Genocide: An Anthropological Reader* (Malden, MA: Blackwell).

Hull, M. (2012) 'Documents and bureaucracy', *Annual Review of Anthropology*, Vol. 41, pp. 251–267.

Linke, U. (2009) 'The limits of empathy: emotional anaesthesia and the Museum of Corpses in post-Holocaust Germany', in Hinton, A.L. and O'Neill, K.L. (eds) *Genocide: Truth, Memory, and Representation*, pp. 147–191 (Durham. NC: Duke University Press).

Morris, R. (1995) 'All made up: performance theory and the new anthropology of sex and gender', *Annual Review of Anthropology*, Vol. 24, pp. 567–592.

Mountz, A. (2010) *Seeking Asylum: Human Smuggling and Bureaucracy at the Border* (Minneapolis: University of Minnesota Press).

Riles, A. (2000) *The Network Inside Out* (Ann Arbor: University of Michigan Press).

Robben, A.C.G.M. (2005) *Political Violence and Trauma in Argentina* (Philadelphia: University of Pennsylvania Press).

Said, E. (1979) *Orientalism*. New York: Vintage Books.

Scheper-Hughes, N. and Bourgois, P. (eds) (2004) *Violence in War and Peace: An Anthology* (Malden, MA: Blackwell).

Shore, C. (2000) *Building Europe: The Cultural Politics of European Integration* (London: Routledge).

Shore, C. and Wright, S. (1997) 'Policy: a new field of anthropology', in Shore, C. and Wright, S. (eds) *Anthropology of Policy: Critical Perspectives on Governance and Power*, pp. 3–39 (London: Routledge).

Shore, C., Wright, S. and Però, D. (2011) *Policy Worlds: Anthropology and the Analysis of Contemporary Power* (London: Berghahn).

Sluka, J. (ed.) (2000) *Death Squad: The Anthropology of State Terror* (Philadelphia: University of Pennsylvania Press).

Taussig, M. (1987) *Shamanism, Colonialism, and the Wild Man: A Study in Terror and Healing* (Chicago: University of Chicago Press).

Weber, C. (1998) 'Performative states', *Millennium: Journal of International Studies*, Vol. 27, No. 1, pp. 77–95.

Wolf, E. (1982) *Europe and the People without History* (Berkeley: University of California Press).

Zaiotti, R. (2011) *Cultures of Border Control: Schengen and the Evolution of European Frontiers* (Chicago: University of Chicago Press).

Žižek, S. (2002) *Welcome to the Desert of the Real* (London: Verso).

4

Compensating (In)Security: Anthropological Perspectives on Internal Security

Alexandra Schwell

'Nobody should feel safe!' This statement comes from an interview conducted in June 2010 with a high-ranking Viennese police officer. We talked about the so-called 'Compensatory Measures' that have been employed by the Vienna police since December 2007 to offset the security deficit that ostensibly accompanied the abolition of border controls with neighbouring countries in Eastern Europe. These measures, the officer told me, consist predominantly of random checks of 'aliens' without grounds for suspicion. Mr Raphael (pseudonym) was also at pains to refute any accusations that Viennese police conduct ethnic profiling, using features such as skin colour and ethnic origin as the sole grounds for suspicion (cf. Goodey 2006; see Republik Österreich 2009). He said it was important that the police do not create this impression and emphasised that he consistently reminded his officers of this, encouraging them to check 'white' Austrians alongside 'foreigners' and thereby ensuring the officers did not make themselves vulnerable to accusations of profiling. His instructions were clear: 'Check everyone! Nobody should feel safe!'

But what is the point of all these controls, checks and surveillance if not to make everybody feel safe? Whose security is being negotiated and traded? Mr Raphael's statement captures the essence of the practices, discourses and policies of internal security in Austria and beyond. He describes a universe of 'good and evil', of differing truths and shared fears. The population can only feel safe when the intended targets of the security measures no longer feel safe. This chapter analyses this '(in)securitisation' process through which socially disputed topics are rendered as security topics from an anthropological perspective.

Security denotes practices beyond the basic human need for protection and comfort in the realm of politics, policies and governmentality. Policies exert an influence on human beings in various ways, by categorising, normalising, educating, taxing, criminalising, healing (or not) and thereby excluding or including them. Policies exert an enormous influence on the options actors have to lead and organise their lives. Simultaneously, there is a certain irony in the fact that policies are apparently successful if they appear to be apolitical. This apparent neutrality and rationality need to be scrutinised: 'Thus, a key task for the anthropology of policy is to expose the political effects of allegedly neutral statements about reality' (Wedel et al. 2005: 37). My analysis follows the research programme of an 'Anthropology of Policy' as described in the contributions in Cris Shore and Susan Wright (1997a) and Shore et al. (2011). This programme is opening up new ways of understanding politics and policies from an anthropological point of view, methodologically and theoretically. Shore and Wright treat policies not as external forces or simply as texts; they argue: 'A policy finds expression through sequences of events; it creates new social and semantic spaces, new sets of relations, new political subjects and new webs of meaning' (2011: 1).

Here, I discuss various approaches used to analyse (in)security. I outline some of the main theoretical features of an anthropology of security and elaborate on them by drawing on my ethnographic material. An anthropological perspective allows for everyday practices to be seen in the light of large-scale macro contexts. Processes that affect whole societies, such as the Europeanisation of policies of internal security, do not take place in isolation, but have local and very practical effects on the level of social action, that in turn retroact on the super-local level. Together they constitute the research field of European internal security. The Compensatory Measures employed by the Vienna police mentioned above will be used as an example of this political and social construction of security. This example illustrates how the opening of the Schengen borders was instrumentalised to increase the police's remit in order to counteract a perceived deficit. Finally, the last section takes a look at the wider social consequences of this process of (in)securitisation.[1]

An Anthropology of Security

Since the attacks of 9/11, the imperative of security has seemed to dominate the way we think about the self and others (see Goldstein 2010b: 487).

Security, of course, is not a fundamentally good or bad thing. A very broad and general definition describes security as the absence of threat (Booth 1991: 319). It can be equated with comfort, a feeling of being at home; it allows for development and leeway. This kind of security certainly seems to be a basic human need. Furthermore, security implies a certain state of social order. According to Michel Foucault (2006: 20), there is a level of security that is perceived as ideal for the functioning of society, which simultaneously defines the 'boundaries of the acceptable'. A secure society is not only the ideal, but simultaneously the condition and also the means to achieve and maintain this order. Accordingly, Gert-Joachim Glaeßner (2002: 4) identifies four levels of meaning of the term 'security': (1) certainty, reliability, absence of danger; (2) security conferred by status and the conservation of social and political conditions; (3) the institutional arrangements to avert internal and external threats; and (4) the integrity of legal interests up to the point of a basic right to security. Depending on whether security is perceived as desirable and a basic need, or the instrumentalisation of insecurity comes into the focus of research, the relevant points of reference and context factors change respectively. Social patterns of interpretation and institutionalisation determine the meaning of security at a given time for a given group of actors. Hence, security cannot be objectified. It is a social construct based on certainties, emotions, trust and intimacy. No one can be indifferent when discussing security as it is in every respect an 'essentially contested concept' (Gallie 1956: passim). As is agued in the introduction to this volume, throughout its history the concept of security has been highly elusive and did not carry a fixed meaning. Yet often anthropological studies tended to treat security as a natural category rather than use it as an analytical category. Generally, the topic of security has not been at the centre of attention of cultural and social anthropology, yet there is a growing interest. Jutta Weldes et al. (1999) attempt to build an interdisciplinary bridge between cultural anthropology and Security Studies as practised in the US branch of International Relations. Mark Maguire (2009) scrutinises the use of biometric devices and techniques; and the contributions in Vida Bajc and Willem de Lint (2011) aim to analyse how private and public life are shaped by the 'meta-frame' of security and surveillance, to name but a few. Furthermore, many authors show that security has a different function and meaning in different contexts, such as Alexandra Kent (2006) with an example in Cambodia and Daniel Goldstein (2010b) in Bolivia. Nils Bubandt uses the term 'vernacular security' to emphasise local rootedness and context-dependency of security perceptions: '"Vernacular security" is an appropriate term for the analysis of different scales of creating imagined communities through a comparison of different but constantly interpenetrating political forms of management of threat and (un)certainty' (2005: 277). Thomas Hylland Eriksen et al. (2010) have a different perspective, asking how the concept of *human security*, which originated in the mid 1990s in the United Nations Development Programme (UNDP), can be successfully applied to anthropology.[2] Majid Tehranian (2004) scrutinises *cultural security* as a specific dimension of *human security* with regard to migration.

Hugh Gusterson (2004, 2007) in turn uses a rather military and state-centred understanding of security in his research on war, militarism and atomic power. Drawing upon Arjun Appadurai (1997), he introduces the concept of the *securityscape* and explicitly opposes anthropological approaches that leave out the state dimension when researching globalisation (Gusterson 2004). He describes a *securityscape* as 'asymmetrical distributions of weaponry, military force, and military-scientific resources among nation-states and the local and global imaginaries of identity, power, and vulnerability that accompany these distributions' (Gusterson 2004: 166). Although the *securityscape* concept has been widely used since, critics warn against the narrow focus on the role of the nation-state and demand for the inclusion of heterogeneous, hybrid and mutually linked actors, both state and non-state, private and public (Albro et al. 2012: 11). Accordingly, this chapter subscribes to this critique and views *securityscapes* as liminal spaces 'where the practices of everyday life are unstable and insecure and where bodies are subjected to routine surveillance and violence' (Wall and Monahan 2011: 240). Furthermore, with the increasing merging of internal and external security, police and the military, *securityscapes* should not be restricted solely to the military domain but should also include other forms of (in)securitisation.

The Concept of Security

Within the European branch of International Relations new security theories have developed in recent years that can be successfully adapted to be used in an anthropology of security (see Goldstein 2010a, 2010b). New theoretical approaches to security analysis within the field of International Relations explicitly dissociate themselves from the *Security* or *Strategic*

Studies of the Cold War, where a narrow-gauge military notion of security prevailed, limited to attack and defence in an armed conflict with another state. In the 1980s, with the development of the peace movement, environmental NGOs (non-governmental organisations) and the end of the Cold War, many authors called for security to be broadened in scope. These New Security Studies developed a social-constructivist concept of security nested between the two poles of militarily defined security, on the one hand, and security as everything people can worry about, on the other hand. Security was thus extended to the civil and social realm, transforming it from an objective fact into a consciously chosen practice. By declaring something to be a security topic, an actor legitimises the use of unusual and extreme means to fight this threat and to reach a higher aim – the main aim is survival (of citizens, the state, a nation, a company, a forest).

The original approach formulated by the so-called Copenhagen School concentrated its focus on the speech act that turns a topic into a security topic and thus creates a state of emergency where normal political rules are suspended (Buzan et al. 1998). Extraordinary threats call for extraordinary measures; their efficiency, however, is only of secondary importance. When the 'audience' in question (the public, voters, etc.) accepts and supports this *securitising move*, the securitisation was successful.[3] The *securitising actor* who announced both threat and remedy, obtains symbolic capital, resources, and legitimacy. Yet the Copenhagen School prefers the reverse, the so-called 'desecuritisation', when securitised topics are removed from the emergency level and reintegrated into normal political action. The Copenhagen School's model and the broadening of the classic concept of security have been criticised by many scholars of security, but they have also been successfully adapted and modified in a constructive way. An understanding of securitisation informed by praxeology, as pursued in this text, not only focuses on states of exception and spectacular measures but also includes the 'diffuse politics of little security nothings' (Huysmans 2011: 372). By this, Jef Huysmans means the practices, actions and devices that do not automatically have an additional meaning in the perception and production of security. They do, however, obtain a specific meaning in the context of the *securityscape*, such as programming algorithms, routine data collection and the unsympathetic gaze of the surveillance camera: 'Yet, these little security nothings are highly significant, since it is they rather than exceptional speech acts that create the securitizing process' (Huysmans 2011: 377). Therefore, I subscribe to Thierry Balzacq's definition of securitisation from a sociological perspective:

an articulated assemblage of practices whereby heuristic artefacts (metaphors, policy tools, image repertoires, analogies, stereotypes, emotions, etc.) are contextually mobilized by a securitizing actor, who works to prompt an audience to build a coherent network of implications (feelings, sensations, thoughts and institutions), about the critical vulnerability of a referent object, that concurs with the securitizing actor's reasons for choices and actions, by investing the referent subject with such an aura of unprecedented threatening complexion that a customized policy must be undertaken immediately to block its development. (2011: 3)

Cultural and social anthropology's specific contribution to the field of Security Studies lies in adding value both theoretically and practically: the discipline's claim to analyse local events as embedded within a wider (national and transnational) context makes it particularly suited to scrutinise questions of security that transcend the local level and need to be analysed reciprocally. An anthropological approach appreciates security as differently experienced and culturally imagined. Both the praxeological approach and the ethnographic methodology are particularly apt to analyse the dynamics of securitisation from an actor-centred perspective.

The Compensatory Measures of the Vienna Police

The Compensatory Measures (CMs) employed by the Viennese police serve as an example of various processes that can be grouped under the term 'securitisation'. The following analysis of CMs illustrates the potential of an anthropology of security: an extraordinary threat is identified by political and police actors who, with reference to an imagined audience, aim to enforce measures that at a first glance seem to address the issue, but at a second glance are not directly linked. The CMs are part of a *securityscape* in a wider sense, as a local expression of a transnational and de-territorialised 'landscape' of security experts, threat scenarios, control technologies and imaginations. As I will show in the following example, four factors are of great importance to an anthropologically informed approach: (1) the context; (2) the tools of securitisation; (3) the strategies and practices of the various actors; and (4) the temporal aspect of the securitisation process.

Compensatory Measures in Context

Mr Raphael is a high-ranking officer of the Federal Police Directorate in Vienna. He is responsible for the organisation of the CMs. He agreed to an extensive narrative interview and provided me with newspaper excerpts, PowerPoint presentations and other material. Mr Raphael began his career outside the police and accordingly claims to have a critical approach to the police service. The interview took place in a very friendly atmosphere, and I am grateful to Mr Raphael for his cooperation and support. The measures implemented by the police and border police relate to the so-called 'Schengen Compensatory Measures'. These encompass measures that were intended to compensate for the abolition of regular border controls between the Member States of the Schengen Area, which were no longer possible with the full implementation of the Schengen Agreement, as the internal borders can be crossed at any location. Following the logic of police and politicians, the abolition of border controls is equivalent to a loss in security: the national border's filtering function needs to be compensated for elsewhere, hence the introduction of 'compensatory' measures. These consist of various tools such as increased personnel at the external borders, harmonisation of visa policy, cross-border police cooperation, increased judicial cooperation and the Schengen Information System (SIS). The Schengen Implementation Agreement and the Schengen Borders Code have removed stationary border controls from Member States' borders, and identity checks in the countries themselves are subject to national legislation (Maurer and Kant 2008: 53).

This is also the case in Austria, where this broad definition of CMs has been narrowed to a very specific interpretation. The measures that are present in the media and public discourse are viewed almost exclusively as compensating for the controls at the Eastern European borders that were abolished in December 2007. It is considered important that any resemblance to border control is avoided. The Federal Ministry of Internal Affairs released the following statement:

> The border controls along the present internal borders are to be substituted by a multi-level alert system which identifies and filters suspicious crime, traffic and migration from the now uncontrolled cross-border traffic. This is then subjected to intense police checks. The geographical extent of this system is not as yet defined. It will take place

on main traffic routes that lead into urban areas. (Bundesministerium für Inneres n.d.: 1 [author's translation])

Both the function and meaning of CMs therefore only become clear in the context of the European security system. Security is, therefore, not an isolated speech act that only occurs when somebody says, 'Security'. Securitisation can only successfully take place within a congenial environment that facilitates the linking and decoding of context and references (cf. Stritzel 2007: 367). Securitisation is therefore the product of a historical process which is always emergent. It implies symbols that only have meaning for those who have the ability to read them. Accordingly, long forgotten dangers such as mad cow disease, the hole in the ozone layer and nuclear war make sense not because of their quantitative probability, but because of their meaning and reception within a specific historical context. Furthermore, processes of securitisation and the relevant actors can differ depending on the respective context or setting, from the sociological or bureaucratic to political or academic, for example (Salter 2008). One group might perceive something as a dramatic problem, while a second group might see it in a completely different light. This becomes especially apparent in the example of (irregular) migration: for some, migration is a natural part of internal security; for others, solely social issues such as the labour market and family policies play a role.

For an anthropological analysis, all of this implies that notions of 'the local' and 'the field' need to be reconceptualised. Policies have a wide scope connecting different actors, discourses and institutions together. They comply with various local conditions and translation processes; political practices are connected to wider contextual social, political and economic processes. Participant observation that focuses on the intrinsic logic of a spatially defined field does not satisfy this complexity; instead, protagonists of an anthropology of policy call for an alternative methodology which traces the links between various places, discourses and social groups that develop within the framework of a policy: '"Studying through" entails multi-site ethnographies which trace policy connections between different organisational and everyday worlds, even where actors in different sites do not know each other or share a moral universe' (Shore and Wright 1997b: 14; see also Feldman, this volume). This has strong implications regarding the choice of a field, since, as Wright (2011: 28) argues, the art of fieldwork consists of choosing sites for research that allow for an understanding of the political processes within the larger field of people, activities and institutions.

If we accept the assumption that, in an anthropology of policy, 'field' and 'site' are not to be equated (Shore and Wright 2011: 12), then the CMs of the Vienna police constitute a 'site' within the wider 'field' of European internal security policy. Hence, CMs can only be understood with reference to their context and history, from the former external Schengen border to the emergent European security architecture. Yet, the CMs have an inherent contradiction as they have to reject their point of reference – border control – since, as stated above, any resemblance to border control needs to be avoided. Furthermore, as this point of reference implies, the target group of the CMs is usually located on the other side of the border. The focus on 'suspicious migration' (see p. 89 above) implies that the CMs police 'clients' consist primarily of non-Austrians or, rather, the choice of clients is shaped by images of the threatening other. This is not an Austrian invention, but rather the result of an Orientalist (Said 1979) and often racist imagination, similar to the imagination of hostile non-European cultures that produces a 'dark vision of threats emanating from life itself' (see Introduction). This finds its expression for instance in the EU's 'blacklist' of countries requiring a visa. Condensed images of the threatening 'East' (see Wolff 1994) and the Balkans (see Todorova 1997) appear that draw upon the specific Austrian situation as a former colonial power in the Habsburg Empire that feels it has been placed under siege by the former crown lands (see Schwell 2012).

Compensatory Measures as Tools of Securitisation

Security imaginations and discourses work because they are translatable into specific political tools and instruments, into the 'policy tools of securitisation' (Balzacq 2008). This can take the form of laws, rules, regulations and databases, but also other tools that codify, regulate and invest human action with meaning. These tools are part of a specific *apparatus*, and they play a highly relevant role as they embody and objectify security practices. Simultaneously, they structure interactions and determine situations, they transport background knowledge regarding threat scenarios and facilitate problem solving: 'Security tools or instruments are the social devices through which professionals of in-security think about a threat. They contribute to the taken-for-grantedness of security practices' (Balzacq 2011: 16). CMs can be perceived as tools of securitisation, because they are not simply politically legitimised bureaucratic institutions in the realm of internal security policy, but the measures, practices and institutions themselves embody a claim to truth (cf. Foucault 1980: 131) and extrapolate it by reproducing the aura of legitimate state action.

In practice, there are three CMs police stations in Vienna which began operations on 21 December 2007, the day of the enlargement of the Schengen Area and the abolition of border controls. They divide the city into three surveillance areas. In addition there is the Operative Centre for Compensatory Measures in Wiener Neustadt. As the Minister of the Interior Mikl-Leitner declared: 'The "best of the best" are deployed here. They will be sent "to the trouble hotspots in the states"' (Amt der Niederösterreichischen Landesregierung 2011 [author's translation]). The emphasis on the quality of the personnel enhances the impression that the centre has a very important mission.

The CMs police stations work under the Department of Organisation and Operations of the Vienna Police. They deal with car theft, drugs and drug-related crime, weapons, forged documents, irregular migration and trafficking in human beings. The CMs police stations are not open to the public. They comprise a total of 75 officers, 50 per cent of whom are permanent staff, and 50 per cent seconded from the states. Most of them are former border guards. The CMs officers' fields of activity are: (1) stop-and-search activities in the greater Vienna area; (2) surveillance of the main transit routes; and (3) surveillance and control of international train traffic, train stations and train intersections. The latter also includes busy metro stations such as the Schwedenplatz. Furthermore, CMs officers participate in special operations and cooperate with other police units and stations when needed. Analysing securitisation via its tools, such as the Viennese CMs, sheds light on how political actors translate intentions into actions. Furthermore, it becomes apparent how a political tool is influenced by social processes. Such tools produce results that are often much more extensive than was originally intended (Balzacq 2008: 76). Accordingly, Shore and Wright (2011: 3) suggest that policies are viewed as 'actants' in the sense of the Actor-Network Theory. Tools of securitisation are decisive when it comes to linking the public to the 'truth' of security experts, as they endow codified knowledge with the aura of what is right, neutral and eternally valid. They both inform and form the actions of various groups of actors.

Actors and Security Practices

Security policies, security measures, laws and regulations are invented by actors, and they are put into practice by these very actors in interaction with other actors. Therefore, these securitising actors are central for an analysis of internal security policies. The CMs officers are an obvious and palpable part of this group, as they are in direct contact with the public. Mr Raphael emphasises the intended proactive nature of the CMs police stations: 'They have to find their work by themselves', not because of directives or after charges have been filed. They do not do investigative work, and they do not act as a result of investigative work. When they come across something, they pass it on to the State Office of Criminal Investigation (Landeskriminalamt). CMs police do not do a desk job: they are field officers. They wear plain clothes and drive unmarked vehicles, with only their badge as a mark of identification. Both the partial visibility and the element of surprise are important police tactics and play an important dramaturgical role for the staging of public efficiency, as will be explained below.

The commanding officer issues the orders; but beyond that the police officers are expected to be proactive. Raphael reports that the best way to find irregular migrants is to go to traffic junctions such as the Schwedenplatz. This provides for 'quantity' – one in five will definitely be 'illegal'. Yet 'quality' – that is, the arrest of a human trafficker – is preferred over 'quantity'. Other areas are better targets in the search for stolen goods and burglars. Raphael says he can tell if a squad is doing a good job if they are looking for the right crimes in the right places. The senior officers rely on the officers' professional ambition to ensure they are doing their job well 'as policemen'. Yet this kind of work inevitably fosters a certain dehumanising perspective that puts migrants into categories like 'quantitatively' and 'qualitatively' valuable.

The CMs officers thus resemble Michael Lipsky's (2010) 'street-level bureaucrats', who not only put policies into action but also produce and negotiate them in interaction with their 'clients'. Thereby the officers not only have specific imaginations and truths about threat scenarios and 'correct' actions, but they also disseminate them in public. The emphasis on the officers' own responsibility highlights in particular the practical aspects of the tools of securitisation, since, as anonymous representatives of the 'monopoly on legitimate use of force' (Weber 2005 [1921]: 39), they should act neutrally and impartially.

Yet the CMs police officers, commanders and senior officers are not the only relevant actors of the CMs. Just like the CMs, they themselves are embedded within the wider field of European internal security and do not act independently. This network consists of security politicians, members of security bureaucracies (ministries, police, judiciary, prisons, etc.), as well as private companies and organisations. Drawing upon Pierre Bourdieu, Didier Bigo locates these securitising actors within a 'security field', a social field where different actors compete for hegemony, resources and influence. Both actors and organisations belong to their respective social, cultural and political environment, and their specific (national) control culture and tradition, shaping their respective habitus (Bigo 2008: 14).

The actors base their credibility on the claim of possessing hidden and privileged knowledge about security threats that they get from sources that are only accessible to and 'readable' by the insider. Hence a strict boundary is drawn between the security expert, on the one hand, and the public and (unknowing) critics, on the other hand. Such professional knowledge exists within the field of security policy and professionals and transcends this security field, aiming to establish itself within wider society. The field produces a 'truth', to borrow conceptually from Foucault, the privileged knowledge of professional and political security actors, which ideally goes unquestioned by the public. It is perceived as legitimate precisely because it originates from experts in the field of security. The less the audience knows about a certain topic, which may, for example, be based on scientific-expert knowledge (nanotechnology) or intelligence (terrorism), the more it will be prone to dramatisation via confirmed and unconfirmed messages (see Vultee 2011: 84). The knowledge and certainties of outside observers are confirmed by the checks on people with dark skin colour at busy traffic junctions: after all, these illegals/drug dealers/criminals wouldn't be checked without good reason. Everyday technologies, practices and negotiations are used for securitisation. Institutions also compete within this security field, where power, resources, prestige and personal careers are at stake (Bigo 2002: 73). 'Extraordinary threats' are given lots of attention by the general public, but an analysis of the practices of security experts allows us to focus on bureaucratic, organisational and other everyday practices which normally go largely unnoticed by the population. Nevertheless, they produce and influence securitisation as much if not more than speech acts about 'states of emergency'.

Apart from the securitising actors of the security field, there are other actors who play important roles but who, in political science approaches, are often subsumed under the notion of the 'audience'. Yet, since Stuart Hall's (1993) ideas on coding and decoding were published, it has become widely accepted that the relationship between sender and recipient is not a one-way street, since a message can be interpreted by a recipient quite differently (and also subversively) than was initially intended by the sender. The same applies to the construction and maintenance of security. Thus, to understand why securitisation is successful (or not), the basic motives of actors in the fields of politics and practical security, as well as within other social fields, have to be taken into account. These social actors cope well outside the security field, but can nevertheless exert an influence, for example by way of voting, forming citizens' action committees or writing letters to newspaper editors.

Therefore, the strategies behind action, motives and intentions have to be included in an analysis that aims to scrutinise why these actors reject, support, promote or even demand a move towards securitisation. As I have shown elsewhere, these can extend beyond the security discourse and touch on other topics like economic welfare and the fear of social downward mobility (see Schwell 2010). Yet this is not to imply that these civil society actors have the same power as the securitising actors of the security field; although the former can subvert the original message and interpret it according to their own preferences, the security experts nevertheless have the authority to set the agenda.

The Staging and Materialisation of Security

CMs promote the use of the police's professional ambition and the 'police eye', that is the professionally trained expert eye of the police. According to Klockars (1980: 39), the police officer perceives his environment within an 'ecology of guilt' and 'reads' it in terms of potential criminals, victims and crime scenes. Moreover, the knowledge about security threats that is produced within the field is actively disseminated: the performative and publicly orientated aspect of the CMs becomes apparent when the media's share of the staging of security and control measures is taken into account.

Raphael tells an anecdote. A team from the Austrian public TV station ORF had planned a report about the CMs police stations. They had decided to film a typical workday of some officers at a Viennese train station.

When Raphael arrived with the TV team, his officers were already in place monitoring passengers. They had seen one man buy eight train tickets, which they considered to be a lot. The man walked towards a group of adults who were then instantly checked by the officers. It was discovered that they were 'illegal immigrants' without residency permits, and the man who bought the tickets their 'aider' and 'abettor'. The team from ORF was astonished and asked Raphael if it was prearranged! He in turn was proud of his officers for doing a good job.

This episode shows the absurdity of the insistence on 'controls without grounds for suspicion' as well as the role of the media in the staging of efficiency and the dissemination of knowledge about security threats. The media play a pre-eminent role in the securitisation of a topic. In particular, sensationalist and tabloid journalism display a tendency to dramatise events. They provide an interpretive framework where the threat imagined by police and actors in the fields of politics and security is disseminated without first having been filtered (see Vultee 2011). The Austrian tabloid media was very vocal about the waves of immigration and burglaries that were expected to happen following the Schengen enlargement in 2007. The impression was given in media reports and letters to newspaper editors that the Austrian population was terrified at the prospect of floods of criminal 'Eastern gangs' waiting to invade their country (see Schwell 2010).

Yet the subjects of this narrative are merely projected; they are not actors with a history, but are rather illegal aliens, Eastern gangs, fraudulent asylum seekers and drug dealers. Similarly, regarding the perceived threat to the USA posed by illegal immigration, Chavez (2008: 42) remarks: 'The Latino Threat Narrative is a social imaginary in which Latinos are "virtual characters"', whose real-life circumstances have little or nothing to do with the knowledge and the truths of the dominant society. This stems from the media coverage to a large extent.

On the other hand, the question remains as to whether the imagined population target group of the tabloid media, but also of populist politicians, is just a projection of these very actors. This imagined population also plays an important role in the case of the CMs, as it was a necessary element for their implementation. This in turn relates to the CMs' explicit reference to the abolition of border controls and the putative security deficit. Hence, Raphael indicates that the initial impetus to introduce the CMs grew from the need to set the population at ease. They make the population happy, and they are an efficient means to fight crime, he says.

This double function thus appears to be the most prominent feature of the CMs: Raphael emphasises that besides their reference to border controls, CMs are an effective means that could have been introduced much earlier. In response to my question as to whether the CMs are literally 'compensatory measures', he replied, 'No, they stand in their own right.' Apparently, the abolition of border controls was the right time and reason for their introduction, but he does not see a direct link with regard to their immediate necessity. Thus the Schengen enlargement offered a great opportunity to install undercover controls under the label of the CMs. A functional need was conjured to introduce measures which otherwise would have been debatable, and even questionable.

The importance of the link between efficiency and the staging of efficiency becomes particularly apparent when we compare the CMs with another popular measure employed by the Austrian police: the so-called 'special crackdowns'. These are particularly loved by the tabloid media. They consist of a roadblock and thorough check of every vehicle, flanked by a lot of flashing blue lights and at least one helicopter. The CMs senior officer does not think much of such missions, describing them as 'political publicity stunts'. Such massive operations, which take place without any relation to a particular event, only serve to allay the population's fears. Besides a few drunken drivers, he says, nobody of relevance is caught in such missions, particularly no one with a serious criminal record. The 'big fish' are informed about the road blockade so quickly, thanks to mobile phones and the internet, that they know how to avoid it.

Yet the difference between undercover and public operations is not as big as it first appears. The 'special crackdowns' and other high-publicity events are measured against success criteria that are not directly relevant to the police, such as the subjective feeling of being secure. Effectiveness is attained by low visibility. Being partially visible, the CMs fulfil a double function. The partial visibility in particular promotes acceptance and the allaying of the subjective feeling of being secure of an imagined target group, the population, as communicated by the media. From the police's point of view, the practical benefit is most important. On the one hand, the check is highly incalculable for the putative wrong-doer, and on the other hand those being checked feel and see its effects, and it portrays a message to outside observers, a signalling function: We are everywhere. We can intervene at any time. For some this is a promise, for others it is a threat. Nobody should feel safe. Everybody can feel safe.

The Temporal Aspect of Securitisation

In the meantime the CMs police stations have become permanent and do not appear to be provisional. Raphael says that neither a positive nor a negative link between crime rate and CMs has been observed, although the ministry keeps saying there is. Furthermore, 'compensation' implies a reaction to an 'exceptional state', and is in place until normality is restored. Yet this is not the case here as, over time, the CMs have become a natural part of police operations. This highlights the habitualisation effect inherent in every securitisation process. What seemed 'extraordinary' at first can soon become 'normal'. Accordingly, an analysis always has to bear in mind two dimensions: the duration of a securitisation and the 'entropy of the public imagination' (Salter 2008: 324). Hence, securitisation is not always followed by de-securitisation. More often a habitualisation effect occurs regarding the handling and the perception of an actual or diffuse threat and how it should be fought. The state of emergency quickly turns into daily routine that is questioned less and less. Actions are professional-ised to a high degree, institutionalised through repetition and transformed into rituals.

The CMs, however, are a constant reminder of the threat that allegedly still exists due to the abolition of the external Schengen border. This is one of the reasons why the CMs are an apt example for tools of securitisation. They embody a specific *apparatus* that expresses a certain imagined threat and frames themes and actors as security problems. Thereby public perception and public action regarding the handling of this security threat are directed along specific lines.

Othering: The Effects of (In)Security

I wish to conclude by throwing some light on the further effects of the process of Othering that result from security discourses and practices. They concern both the images of self and others in mainstream society and those of securitised and securitising actors. *Securitising actors*, such as the experts of the security field, including the CMs officers, always are an inseparable part of the field. The truths and certainties within the field produce certain effects that in turn develop specific routines and practices. The officers' habitus is shaped by their position and their organisation's position within the field as well as by the relations with other actors in the field. Furthermore, actors are not only active in one single field. As Bourdieu (1996) has shown, the thinking of political actors is structured by the fact that they are partaking in the political field and its *illusio*. This is not necessarily to imply that political actors fully believe in the stories and myths they disseminate about migrants, Islamists etc.:

> Nonetheless, they cannot call into question those myths about state, about the integrity of the people, because the myths are the way they frame their everyday explanation of the political and social world and the way they see their own struggles and values. Even the most cynical among them do not have another framework in which to speak about the state and security. (Bigo 2002: 69)

Furthermore, the security measures have strong repercussions in the political field which legitimises and reproduces the 'regime of truth' as they are translated into political programmes, statements, laws and regulations.

Moreover, processes of securitisation always have an impact on the societies in which they take place. This goes beyond the acute threat and the fight against it. Habitualisation, naturalisation and institutionalisation mean that security measures are increasingly less questioned, and become integrated into everyday life. When more and more parts of society are regarded as suspect, the state of emergency increasingly becomes the routine. The cost–benefit ratio of security measures is scrutinised less and less and they become ends in themselves.

Finally, habitualisation is followed by an internalisation of the rules. These are set in place by the security measures and demand obedience – securitisation as governmental practice (Pram Gad and Lund Petersen 2011: 319). Technical means, like video-surveillance, are apt to fundamentally change the perception of everyday life, even (or particularly) when they are not present, for example turning a space without surveillance into an apparently dangerous place.

Finally there are the *securitised actors*, the putative terrorists, criminals, those who refuse to integrate and drug dealers, that is, the CMs' clientèle. The effects of the security discourse and practice concern them immediately as they are the primary focus of securitisation as a policy of Othering and exclusion. Likewise, Werner Schiffauer (2007: 370) points to the unintended consequences of the governmental policy to prevent terrorism, which seems to target members of the Muslim community.

This policy, he argues, leads to a growing distance between Muslims and mainstream society and undermines trust in the rule of law. It weakens reformers within the communities and renders integration by participation impossible.

Thus security is not only relevant for the 'suspicious' and the 'insecure' groups. Security is an expression of the practice of the 'governmentality of unease' (Bigo 2002) and constitutes an inseparable discursive and practical interrelation of all the actors involved. As I have outlined in this chapter and my analysis of the CMs and their practical and discursive role for securitisation processes, it is here that an anthropology of security can step in.

Notes

1. An earlier version of this chapter was published in German (Schwell in press). I use (in)securitisation to emphasise the process that turns a safe/self-confident social group (population) into one that is characterised by a strong feeling of (subjective) insecurity. The German version reads '*Ver-Unsicherung*'. Whereas securitisation refers to the issue that is securitised, I refer to the 'audience-as-actor' that feels increasingly insecure.

2. In contrast to an 'anthropology of security' that is the focus of this chapter, there is the so-called *security anthropology* that relates to a predominantly US-American discussion focusing on the question of whether it is ethical for anthropologists to work for government and military institutions and provide them with information about the populace in war zones. Gusterson (2007: 164) calls this specific way of doing 'applied' anthropology *weaponising culture*.

3. The 'audience' is one of the central concepts in New Security Studies; yet both the role and agency of the audience are subject to discussion. An anthropological and actor-centred perspective can hardly subscribe to the implications this notion of audience yields; therefore, as I show, it is also possible to treat the audience as an actor with agency.

References

Albro, R., Marcus, G., McNamara, L.A. and Schoch-Spana, M. (2012) 'Introduction', in Albro, R., Marcus, G., McNamara, L.A. and Schoch-Spana, M. (eds) *Anthropologists in the SecurityScape. Ethics, Practice, and Professional Identity*, pp. 7–14 (Walnut Creek, CA: Left Coast Press).

Amt der Niederösterreichischen Landesregierung (2011) LH Pröll und BM Mikl-Leitner eröffneten 'Operatives Zentrum für Ausgleichsmaßnahmen' in Wiener Neustadt. Press release 30 August, APA OTS.

Appadurai, A. (1997) *Modernity at Large: Cultural Dimensions of Globalization* (Minneapolis: University of Minnesota Press).

Bajc, V. and de Lint, W. (eds) (2011) *Security and Everyday Life* (New York: Routledge).

Balzacq, T. (2008) 'The policy tools of securitization: information exchange, EU foreign and interior policies', *Journal of Common Market Studies*, Vol. 46, No. 1, pp. 75–100.

—— (2011) 'A theory of securitization: origins, core assumptions, and variants', in Balzacq, T. (ed.) *Securitization Theory: How Security Problems Emerge and Dissolve* (London: Routledge).

Bigo, D. (2002) 'Security and immigration: toward a critique of the governmentality of unease', *Alternatives*, Vol. 27, pp. 63–92.

—— (2008) 'Globalized (in)security: the field and the ban-opticon', in Bigo, D. and Tsoukala, A. (eds) *Terror, Insecurity and Liberty: Illiberal Practices of Liberal Regimes, the (In)Security Games*, pp.10–48 (London: Routledge).

Booth, K. (1991) 'Security and emancipation', *Review of International Studies*, Vol. 17, No. 4, pp. 313–326.

Bourdieu, P. (1996) *The Rules of Art: Genesis and Structure of the Literary Field.* London: Polity Press.

Bubandt, N. (2005) 'Vernacular security: the politics of feeling safe in global, national and local worlds', *Security Dialogue*, Vol. 36, No. 3, pp. 275–296.

Bundesministerium für Inneres (n.d.) *Möglicher Assistenzeinsatz des Bundesheeres nach Abbau der Schengen Außengrenze – Grundsätze für den militärischen Aufgabenbereich.* Vienna.

Buzan, B., Wæver, O. and de Wilde, J. (1998) *Security: A New Framework for Analysis* (Boulder, CO: Lynne Rienner Publishers).

Chavez, L.R. (2008) *The Latino Threat: Constructing Immigrants, Citizens, and the Nation* (Stanford, CA: Stanford University Press).

Eriksen, T.H., Bal, E. and Salemink, O. (eds) (2010) *A World of Insecurity: Anthropological Perspectives on Human Security* (London: Pluto Press).

Foucault, M. (1980) 'Truth and power', in Gordon, C. (ed.) *Power/Knowledge: Selected Interviews and other Writings 1972–1977*, pp. 109–133 (New York: Pantheon).

—— (2006) *Geschichte der Gouvernementalität 1: Sicherheit, Territorium, Bevölkerung: Vorlesung am Collège de France 1977/1978* (Frankfurt am Main: Suhrkamp).

Gallie, W.B. (1956) 'Essentially contested concepts', *Proceedings of the Aristotelian Society*, Vol. 56, pp. 167–198.

Glaeßner, G.-J. (2002) 'Sicherheit und Freiheit', *Aus Politik und Zeitgeschichte*, Vol. 10–11, pp. 3–13.

Goldstein, D.M. (2010a) 'Security and the culture expert: dilemmas of an engaged Anthropology', *PoLAR: Political and Legal Anthropology Review*, Vol. 33, No. s1, pp. 126–142.

—— (2010b) 'Toward a critical anthropology of security', *Current Anthropology*, Vol. 51, No. 4, pp. 487–517.

Goodey, J. (2006) 'Ethnic profiling, criminal (in)justice and minority populations', *Critical Criminology*, Vol. 14, pp. 207–212.

Gusterson, H. (2004) *People of the Bomb: Portraits of America's Nuclear Complex* (Minneapolis: University of Minnesota Press).

—— (2007) 'Anthropology and militarism', *Annual Review of Anthropology*, Vol. 36, pp. 155–175.

Hall, S. (1993) 'Encoding, decoding', in During, S. (ed.) *The Cultural Studies Reader*, pp. 90–103 (London: Routledge).

Huysmans, J. (2011) 'What's in an act? On security speech acts and little security nothings', *Security Dialogue*, Vol. 42, No. 4–5, pp. 371–383.

Kent, A. (2006) 'Reconfiguring security: Buddhism and moral legitimacy in Cambodia', *Security Dialogue*, Vol. 37, No. 3, pp. 343–361.

Klockars, C.B. (1980) 'The Dirty Harry problem', *Annals of the American Academy of Political and Social Science*, Vol. 452, pp. 33–47.

Lipsky, M. (2010) *Street-level Bureaucracy: Dilemmas of the Individual in Public Services* (New York: Russell Sage Foundation).

Maguire, M. (2009) 'The birth of biometric security', *Anthropology Today*, Vol. 25, No. 2, pp. 9–14.

Maurer, A. and Kant, M. (2008) 'Vergrenzung des Inlands: Von der Schleierfahndung zur neuen Bundespolizei', *Bürgerrechte & Polizei/CILIP*, Vol. 89, No. 1, pp. 52–57.

Pram Gad, U. and Lund Petersen, K. (2011) 'Concepts of politics in securitization studies', *Security Dialogue*, Vol. 42, No. 4–5, pp. 315–328.

Republik Österreich, P. (2009) *Anfrage der Abgeordneten Korun, Pilz, Freundinnen und Freunde an die Bundesministerin für Inneres betreffend 'Rassenkontrolle' durch die Wiener Polizei. Eingelangt am 23.09.2009.* www.parlament.gv.at/PAKT/VHG/XXIV/J/J_03075/fnameorig_168661.html.

Said, E. (1979) *Orientalism* (New York: Vintage).

Salter, M.B. (2008) 'Securitization and desecuritization: a dramaturgical analysis of the Canadian Air Transport Security Authority', *Journal of International Relations and Development*, Vol. 11, pp. 321–349.

Schiffauer, W. (2007) 'Nicht-intendierte Folgen der Sicherheitspolitik nach dem 11. September', in Graulich, K. and Simon, D. (eds) *Terrorismus und Rechtsstaatlichkeit Analysen, Handlungsoptionen, Perspektiven*, pp. 361–375 (Berlin: Akademie Verlag).

Schwell, A. (2010) 'The Iron Curtain revisited: the "Austrian way" of policing the internal Schengen border', *European Security*, Vol. 19, No. 2, pp. 317–336.

—— (2012) 'Austria's return to Mitteleuropa: a postcolonial perspective on security cooperation', *Ethnologia Europaea*, Vol. 42, No. 1, pp. 21–39.

—— (in press) '"Niemand darf sich sicher fühlen!" Anthropologische Perspektiven auf die Politik der Inneren Sicherheit', in Adam J. and Vonderau, A. (eds) *Formationen des Politischen: Anthropologie politischer Felder* (Bielefeld: transcript).

Shore, C. and Wright, S. (eds) (1997a) *Anthropology of Policy: Critical Perspectives on Governance and Power* (London: Routledge).

—— (1997b) 'Policy: a new field of anthropology', in Shore, C. and Wright, S. (eds) *Anthropology of Policy: Critical Perspectives on Governance and Power*, pp. 3–39 (London: Routledge).

—— (2011) 'Conceptualising policy: technologies of governance and the politics of visibility', in Shore, C., Wright, S. and Però, D. (eds) (2011) *Policy Worlds: Anthropology and the Analysis of Contemporary Power*, pp. 1–25 (New York: Berghahn).

Shore, C., Wright, S. and Però, D. (eds) (2011) *Policy Worlds: Anthropology and the Analysis of Contemporary Power* (New York: Berghahn).

Stritzel, H. (2007) 'Towards a theory of securitization: Copenhagen and beyond', *European Journal of International Relations*, Vol. 13, pp. 357–383.

Tehranian, M. (2004) 'Cultural security and global governance: international migration and negotiations of identity', in Friedman, J. and Randeria, S. (eds) *Worlds on the Move: Globalization, Migration, and Cultural Security*, pp. 3–22 (London: I.B. Tauris).

Todorova, M. (1997) *Imagining the Balkans* (Oxford: Oxford University Press).

Vultee, F. (2011) 'Securitization as a media frame: what happens when the media "speak security"', in Balzacq, T. (ed.) *Securitization Theory: How Security Problems Emerge and Dissolve*, pp. 77–93 (London: Routledge).

Wall, T. and Monahan, T. (2011) 'Surveillance and violence from afar: the politics of drones and liminal security-scapes', *Theoretical Criminology*, Vol. 15, No. 3, pp. 239–254.

Weber, M. (2005 [1921]) *Wirtschaft und Gesellschaft: Grundriss der verstehenden Soziologie* (Frankfurt am Main: Zweitausendeins).

Wedel, J.R., Shore, C., Feldman, G. and Lathrop, S. (2005) 'Toward an anthropology of public policy', *Annals of the American Academy of Political and Social Science*, Vol. 600, pp. 30–51.

Weldes, J., Laffey, M., Gusterson, H. and Duvall, R. (eds) (1999) *Cultures of Insecurity: States, Communities, and the Production of Danger* (Minneapolis: University of Minnesota Press).

Wolff, L. (1994) *Inventing Eastern Europe: The Map of Civilization on the Mind of the Enlightenment* (Stanford, CA: Stanford University Press).

Wright, S. (2011) 'Studying policy: methods, paradigms, perspectives', in Shore, C., Wright, S. and Però, D. (eds) *Policy Worlds: Anthropology and the Analysis of Contemporary Power*, pp. 27–31 (New York: Berghahn).

5

Petty States of Exception: The Contemporary Policing of the Urban Poor

Didier Fassin

The question of the state of exception and its variation as a state of emergency has recently made an improbable comeback in public debate and academic literature. Improbable, considering that it is generally acknowledged that, after the end of totalitarianisms and the fall of most dictatorships, the contemporary world, especially in the West, seems to be going through relatively democratic times. The return of the exception is the result of two distinct albeit partially related phenomena: one intellectual, the other historical. On the one hand, political theorists and legal scholars have rediscovered the work of Carl Schmitt (1985 [1922]), in particular his political theology and his definition of sovereignty as the power to decide on the exception; this rediscovery is not without ambiguity and the German philosopher, known for his Nazi affinities, has been adopted by both extremes of the ideological spectrum in the intellectual realm. A milestone in this revival has been Giorgio Agamben's (2005 [2003]) reappraisal of the Schmittian theory and his controversial affirmation that the camp is the paradigm of our modernity. On the other hand, political events and legal situations have been assimilated and often denounced as contemporary forms of exception (Armitage 2002); the passing of the Patriot Act signed by George W. Bush in 2001 and partially confirmed by Barack Obama in 2011, which substantially expands the discretionary power of law enforcement and authorises indefinite detention of suspect aliens, and the publication of the Torture Memos written by John Yoo in his position as Deputy Assistant Attorney General at the Department of Justice to provide a legal justification for the so-called 'enhanced interrogations' are high on the list of such facts. The inflation of the concept and its translation into actuality have thus led many analysts to adopt as their motto, either interrogatively or assertively, Walter Benjamin's (2003 [1922]: 392) prophetic sentence according to which 'the "state of emergency" in which we live is not the exception but the rule'. The sense of tragedy which underlies this statement and the discussion of the exception in general, with its implicit reference to the pre-Second World War era in particular, may nevertheless be misleading in our interpretation of contemporary configurations (Fassin and Vasquez 2005). Indeed, the trivialisation of the concept raises theoretical as well as ethical issues and we ought to be cautious and sparing in its use to analyse current realities.

With this concern in mind, I propose in this chapter the phrase 'petty state of exception' to depict the state of affairs characterised by the intensive policing of the urban poor. There is a hint of irony in my choice of this expression and one could even suggest that the petty state of exception is to the state of exception what the petty bourgeois is to the bourgeois. What I designate through this notion is the temporally, geographically and juridically limited forms of non-respect of the rule of law within democratic regimes. I am interested in the moments when and the places where partial suspension of legal procedures and normal practices affect certain populations, which are predominantly disadvantaged, marginalised and racialised. Democracy is still functioning but not everywhere and not for everyone. The democratic illusion works because the majority is unaware or unwilling to be aware of the conditions imposed on minorities. Actually this may be the way in which democratic regimes commonly operate – with petty states of exception. Paraphrasing Benjamin, one could say that these are not the exception but the rule. The interesting paradox of this exception is that it is presented as a response to problems of security in urban areas, but as I will show, it actually contributes to produce or exacerbate the sentiment and the reality of insecurity.

My analysis is grounded in the ethnographic research I conducted between the spring of 2005 and the summer of 2007 in the largest police district in Paris region. The corresponding conurbation, of approximately 200,000 inhabitants, includes middle-class residential areas and housing estates, several of which are administratively classified as 'sensitive urban zones' on the basis of social criteria of deprivation, with the consequence that they are provided state support. The population as a whole is characterised by unemployment and poverty rates, percentages of school dropouts and aided households, and proportion of immigrant families that are all above the national or regional average. Criminality in these areas is also higher than in the rest of the country. In this regard, two facts are deserving of special attention, due to their implications for the interpretation of policing practices: contrary to what is generally believed and publicly declared, in France according to official statistics, first, serious crimes, especially homicides and robberies, have significantly and regularly decreased over the past half-century, and, second, housing estates, often stigmatised for their insecurity, experience no more violations of the law than their surrounding urban areas. In the precinct, police forces comprise various units, most of which are dedicated to public security and deployed for patrolling neighbourhoods. It is with these units that I have spent most of my research, cruising by day and by night across the twelve towns that compose the conurbation. As is the case for all large urban districts, in addition to the teams of uniformed officers driving marked cars, there was an anti-crime squad with plain-clothes officers in unmarked vehicles supposed to catch criminals red-handed. Founded in the mid 1990s by the populist Minister of the Interior Charles Pasqua, these special units are particularly dreaded by the population for their verbal and physical aggressiveness. Since their creation, they have been directly involved in most incidents entailing the death of young men that have iteratively triggered urban disorders.

Unrest

On 27 October 2005, late in the afternoon, a group of adolescents from Clichy-sous-Bois, a town east of Paris, were heading home after a football match in a neighbouring town when they heard the wail of a police car siren (Mauger 2006). They noticed youths running in the opposite direction and saw officers of the anti-crime squad charging towards them with Flash-Balls, weapons that fire 'non-lethal' rubber ammunition. They were frightened and fled. Although they had done nothing wrong, they anticipated on the basis of previous experiences with these units that they would be stopped and searched, probably taken to the police station for questioning, possibly held in custody overnight; eventually their parents would be called to pick them up and they would certainly be punished for being arrested and causing the family trouble. Besides it was Ramadan, they were hungry and thirsty, and they did not want to miss the festive breaking of their fast. As they were fleeing three of them found themselves in front of an electric transformer. Ignoring the warnings of danger, they entered. A few minutes later they were electrocuted by a 20,000 volt current. Fifteen-year-old Bouna Traore and 17-year-old Zyed Benna died. The two were from Mauritania and Tunisia respectively. Their fathers worked as garbage collectors in Paris. Seriously burnt, their friend Muhittin Altun survived. His family was Kurdish and from Turkey, and his father was an unemployed mason. The three friends lived in the same housing estate of a town confronted by major problems of poverty.

The following night, informed of the tragedy, several dozen angry youths burned cars and attacked police officers and firefighters. The next day, however, a peaceful protest was organised by local organisations in memory of the two adolescents with a slogan that would become a leitmotiv for further mourning: 'Dead for nothing'. In reaction to these events, the Minister of the Interior, Nicolas Sarkozy, explained to the press that three 'thieves' who were not 'chased' by the police had died as they hid in a power substation. Thus, instead of expressing his compassion towards the families, he accused the adolescents and treated them as suspects (it would later be established that they had not participated in any criminal activity), and rather than requesting an investigation as is normally the case in such situation, he absolved the police of all responsibility (further inquiry proved that officers had run after the adolescents as far as the transformer and had done nothing to prevent the accident). The minister's allegations followed two polemical public statements. On 20 June, after the death of a child shot by a stray bullet in a housing estate of La Courneuve, he declared that he would 'cleanse the estate with a high-pressure hose'. On 23 October, during a visit to the esplanade of Argenteuil, he hailed a woman watching from her window, promising that he would 'rid the town of its scum'. The accumulation of aggressive and dismissive utterances against the youth from disadvantaged neighbourhoods triggered further riots, which in turn prompted further responses from the police.

In these tense times, the explosion of a tear gas grenade in the mosque of Clichy-sous-Bois during the evening prayer just three days after the death of the adolescents and after years of what was perceived as a systematic stigmatisation of Muslims, was considered the ultimate provocation and led to the rapid spread of disturbances in the housing estates all over the country. Within a week, 300 towns were affected: instead of direct confrontations between youth and the police, the protests involved setting fire to private cars or sometimes official buildings. Rather than being violent, they were spectacular. On 9 November, even though the statistics indicated a substantial decrease in these incidents, the Prime Minister, Dominique de Villepin, in a political escalation with the Minister of the Interior, his rival for the leadership of the Gaullist party, paradoxically decreed a state of emergency, using for the first time a legislation passed in 1955, at the beginning of the war in Algeria – the symbolism of this act did not go unnoticed. Then on 14 November, in an address to the nation President Jacques Chirac solemnly acknowledged for the first time that the inequalities and discriminations experienced by youths of immigrant origins were the deep-seated causes of the unrest and more generally of the 'crisis of identity' that the country was going through. Meanwhile, the popularity of Nicolas Sarkozy in the opinion polls reached its highest level ever. Despite the fact that the riots were by then almost over, with no more than sporadic burning of cars in housing estates, the state of emergency was extended for almost two months, until 3 January, when it was ended by a presidential decree. Meanwhile, a long judicial battle was beginning. On 20 September 2013, in a provisional conclusion to a series of lawsuits, the appeal judges sent the officers involved in the chase of the youths back to court in spite of the public prosecutor's request to close the case.

Contrary to the impressive iconography displayed by the international media, the urban disorders were remarkably self-limited, both sides having avoided physical confrontation. When I asked the commissioner of the precinct where I was conducting my research about how the riots had been experienced by his personnel, he replied:

What riots? What do you mean? We need to know what it is we're counting here: cars or violence? If we're talking about cars, there were a few dozens. If we're talking about violence, there was hardly any. But the media only counted the burned-out cars. It was actually very calm here.

He was right in emphasising the role of the media in the propagation of images, figures and comments which caused much of the anxiety felt both in France and abroad. Indeed, on the first anniversary date of the death of the two adolescents, journalists were eager to announce new disturbances, which never occurred. It was instead two years later that riots took place. But these were not to honour the memory of the two victims of Clichy-sous-Bois.

On 25 November 2007, in Villiers-le-Bel, a town north of Paris, two adolescents, Moushin Sehhouli, age 15, and Laramy Samoura, age 16, riding a motorbike were killed in a collision with the vehicle of an anti-crime squad. Convinced that the police deliberately caused the accident, dozens of youths from a neighbourhood that had endured the permanent pressure of police patrols for years engaged in violent protests, seriously wounding the commissioner who had arrived at the scene. Fearful that the disturbance might fan out to the rest of the country as was the case two years earlier, the government immediately deployed several hundred officers to the housing estate where the two adolescents had died and this time avoided making any derogatory remark regarding the victims that would risk worsening the situation. But the overwhelming presence of the police in the cordoned-off area exacerbated the tensions and generated confrontations. Officers were hit by rifle pellets shot in the dark. Cars, shops, the public library and the police station were burned. However, the events remained limited to the town and were controlled in only a few days, with numerous youths arrested. The newly elected President Nicolas Sarkozy, speaking to law enforcement officers, commented that the unrest 'had nothing to do with a social crisis, but everything to do with hooliganism'. In contrast to his predecessor, he refused to ascribe a political signification to the events.

The unrest was followed by an interminable legal process, with two distinct lines of enquiry. The first investigation concerned the accident. Although the public prosecutor declared immediately after the event that the two teenagers were solely responsible for it, further probing revealed that the car had been speeding, that the police had tried to obfuscate what had actually happened, and that the assertion that the vehicle had been vandalised by the inhabitants of the estate only served to avoid attributing its condition to the collision. Two years later the case was dismissed. An appeal was lodged, and six years after the event, the driver received a six-month suspended sentence. Since such a punishment is quite rare for a law enforcement agent in France, the decision indicates that the court had serious doubts about the unintentional character of the accident. The second investigation dealt with the violence against the police. Considerable means were used to gather testimony from the inhabitants against the culprits, especially those involved with the gunshots. Four months after the fact, early one winter morning, an impressive police operation was conducted by 1000 helmeted and heavily armed officers in the presence of dozens of journalists to spectacularly and brutally arrest 37 suspects. A commissioner who commanded part of this operation later told me that he did not understand why law enforcement agents were so aggressive: 'Why do they have to break doors to apprehend someone when it suffices to knock and people open?' In the days that followed, most of those arrested were released for lack of evidence. Eventually, three years after the riot, despite the lack of evidence and on the sole basis of questionable testimony (most of it from anonymous regular police informants in exchange for rewards, the only witness who had openly denounced suspects having retracted after admitting he had been pressured by officers and the prosecutor), five youths received sentences of 3–15 years in prison. Unlike in the 2005 riots, this time it was not the two dead adolescents who were the victims, but the police.

The 2005 events, and to a lesser degree those of 2007, have revealed the social and racial tensions affecting the *banlieues*, that is, the outskirts of the main cities, and more specifically the *cités*, in other words, the housing estates where working-class families mostly from North and Sub-Saharan Africa are concentrated, to the nation and probably to the world (Fassin and Fassin 2007). While the issues related to unemployment, inequality, segregation, discrimination and withdrawal of the welfare state from these territories have been legitimately acknowledged as the profound reasons for the protests, the question of the relationships between the police and the population has hardly been addressed. In contrast to what has happened in the United States or the United Kingdom after similar, albeit often more deadly events, there has been no parliamentary commission or independent investigation to inquire about the facts and their immediate determinants – and therefore no acknowledgement of the importance of the problem and no reform envisaged to solve it. Although dozens of urban disturbances have followed violent interactions between law enforcement agents and housing estates inhabitants over the past three decades, often involving the death of one or several youths, the topic has been overlooked, if not outright denied.

And so it was thus that an identity check of a woman wearing a *niqab* while walking home with her baby, mother and husband on 20 July 2013, in Trappes, devolved into the arrest of the couple, who are said to have resisted the check. Shortly afterwards, inhabitants who had witnessed the violent altercation attacked the police station, throwing stones at the building. As reinforcements arrived, an adolescent watching the scene was hit in the face by a Flash-Ball shot and taken to the hospital, only to be told that he had probably lost an eye. The immediate reaction of the public relations services of the Minister of the Interior was to invoke the legislation recently passed prohibiting the *niqab* and the necessity for everyone to respect the law of the Republic, a stance that receives wide support in the country. However, the couple, both new converts to Islam, publicly expose that actually they have been stopped and fined on several occasions already but never experienced any difficulty. This time, they explain, it was the aggressiveness of the officers towards the woman and her mother that triggered the indignant reaction of the husband. In the following days, however, most media adopted the official position, interpreting the unrest as a problem of secularism rather than of police behaviour.

Inquiry

The research I conducted on law enforcement started six months before the 2005 riots and ended six months before the 2007 unrest (Fassin 2013 [2011]). It is therefore inscribed in between these two important events of the previous decade. Yet, rather than these intermittent explosions of violence, it was the routine interactions officers have with residents of the disadvantaged neighbourhoods that interested me when I started my research. The lack of ethnography of law enforcement in France, due to difficulties in obtaining the necessary permissions to gain access to the field, but also to the habitus of criminologists more inclined to work with questionnaires and interviews, has left the question of what is it that the police are doing almost entirely unanswered. It is, however, the approach used during the daily and nightly patrolling that could provide the keys with which to unlock and understand the outbursts that were usually described as purely irrational and inexplicable, and, perhaps even more important, could give a sense of what it is to live in areas subject to intense policing.

Seen through the lens of law enforcement agents, the *banlieues* are a strange and hostile world. Since more than 80 per cent of police officers come from rural areas and small towns, they have no experience with large urban contexts. The national recruitment and organisation of the institution mean that their first postings correspond to those precincts which veterans least want to serve in, in practice always the outskirts of big cities where France's 'sensitive urban zones' are concentrated. During their training in the academy, these districts are depicted to them as a 'jungle' and their residents as 'savages', both being associated with racialised and belittling stereotypes. As a result they approach the housing estates with mixed feelings of animosity and anxiety, soon reinforced by the comments of their older colleagues. But far from the intense activity of catching 'thieves and thugs', as they often say, they discover the boredom of long hours of patrolling in vain.

Here, for instance, is the account of an ordinary evening. Early in the shift, the radio announces that a man has been seen climbing the wall surrounding a supermarket in a housing estate. Two crews of the anti-crime squad are dispatched. As we arrive in the vicinity of the place where the break-in is supposed to have occurred, the driver of the car I am in decides not to approach the store directly in order not to attract any attention and parks his vehicle at a distance. Trying to find our way back to the site of the incident, we get lost in a dead-end alley and must retrace our steps. We finally get near the supermarket 20 minutes after the call and hide for a while behind a tree, scrutinising the surroundings in the cold winter night. At some point, the silence is suddenly broken by the loud noise of the walkie-talkie that one of the officers forgot to switch off. His colleagues curse at him in a low voice. However, they are now aware that they are wasting their time. The burglar, if he ever existed, is probably long gone. The officers leave the place. As they walk back to their car, they encounter four adolescents with sports bags hurrying through the empty street. They stop them and roughly ask what they are doing. The teenagers explain that they are going home after their handball training. They are nevertheless checked, searched and admonished for being outside that late. The officers eventually get to their car and continue their cruising through the quiet neighbourhoods. After midnight, a radio call sends them to a house for a domestic dispute, but when they arrive on site, the couple seems to be reconciled. The rest of the night is completely eventless. The train stations and the housing estates, which are the usual places for patrolling, seem deserted, denying the police even the occasional interaction with their preferred publics: immigrants and youths.

As is clear through this brief depiction, patrol work comprises two activities: responding to phone calls from citizens and taking the initiative in interactions with the population. Reactive policing is limited by the scarcity of demand. The reasons for it are complex: not only is serious crime in decline, but it is also often difficult to catch a perpetrator in the act. An officer told me that during the seven years he had spent in this district – which is supposed to have higher criminality rates than the rest of the region – he had only arrested one burglar red-handed. Proactive policing therefore becomes the alternative. It consists in checking and searching individuals in public places. Such practices are legally regulated.

The Code of Penal Procedure distinguishes two possibilities: investigative, when there exists a suspicion of breach of the law, and administrative, under the vague rationale of crime prevention. Despite this quite extensive definition, not all stops and searches are legal, as the Constitutional Court has made clear. Yet officers generally consider that 'in theory, we have to follow strict rules, but in practice, we can do what we want'. Besides, their superiors are extremely tolerant with regards to forms of law enforcement. In the words of a commissioner: 'It's illegal, but we do it all the time.' Similarly, searches are strictly limited by the legislation to occasions when there is a reasonable suspicion of an offence, but in fact are systematically conducted as a complement to the check.

Although the stops and searches have existed for a long time, their frequency has dramatically increased in recent decades. First, the introduction of the 'administrative check' into the legislation in 1994 has given a wide margin of freedom to officers in the exercise of their discretionary power in that matter. Second, the implementation of the 'politics of numbers' in 2002 has provided strong incentives to intensify these practices as a way to fulfil arrest quotas. Nicolas Sarkozy implemented the latter policy, whereas his political mentor, Charles Pasqua, introduced the former. Establishing quantified objectives that were unattainable in terms of serious crime given its limited occurrence and accessibility had remarkably perverse effects. In the precinct where I carried out my research, not being able to achieve their monthly 30 arrests, the officers used what they called 'adjustment variables'. They were of two kinds: infractions of the drugs law and infringements of the immigration legislation. Practically this meant, as the officers would phrase it, 'arresting dopeheads and illegals'. Both targets were easy prey and both actions were profitable for the police, since they increased their clearance rate.

To arrest marijuana users, searching young people at random would theoretically suffice, since it is estimated via national surveys that among 17-year-olds one out of every ten is a regular consumer. However, it was clear that the quest for these offenders was extremely selective. High school and university students were almost never checked and searched, and when – exceptionally – they were, if a small quantity of drugs was found, the police let them go with a mere warning. By contrast, the housing estates and certain sites where the youth from disadvantaged neighbourhoods met were systematically visited and those loitering in the public spaces or the entrance halls of buildings often stopped and frisked. When marijuana was found, officers had the option to take the offender into custody or not, using their discretionary power. Their decision depended on the number of arrests they had been able to make in the course of the month, the proximity of the end of their shift, their mood at the moment, the attitude of the youth and an implicit mental classification based on previous encounters or simply a generic assessment that he was 'a bastard' who should be taught a lesson. The arbitrary character of the punishment and the provocation that frequently accompanied it, with disparaging or insulting comments and needless use of physical force, sometimes led to protests or even resistance, which immediately served as a pretext to throw the young man violently to the ground to handcuff him and generated the charge of 'outrage and rebellion against a person representing public authority'. Encouraged by the Ministry of the Interior, which even paid lawyers to represent the officers concerned, there had been an inflation of such offences at the national level. Everyone in the institution knew that it had become, in particular, a way of covering up police brutality, since the offence often served to counter a possible complaint by the victimised suspect and eventually, in court, the word of the officers would carry more weight than the word of the offenders claiming physical abuse. The head of the precinct told me that he knew that officers who had the most cases of outrage and rebellion were the most violent of his men.

For undocumented immigrants, the procedure was not much more complicated. The obsessiveness of successive governments on the issue of immigration had reached a climax at the time of my research with the establishment of annual quotas of deportations. Because a large proportion of the foreigners thus apprehended were later released by magistrates due to irregularities, the hunt for illegal immigrants had to be intensive in order to produce about four times more arrests than the desired number of deportations. Officers were sometimes summoned for special operations in train or metro stations consisting of the selective checking and searching of individuals, mostly men, with physical traits or clothing suggesting their foreign origin. More often, using the same criteria based on the external appearance, they would stop people in public spaces and verify their residence permit. Such racial discrimination, which had been denounced by human rights organisations ten or twenty years earlier as unacceptable, was then almost normalised. Rather than contesting it, commissioners would justify its use as the only way to meet their obligations. Occasionally courts would annul the detention of immigrants arrested on these grounds, but the practice was so actively supported by the government that it nevertheless continued.

The politics of numbers and the corresponding policy of check and search, associated with the creation of special units, have thus become, within three decades, a signature of contemporary forms of urban policing in France, as well as in other countries and places, most famously New York City, where the practice of stop and frisk has raised concerns among activists and led to lawsuits. One might view it as paradoxical that the institution in charge of law enforcement should have made unlawful practices the core of its action in disadvantaged neighbourhoods. Not only are checks, searches, arrests and handcuffing carried out for illegal reasons or using illegal methods, but also the very principle of social targeting and racial discrimination that exists within the force exercised by police is decidedly unconstitutional. The argument used to justify this evolution has been the protection of the public order against criminals. The troubling fact is, however, that the implementation of these measures of exception against certain areas and groups is precisely what has caused the most impressive riots that the Western world has seen in recent decades, from Watts in 1965 to London in 2011. This was no surprise to my interlocutors in the field. One commissioner, who had been the regional head of public security and as such responsible for the local restructuring of the anti-crime squads, explained to me that frequently, because of their aggressiveness, these 'packs caused, rather than solved, problems when they went out on patrol' in housing estates.

The efficacy of these special units and, more generally, of the police forces operating in the disadvantaged neighbourhoods, is not what one imagines it to be. The statistics they produce, which the Ministry of the Interior then proudly exhibits, do not correspond to the expectations of the population in terms of security or to the aspirations of the officers when they entered their profession. Instead of serious crime, they principally represent misdemeanours with little impact on the life of most citizens, such as the use of marijuana or the lack of immigration documents. In fact, within the upper and middle classes, many children may have had experience with the former offence while some families may employ persons confronted with the latter issue. The form of urban policing that I have described therefore serves less to preserve the public order than to impose and maintain a social and racial order. By their presence in these places and their harassment of these populations, law enforcement agents contribute to the inculcation of the idea that each one must remain in his or her place. Working-class populations of immigrant origin living in housing estates can be treated with impunity in a discriminatory and humiliating way. Protesting and resisting unfair practices is doomed to be turned into outrage and rebellion against a person representing public authority. In disadvantaged neighbourhoods people know the rules of the game. To circumvent them, they generally use the 'weapons of the weak', as James Scott (1987) terms it, cunning rather than force, avoidance rather than confrontation, silence rather than retort. Occasionally, however, when the injustices become unbearable, in particular when they lead to the death of one or several youths, explosions of violence may occur, which can only make sense – even political sense, though this is generally denied – in light of what happens on a daily basis.

Conclusion

In the contemporary world, petty states of exception are not only more numerous but also more threatening for democracies than is the grand state of exception in its Schmittian or Agambenian definition. The threat is not so much the urban disturbances that occasionally disrupt the apparently peaceful flow of events, as it is the slow decline of the foundational values of democracy. The non-respect of the rule of law in certain territories and for certain categories, and the breach of the social contract grounded on the principles of equality and justice, which entails a differential treatment of socially stigmatised, racially discriminated, economically marginalised and politically excluded groups, undermine the cohesion and perhaps even the meaning of a common world. But in times of anxieties about security, both external and internal, societies tend to be tolerant regarding abuses that are viewed as the collateral damage of policies supposedly intended to protect them. This is where the mystification resides. Indeed, urban policing, as it has been intensively developed in recent decades, mainly serves a different purpose. Rather than preserving the public order, it perpetuates and consolidates a social order. Thus, while inequalities have considerably increased in the past 30 years in France, as has been the case in many other countries, the police make sure that everyone is reminded of his or her social position, whatever the cost for democracy.

Acknowledgements

The investigation on which this chapter is based has been supported by an Advanced Grant of the European Research Council. I am grateful to the commissioner who let me conduct my ethnographic study and to the officers who accepted my presence even when it allowed me to observe practices quite distant from the ideals of their profession.

References

Agamben, G. (2005 [2003]) *State of Exception* (Chicago: University of Chicago Press).

Armitage, J. (2002) 'State of emergency: an introduction', *Theory, Culture & Society*, Vol. 19, No. 4, pp. 27–38.

Benjamin, W. (2003 [1942]) 'On the concept of history', in Eiland, H. and Jennings, M.W. (eds) *Walter Benjamin: Selected Writings, vol. 4, 1938–1940*, pp. 389–400 (Cambridge, MA: Harvard University Press).

Fassin, D. (2013 [2011]) *Enforcing Order: An Ethnography of Urban Policing* (Cambridge: Polity Press).

Fassin, D. and Fassin, É. (2007) *De la question sociale à la question raciale? Représenter la société française* (Paris: La Découverte).

Fassin, D. and Vasquez, P. (2005) 'Humanitarian exception as the rule: the political theology of the 1999 Tragedia in Venezuela', *American Ethnologist*, Vol. 32, No. 3, pp. 389–405.

Mauger, G. (2006) *L'Émeute de Novembre 2005: une révolte protopolitique* (Bellecombe-en Bauges: Éditions du Croquant).

Schmitt, C. (1985 [1922]) *Political Theology: Four Chapters on the Concept of Sovereignty* (Cambridge, MA: MIT Press).

Scott, J. (1987) *Weapons of the Weak: Everyday Forms of Peasant Resistance* (New Haven, CT: Yale University Press).

6

Counter-terrorism in European Airports

Mark Maguire

'I suppose', thought Razumov, 'that if I had made up my mind to blow out my brains on the landing I would be going up these stairs as quietly as I am doing it now.... Thus, too, when the mind is made up. That question is done with. And the daily concerns, the familiarities of our thought swallow it up – and the life goes on as before with its mysterious and secret sides quite out of sight, as they should be. Life is a public thing.'

– Joseph Conrad, *Under Western Eyes*, 1911

'If you want to act you have to close the door on doubt' – said a man of action. 'And aren't you afraid of thus being *deceived*?' – replied a man of contemplation.

– Friedrich Nietzsche, *Daybreak*, 1881

The 'critical anthropology of security' (Goldstein 2010) has an important role to play in the study of European securitisation processes. Because of the historically informed global perspectives that it may bring, the critical anthropology of security has the capacity to shake the common-sense and taken-for-granted ways of the world, showing them to be contingent and always embedded in cultural weaves. Moreover, because of its ethnographic attention to lived experiences of security, anthropological perspectives may throw new light on contemporary apparatuses and anticipations of the future in situated and critical ways. All of this is shown when one examines counter-terrorism measures in European airports.

Anthropological work on terrorism has generally arisen from ethnographic fieldwork among religious, indigenous or ethno-national resistance movements and has refused narrow-gauge and ideological definitions of terrorism.[1] Rather, anthropologists study terrorism as both an empirical reality and a cultural construct, but a cultural construct with reality-making powers (Zulaika and Douglass 1996). To elaborate, one may turn to Edmund Leach's *Custom, Law and Terrorist Violence* (1977). Terrorism, Leach argues therein, 'is an activity of fellow human beings and *not* of dog-headed cannibals' (1977: 32). If one takes terrorism to denote horrific acts emanating from a realm beyond civilised rationality then one inevitably conjures inhuman enemies and permits exceptional measures to combat them. The outcome, according to Leach, is that 'counter-terrorism becomes, in a bizarre sense, a religiously sanctioned duty' (1977: 32).

Leach's provocations are worth revisiting because he anticipates current discussions of the biopolitics of terrorism through myth-making and second-order mediations, identifying how real or imagined threats are configured as dangers to life itself posed by other-than-human beings (Strathern et al. 2006; Foucault 2007; Sluka 2008).[2] But Leach's early commentary also calls attention to the cultural and geo-political conditions for the possibility of recognising and labelling terrorists. For example, in 1985, US President Ronald Reagan paraded on to the White House lawn and introduced 'the moral equivalents of America's founding fathers' to the media. The turbaned gentlemen he introduced were the leaders of the Afghan Mujahideen (Ahmed 2010: 126). When the Cold War's security apparatuses readjusted to face the 'War on Terror', threats had to be produced, versions of the past had to be elided or reimagined, and dark visions of the future had to be articulated. Thus, in his 'axis of evil' speech, President George W. Bush erased the history of US involvement in Afghanistan and rendered it as an incubator for the viral spread of 'thousands of dangerous killers, schooled in the methods of murder ... spreading throughout the world like ticking time-bombs set to go off without warning' (CNN 2002).

Anthropologists do not simply avoid narrow definitions of terrorism but, rather, seek to situate those acts amid geo-politics and in the context of the more destructive phenomena of 'state terrorism' – all too often organised and supported by Western governments and their client states. Terrorism, situated thus, is a thoroughly cultural concept, and real or imagined terrorists are thoroughly cultural beings. However, this is not just an academic position: the cultural dimensions of how one understands terrorism and recognises terrorists are matters close to the heart of many security agencies and skilled counter-terrorism officers. Indeed, I aim to show that counter-terrorism is not simply a covert war against real or imagined threats but, rather, a battleground in which different but related interests are struggling over the securitisation of life itself.

This chapter is about the cutting-edge counter-terrorism measures in European and North American airports. The aviation corridors between North America and Europe are 'vital systems' (Collier and Lakoff 2008a, 2008b) within the global economy and have shown themselves to be vulnerable to attack. Despite this, however, the history of airport security is a story of piecemeal and often reactive securitisation. It is important to recall, for example, that during the 1960s there were approximately two attempted airplane hijackings per month in the United States of America. It was only when hijackers threatened to crash a plane into Oakridge Nuclear Facility in 1972 that serious efforts were made to search all airline passengers.[3] Hundreds of guns were confiscated in North American airports during 1973 following the introduction of bottlenecks, baggage x-ray equipment and metal detectors. Moreover, it was not until the 1980s, in the wake of terrorist incidents in Europe, that passenger-to-baggage matching began to take place in a systematic fashion.

Today, in the wake of 11 September 2001, airport security is a magnet for societal fears and the target of enormous research and development spending. But, despite an international drive towards standardisation (ICAO 2010), these security laboratories remain diverse places. In some EU Member States one may encounter skilled security operators, while in other jurisdictions one may encounter poorly paid baggage screeners who complain of derisory training and inadequate supervisory support. In the US, partly because of the role of the federal government, great emphasis is placed on standardisation and on finding dependable technological solutions.[4] The US Department of Homeland Security (DHS) operates a vast security apparatus within which the Human Factors Division alone is concerned with areas ranging from technological identification systems, such as those based on biometrics, to experimental systems designed to capture the most elusive aspects of human behaviour. However, across this broad range of activities there is a common drive towards finding scientifically validated solutions. As one research participant, a US-based counter-terrorism expert, put it, 'These days, the government wants a box that you can plug in anywhere, that gives you a green light and a red light' (Interview 2012).

Counter-terrorism in airports is a realm of experimental scientific research and development, a landscape characterised by secrecy, complex institutional features, and cultural formations (see Masco 2010). But it is also a lived space in which security personnel see themselves operating in high-risk environments in which human error exists alongside possible new weapons that have yet to be imagined. Many security officers are innovative and take their roles as seriously as one could possibly imagine. Today's terrorists are understood to be prepared to die during attacks that aim to maximise fatalities, and beyond the security promised by high-tech solutions there remains an enduring respect for the skilled senses of officers and the 'art' of hunting dangerous persons. This chapter begins by describing the ramifications of a terrorist incident in the wake of 11 September 2001.

The Real Thing

On 21 December 2001, Richard Reid, a British citizen, attempted to board a flight from Paris to Miami, Florida. Reid had no checked luggage and his dishevelled appearance and distracted attitude aroused the suspicions of airline passenger screeners. Concerned, but without evidence of wrongdoing, airline staff reissued his ticket for the following day. On 22 December, Reid returned to Roissy-Charles De Gaulle and boarded American Airlines flight 63. As the aircraft flew over the Atlantic, passengers complained of a strong burning smell. Hermis Moutardier, a flight attendant, found Reid attempting to light a match and cautioned him. Minutes later, Moutardier noticed that he had slumped over. Reid grabbed at her when she approached him. It became apparent that he was attempting to light a fuse trailing from one of his shoes. After a brief struggle, he was subdued by attendants and passengers until doctors on board managed to sedate him using the contents of the emergency medical kit. The aircraft was diverted to Boston's Logan International Airport, whereupon Reid was removed safely and taken into custody. Forensic analysis, though not conclusive, indicated live explosives that if detonated could have killed all 197 passengers and crew. It is likely that the lives of flight 63's passengers were saved by Reid's overnight delay in rainy Paris and some amount of foot sweat.

As time went by, more and more information about the so-called 'shoe bomber' emerged, from his troubled upbringing in London to his conversion to Islam in Finsbury Park Mosque. He pleaded guilty to multiple charges in 2002 and was handed down three consecutive life sentences the following year. Reid's attack spurred new security measures such as footwear scanning in US airports (though the explosives used by Reid cannot be detected by x-ray). Moreover, questions were being asked about research into suspect populations and suspicious behaviours. Commentators in the international media puzzled over the incident – had security measures actually worked in the sense of at least delaying Reid, or was this to be understood as failure, which would inevitably be followed by more tough talk and the inevitable inconveniences of purely performative 'security theatre' (see Schwell in this volume)? But the reactions inside the world of counter-terrorism were profound.

As soon as Richard Reid began his 2001 attack on flight 63, Boston-Logan was put on high alert. A large team of security and public safety officials immediately assembled with the aim of taking Reid and any possible accomplices into custody and screening the aircraft for other threats.[5] Among them was Tony (pseudonym), a celebrated detective and security expert. At one point, Tony stood just a few feet from Reid. He reflected: here was 'the real thing', a terrorist with a never-before-seen weapon who was prepared to die in order to cause the maximum loss of life. He replayed the events in his mind, always returning to the crucial issue of the materiality of terrorism. Existing screening methods, he began to realise, were fixated on suspicious objects and suspect identities – things out of place; documents that were not in order; arrangements of persons and things. But Reid was the problem and not his passport or his shoes. How could one truly identify Richard Reid? What *kind* of person was he?

Tony was by no means the first to stray into this uncertain realm. Jean and John Comaroff remind us that modernity has, at one and the same time, a deep fascination with crime statistics, forensic science and the 'art' of the intuitive detective (Comaroff and Comaroff 2006). This is evident in a long line of real and fictional detective literature, from the redoubtable Allan Pinkerton to Conan Doyle's Sherlock Homes. These figures exemplified scientific policing through second-order mediations and yet could also operate at a different level. Indeed, the history of modern policing is often told as a passage from confusion and obscurity to science and order, but that same history reveals a hidden transcript about deception and skilled vision. Thus, when Tony gazed at Richard Reid and wondered whether or not extant security systems were overly focused on the materiality of terrorism he was raising fundamental questions about how one sees suspect behaviours.

There is also an important line of philosophical thought on this theme. Jeremy Bentham's 'Indirect legislation' (1838 [1792]) addressed ways to police those mobile persons who were outside of the gaze of societal institutions. 'Who are you, with whom I have to deal?' Bentham wondered, choosing to focus on recognition by means of identification methods (see Maguire 2010). Bentham's self-proclaimed genius for legislation was directed towards *arrangements* of persons and things such that recognition would lead to control and the amplification of the positive qualities of mobility. However, Bentham also addressed unknown qualities: people who could not be recognised and who could elude the gaze of good government, disturbing the very relations between evidence, truth and deceit. Later, especially in *Daybreak* (1997 [1881]), Friedrich Nietzsche recovered these questions from utilitarian concerns. He attended to the ocular and relational conditions for deception, self-deception, dissimulation and security. 'We are like shop windows,' he tells us, 'in which we are continually arranging, concealing or illuminating the supposed qualities others ascribe to us – in order to deceive ourselves' (1997 [1881]: 172). He asked a rhetorical question that still resonates today: 'Why does man not see things?' 'He is himself standing in the way: he conceals things', Nietzsche answers (1997 [1881]: 203; see also Freud 1965). What we find here is an extraordinary glimpse of an affective and relational field of communication flows. Bentham sought clarity through second-order mediations; Nietzsche sought out the very contradictions and multiform relations of deceit and detection that appear tantalisingly within and perhaps prior to those mediations.

When looking at Reid, then, Tony was confronted by a particular and complex set of problems that are as old as modernity itself. His frustration with the materiality of counter-terrorism was a frustration with forms of knowledge that attempt to produce security through the management and arrangement of persons and things. He recognised that important security measures, such as the necessity to carry a standardised identity document, would never penetrate far enough. 'Identity is not your name – it's your beliefs and intent' (Interview 2012). What Tony was searching for was a synthesis of science and intuition that could police at a different level of life itself.

Tony spoke with the incident commander for Reid's arrest at Boston-Logan who suggested that airport narcotics interdictions might be modified in some common-sense way to achieve counter-terrorism ends. He began to make connections and gather ideas together *bricolage*-like. But a door of doubt remained open. He wondered how one might deem a new interdiction method to be a success or a failure? After all, terrorist attacks are extremely rare. And even if one had an ostensibly successful interdiction method in place would one know *why* it was successful? During an interview he described how he scoured 'every shelf in Barnes and Noble – history, geography, psychology, anthropology – searching for jewels of information' in order to develop 'a synthesis of experience and science'. He understood that counter-terrorism is situated in an uncertain realm – but it is still necessary to act. What was needed was a relatively inexpensive system that drew on security officers' experiences and existing skills and could be integrated into normal port-of-entry policing. He began to develop such a system, knowing that there were bigger questions yet to be asked. The man of action closed the door on doubt. The result was the Behaviour Assessment Screening System (BASS), which began life in Boston-Logan and soon mutated into the $1 billion-per-annum Screening Passengers by Observation Technique (SPOT) programme. And it is noteworthy that similar programmes emerged simultaneously in the Netherlands and in an even more advanced form in Israel.

It is not appropriate to give a full account of counter-terrorism programmes such as BASS – to do so would raise ethical, confidentiality and security issues. Instead, I discuss counter-terrorism systems in necessarily abstract ways based on a brief period of access to classroom-based counter-terrorism training and live field deployments in the UK during December 2011. This work was augmented by more than twelve months spent doing desk-based research and interviewing key figures in counter-terrorism, such as Tony. This is extraordinary access to sensitive training and material, but fieldwork was limited by the standards of anthropology. Consequently, my reflections are tentative. Below, for example, I open discussions of 'skilled vision'. But I was not present in the 'field' for long enough to confirm the relationships between skills displayed and the professional careers that gave rise to those skills. Moreover, the individuals who participated in the training were drawn from different security services. Few participants were known to one another prior to training, though informal conversations and shared humour quickly 'positioned' participants. Some individuals, however, never shared their professional backgrounds. Like Gregory Feldman in his contribution in this volume, I see the anthropology of security demanding critical reflections on anthropological concept work and research practices, especially our understandings of the local.

Detecting the Normal and the Abnormal

Can you guess? But, then, you don't know why. Was it a double blink? No? Maybe he was just *a wee bit odd* …

– Counter-terrorism expert, 2011

Counter-terrorism training programmes aim to find ways to detect, disrupt and deter potential terrorists, (ostensibly) mindful of relevant anti-terrorism legislation and privacy and civil liberties laws. Security officers study historical patterns of terrorism and appreciate that attacks will often include reconnaissance missions, counter-surveillance measures or a variety of botched acts. Preparedness is therefore fundamental to any security system's capacity to disrupt and deter (see Collier and Lakoff 2008b). But, how exactly does one prepare counter-terrorism officers to detect unknown suspects?

It is important to understand that the key problem presenting itself to counter-terrorism is one of numbers. Heathrow Airport, for example, handled over 65 million passengers in 2010 alone and is the place of work for over 75,000 people at any one time. Even though people who move through Heathrow will have to pass through layers of individuating security, from document to biometric checks, crowds remain a problem. Moreover, because security is designed into airports in the form of lines of sight, bottlenecks and chokepoints, space will discipline individual behaviours. Airports are machines for producing certain types of 'normal' behaviours and reactions. So, how does one see 'abnormal' behaviours, and how does one recognise them for what they are? Beyond preparedness, two pillars have emerged in counter-terrorism, especially since 9/11. The first pillar is exemplified by the high-tech surveillance systems, which will be described further below. Those systems rest upon the core assumption that crowds have distinct patterns or baselines, and someone who acts outside the 'normal' range of behaviour should be 'red-lighted' by the technology. But, according to Markarian et al.:

Machines are very good at measuring data and alerting when an input is within a certain *range*. However, they are not good at *inferences* regarding that data. Knowing the difference between someone acting strangely because they are late and worried they will miss their flight or because they are intending to blow themselves up on the flight is not easy for a computer to do. (2011: 246, emphasis added)

The second pillar of counter-terrorism emphasises the importance of making *inferences* based on clusters of behaviours and characteristics. This is an area of expertise that seems closer to art than to science, closer to the skills of the hunter than to the ranges programmed by the computer scientist. But, as one research participant put it: 'There is no better super-computer in the universe than the human' (Interview 2012).

During counter-terrorism training it is common to examine CCTV footage. Many of those who undergo training are experienced security professionals, and few have any difficulty in quickly identifying suspicious behaviours. But counter-terrorism training attempts to bring quasi-scientific methods and professional experience together. Participants are encouraged to identify baseline behaviours in groups and larger crowds, and learn to appreciate the ways in which one may deviate from the norm. In essence, abnormal behaviour detection methods are about understanding what is normal before jumping to conclusions about what is abnormal. As one training officer with over 25 years of experience put it: 'Know what is right and then you'll see what is wrong' (Observation records 2011).

Take for example the following composite scenario drawn from ethnographic records. A flight lands and holidaymakers flood into the arrivals area of an airport. A woman stands out. It is not that she is dressed in a different way, but, rather, she shows a cluster of signs that indicate deviation from the baseline. She moves at a different pace to the other travellers, occasionally slowing and turning as if looking for another passenger. She looks at her phone but neither texts nor talks on it. As she approaches a security checkpoint, she begins to look nervous. It would be easy to look at this scenario and dismiss screening as the paranoid gaze of security officers. The security gaze may have been provoked by the woman moving at a different pace to everyone else, displaying 'suspicious' behaviours and possible covert ties, but a second glance may pick up a clue which may reveal that the same woman is awaiting an important call and therefore is walking quickly and in a distracted manner. Her partner, on the other hand, is progressing more slowly, insensitive to her worries. She may have appeared nervous on seeing a security checkpoint, but only because of the further delays this may represent. This woman's machine-readable behaviours may have been outside of the baseline *range*, but machines are not good at *inferences*. Like most travellers, this woman poses no risk whatsoever. 'Abnormal' behaviours, as a cluster of characteristics, are simply signs of mental effort, memory, stress and emotions, the stuff of human beings' everyday lives. To clarify, we may reach for a philosophical insight from Georges Canguilhem via Paul Rabinow, 'An anomaly is not an abnormality' (quoted in Rabinow 1996: 84). Therefore, the training of the security officer's gaze might be understood as an apprenticeship in exercising 'skilled vision' (see Hertzfeld 2009). Skilled vision in this context denotes the trained senses attending to and distinguishing between the normal behavioural anomalies of vital life and the abnormal behaviours and reactions that indicate maleficence.

But one must ask: are we simply dealing with potentially biased and entirely subjective decision-making by security staff? Several social scientists dismiss abnormal behaviour detection as a pseudo-social-scientific mask that hides dehumanising and racialising border control. Criminologist Anna Pratt describes behavioural detection on the Canadian border as:

> a cocktail of different low-level administrative knowledges that derive from quasi-scientific frameworks ... expert intelligence and second-hand social psychology on deception detection, but also through on the job knowledge such as that gained individually through experience, informants, gossip and quasi-magical intuition ... intertwined with moralistic and racialised knowledges. (2010: 462)

But borders and security zones are policed by means of layers of security. The systems deployed by those trained in counter-terrorism do not simply involve gazing at people and forming conclusions. Critical evaluations of border control are of great importance, but, understandably, such evaluations are often carried out at a distance and are thus distorted (cf. Adey 2009: 280–283).[6]

Of course, describing a counter-terrorism programme in terms of skilled vision should not be construed as an attempt to glorify it. Rather, better understandings of actually existing practices may lead to better appreciations of context and better critical evaluations. Today, there is an obvious need to develop critical anthropological perspectives on the counter-terrorist security apparatus – a *critical* anthropology of security requires concept work, tools and research practices. Therefore, I use 'skilled vision' simply as an exploratory tool to uncover an animated system in which perception and attention are imbricated by other senses, ideological formations and styles of reasoning (see also Grasseni 2009: 1–23 passim). It is difficult if not impossible to track the emergence of professional skills in the careers of counter-terrorism officers, because they may be drawn from different branches of the security services and may reveal little even to each other. However, they do develop skills as co-participants in complex, asymmetrical and affective fields of attention and knowledge. Simply stated, counter-terrorism training involves encouraging officers to see anew and to appreciate the mind's ability to attune to non-rational indicators. One may elaborate on this by turning to the research literature on deceit detection.

Studies of deceit detection have shown time and again that the average person has an ability slightly greater than chance to identify deception, because deceit, deception and lies are imbricated with everyday life and, thus, embedded in emotions and memory processes. Moreover, research involving security professionals such as police officers has shown that they are often no more or less accurate than members of the public at detecting deceit. But there are notable exceptions. Research on members of the US Secret Service indicates that, as a group, they are highly skilled in deceit detection and highly attuned to non-verbal signs (Ekman and O'Sullivan 1991). Such agents spend much of their time gazing upon crowds of people, searching for clusters of characteristics that go beyond the normal baseline range. These agents gaze upon people under stress, who exert mental effort and exercise memories and emotions, but who generally pose no threat whatsoever. But while members of the US Secret Service may well possess remarkable individual skills, contemporary counter-terrorism systems are not wholly reliant virtuoso performances.

Leach (1977) argued that we must understand terrorists as cultural beings engaged in cultural acts, but what is interesting about counter-terrorism today is that, despite the fear-inducing nightmares reproduced endlessly, many counter-terrorism screening programmes have to acknowledge the humanity of their real or imagined enemies – this is a precondition for successful screening. Indeed, experts understand terrorism to be a fundamentally human set of actions that require deception and often great mental effort. Therefore, when engaged in reconnaissance, counter-surveillance or an actual terrorist act, individuals with hostile intent will tend to break baselines, behave abnormally *and* be unable to fully disguise their hostile intentions. To paraphrase Sigmund Freud, betrayal will ooze out of them at every pore. But what form does that betrayal take exactly? The critical issue in counter-terrorism operations, then, is to create the conditions whereby skilled vision can distinguish between the normal behavioural anomalies of vital life and the abnormal behaviours and reactions that indicate maleficence.

While they are not surveillance operations, counter-terrorism deployments in airports are not passive. Rather, such deployments involve active interventions in spaces and among crowds with the intention of disrupting baseline behaviours, and then, 'Only by looking will you see' (Interview 2011). These disruptions take the form of what one might call security statements, which often operate by means of key cultural symbols. Officers watch the crowd. Often nobody reacts; or someone seems curious, but that's it. On other occasions, an individual will very obviously pick out the members of the security team. Counter-terrorism officers often speak of these moments, noting that the individual in question will generally turn out to be an active or former member of the military or police services – the gaze returned. However, with striking regularity, an individual may be observed who is displaying clusters of suspicious characteristics; an individual whose cues do not suggest that their abnormal behaviour is simply the result of harmless levels of stress or anxiety. Counter-terrorism training is about providing the conditions whereby potentially threatening abnormal behaviour comes into view, and in those situations officers are trained to respect their *interest* in those behaviours.

The conditions for the possibility of counter-terrorism screening may well be the phantasmagoria of fear and suspicion in the realm of security post-9/11, but this should not distract us from careful analysis of the available information on those systems. Unsurprisingly – and I would argue worryingly considering the level of internal debate and lack of verification – counter-terrorism screening systems are generally regarded by security agencies as success stories (see GAO 2010). In 2011 the DHS's Larry Willis gave testimony to the US House of Representatives on the effectiveness of Transport Security Agency (TSA) behavioural screening against random screening of tens of thousands of passengers by non-trained staff.[7] He argued that a 'high-risk' traveller was nine times more likely to be identified by trained screeners versus random screening and that this could be achieved while not unduly inconveniencing 'legitimate' travellers (see Willis 2011). If one follows Michel Foucault's tentative summation of security as 'a matter of maximising the positive elements ... and of minimising the risky and inconvenient' (2007: 35), then it appears that low-tech and relatively inexpensive behavioural screening suits the moment. Nonetheless, we must also question what is characterised as 'high risk'. There is good evidence to suggest that the majority of persons stopped in counter-terrorism interdictions are guilty of only minor offences. Moreover, Hertzfeld (2009: 208) reminds us that the training of skilled vision – and this is surely true of counter-terrorism –includes the transmission of attitudes, attention and common-sense values. What, one may ask, are the relationships between counter-terrorism screening and profiling? The example of the UK provides an illustrative example of the complex relationships between the law, the enforcement of the law and the more shadowy realm of counter-terrorism.

Section 44 of the UK Terrorism Act, 2000 amplified the police's powers to 'stop and search' members of the public. Since 2000, the misuse of anti-terrorism legislation has been the subject of much public discussion. Human Rights Watch, for example, called attention to the seven-fold increase in recorded stops from 2007 to 2009 alone, and the remarkably few resulting terrorist prosecutions. Moreover, all the evidence during that period indicates severe threats from far-right groups and 'residual' terrorism in Northern Ireland, and yet people categorised as 'Blacks' or 'South Asians' are far more likely to be stopped than so-called 'Whites'. Shockingly, in 2009 Lord Carlile of Berriew, QC, chided the UK's police services for increasingly stopping 'Whites' in order to balance the statistics (see Slack 2009). In 2010, the European Court of Justice added its voice, specifically attacking policing decisions, 'based exclusively on the "hunch" or "intuition" of the officer concerned' (ECJ 2010: 83–84). These and other criticisms resulted in a curtailing of police powers in 2011 pursuant to the Terrorism Act 2000 (Remedial) Order 2011. But the evidence that there are unreasonable stops and ethnic profiling in day-to-day UK policing is one matter – and, as Didier Fassin shows in his contribution to this volume, it is certainly an important matter in Paris also. But here I am interested in addressing the link, if any, between profiling and screening by counter-terrorism officers.

Counter-terrorism training for secure ports of entry has become common since 2010. The BASS system, and the research literature it rests on (see Simcox et al. 2011), recognises that terrorists do not fit crude profiles and that a whole series of behavioural characteristics must be present as 'informed considerations' prior to stopping and questioning a traveller. What data there is from the UK shows little evidence of conscious ethnic/racial profiling, though there is evidence that certain populations perceive themselves to be unfairly targeted (see Anderson 2011: 79; Choudhury and Fenwick 2011). In Northern Ireland, a devolved policing jurisdiction with a 'severe' threat level from residual terrorist groups and a perceived backdoor route to the UK, Section 44 stop-and-search powers were curtailed in 2010, but recognition was given to the unique situation there. No data on the outcomes of counter-terrorism interdictions are available for Northern Ireland, and internal reviews do not suggest prevalent 'profiling' on the basis of skin colour (see Carlile 2010: 41).

While researching both historical and contemporary detection, I constantly encountered ideas about 'intuition', 'hunches' or 'the cop's nose'. Contemporary methods of counter-terrorism training attempt to convert this iffy, experience-based professional culture into skilled vision by zeroing in on a particular level of life itself, ostensibly minus the biases. The counter-terrorism training of that vision must reference, explicitly, potential grounds for interdictions. This whole realm remains elusive, and in the contemporary moment elusive is not good enough. It should be no surprise, then, that there are powerful interests pushing for greater use of technology alongside and perhaps instead of skilled officers. New database and imaging technologies, together with advances in face recognition and deceit detection methods, are now promising computer screening at this same elusive level of life itself.

A Green Light and a Red Light

Seven years after the so-called 'shoe bomber' incident, and after many leaks in security and media circles, the US DHS released an impact assessment of the new Future Attribute Screening Technology (FAST), one of the first publicly available glimpses into their high-tech counter-terrorism system. FAST is a mobile and informated security environment that can be rolled out in airports or for special events. It promises to screen individuals by means of non-intrusive sensors that record and analyse video, audio, respiration, cardiovascular reactivity, bodily secretions, eye movement, facial features and facial expressions, and readings of the skin's electrical resistance. The core idea is that this array of sensors is capable of detecting 'malintent'. 'Malintent' denotes the intent to cause harm. The theory of malintent, such as it is, holds that individuals who intend to cause harm will display particular behavioural and/or physiological cues depending on the nature, timing and consequences of the planned event. If an individual who intends to cause harm passes through FAST the system should 'red-light' the individual and give security operators some sense of the threat level. And, should a security operator decide to further question an individual, the system includes an area for questioning and even micro-facial expression scanning.[8] FAST offers security in the form of 'code/space' wherein life itself becomes machine-readable via software (see Kitchin and Dodge 2011). The software-mediated environment that is FAST is composed of ostensibly separate technologies, knowledge and styles of reasoning that have been brought together and must now work as a functional and nested entity – FAST is, quite literally, an assemblage.[9]

Mainstream media and scholarly publications have pored over any new information on the system. For example, in a widely cited article in *Nature* magazine, Sharon Weinberger drew comparisons 'with the science-fiction concept of "pre-crime", popularised by the film *Minority Report*' (2011: 412). What is the scientific basis of the theory of malintent? Indeed, is it possible to talk about science, as such, if everything is hidden from view, like the experiments of a medieval alchemist? What is known is that in 2009 the former MIT research company, Draper Labs began to test the system, first by peer review and then in a live deployment. Volunteer participants at an exhibition were recruited for a vague security experiment. Some were given disruption items to smuggle into the exhibition; others had to search the hall for a hidden device and set it off. The two types of study participant, together with members of a control group, entered the space in single file via a security checkpoint. A guard asked them questions while the battery of sensors measured their reactivity. The results are classified, but the whole experiment was judged to be a success.

Within the assemblage that is FAST there exists another techno-scientific assemblage in the area of facial expressions and deceit detection. Indeed, research into the expression of emotions is one of the most striking and innovative interdisciplinary areas today. Frank et al. explain:

A lie conceals, fabricates, or distorts information; this involves [for example] additional mental effort.... Lies can also generate emotions, ranging from the excitement and pleasure of 'pulling the wool over someone's eyes' to fear of getting caught to feelings of guilt. Darwin first suggested that emotions tend to manifest themselves in the facial expressions, as well as in the voice tones, and that these can be reliable enough to accurately identify emotional states. Research has since shown that for some expressions – e.g., anger, contempt, disgust, fear, happiness, sadness/distress, or surprise – cultures throughout the planet recognise and express these emotions in both the face and voice similarly. (2010: 2–3 passim)

Frank et al. argue that a counter-terrorism system is likely to pick up specific signals from a person with malintent. Moreover, counter-terrorism officers can be trained to 'push buttons' during interviews and follow emotional threads in order to elicit responses which are then open to real-time and automated deceit detection from involuntary facial expressions. However, Paul Ekman, the father of lie-detection psychology, has yet to be convinced: 'You can't, in my view, simulate a terrorist', he said (Wright 2009: n.p.). Ekman insists that much more needs to be known about the art and science of deceit detection before we can rely on a system like FAST. But one must go farther than this. Key issues emerging from research on counter-terrorism training indicated that abnormal behaviour detection should not be conflated with deceit detection. Deceit detection offers an ostensibly scientific domain amenable to affective computing systems such as FAST, but it is by no means clear that abnormal behaviour detection involves counter-terrorism officers detecting micro-facial expressions indicative of deceit. Instead, we see an elusive kind of training which focuses on the interest aroused by potentially threatening or potentially dangerous persons and the recognition of threat or danger for what they are.

The technologies of counter-terrorism are spreading. Take for example the Security of Aircraft in the Future European Environment (SAFEE) project. SAFEE includes a sensor-based Onboard Threat Detection System that seeks to identify abnormal behaviours and read them as 'suspicious', 'threatening', 'aggressive', etc. Clearly, science is inseparable from cultural formations. To programme software to recognise a baseline *range* for aggression is one thing, but what exactly is 'suspicious'? Anthropology can speak to these issues; but anthropology must offer more than instrumental knowledge for the security sector. The critical anthropology of security can speak to the agency of technologies and the unintended consequences of their use in multiple settings, but a truly critical anthropology of security must challenge the conditions for the possibility of (in)securitisation and the reconfigurations of life itself in security domains. Clearly, for example, there is a need to critically evaluate the enormous spending on counter-terrorist systems and infrastructures especially because of the obvious technological fetishism. But technological flaws are often configured as the 'bleeding edge' of later scientific excellence. What is at stake, then, is the question of what exactly are points of contestation in the undergirding techno-scientific sensibilities, political rationalities and styles of reasoning.

Conclusions

When the Cold War's security apparatuses readjusted to form post-Cold War counter-terrorist apparatuses this involved reconfigurations of many domains of life. The biopolitical government of populations through expert management of unease (Bigo and Tsoukala 2008) has shifted in the contemporary moment, inaugurating new ways of imagining, preparing for and pre-emptively acting in the near future. Great emphasis is now being placed on vital systems – often described as critical infrastructures – over and above more traditional configurations of nation-state security, territory and populations. And new techno-scientific developments are shaping and being shaped by 'expert' efforts to explore human life in security contexts.

This chapter focused on the tensions between the 'skilled vision' of counter-terrorism officers and the techno-scientific solutions that are mushrooming in European and North American airports. This is not a story about skilled men and women battling bravely against threats and, at the same time, the progressive intrusion of machines into their professional lifeworlds. Rather, I offer a snapshot of the emergent and contested styles of reasoning and modes of action within the counter-terrorism apparatus. Tensions exist between ways of understanding 'baseline' human behaviours, the quality of human- or computer-mediated inferences, and the value held in or ascribed to professional skills versus standardisation. However, we must also recognise significant tensions arising because of the problematisation of life itself: contemporary security apparatuses problematise the normal, the anomalous and 'abnormal' aspects of vital life.

Just as the Cold War national security apparatus provided fertile grounds for scientific innovation, counter-terrorism today provides the conditions for some professionals, experts and techno-scientific players to ask 'big questions' and to innovate in well-funded and often well-supported environments. But as we learn enough to understand and critically evaluate the professional skills and disturbing high-tech innovations in the realm of counter-terrorism, we must also ask 'big questions' about the *uses* of empathy and the limits of professional and techno-scientific compassion, the ethics of security innovation and the taken-for-granted assumptions in this realm (see also Feldman in this volume). While anthropological perspectives may provide new and experience-rich insights into the realm of counter-terrorism, one must not equate a critical anthropology of security with deployments of ethnographic methods in security settings. To do so would be to canalise anthropology's contribution as a narrow-gauge form of user experience research. Rather, anthropological research practices and concept work should contribute to understanding the historicity of actually existing (in)securitisation, and critical anthropological perspectives may include consideration of realistic alternatives to expensive technology and secretive policing.

Notes

1. 'Terrorism' refuses handy definitions. Indeed, it is noteworthy that historians describe the period 1870 to 1914 as the 'golden age' of terrorism (see Chaliand and Blin 2007).
2. Following Feldman (2005:224) I use the term 'second-order mediations' to denote the indirect mediation of actors' efforts to satisfy their needs. Second-order mediations, in Feldman's erudite discussion of the term, are closely bound to alienation and estrangement, because an actor may lack direct or, indeed, any access to that realm.
3. The plane was hijacked by US citizens facing criminal charges.
4. We should not be surprised to note that a 2005 Department of Homeland Security report to the US Congress revealed that airport baggage screeners failed to detect 13 per cent of potentially dangerous objects during tests conducted in 1978. In 1987 similar tests showed that screeners failed to detect 20 per cent of dangerous objects despite massive technological advancements and correcting for traffic volume.
5. Kerry B. Fosher notes that while Reid was subdued on board, the interagency response teams could not assume that he had been disarmed (or that he was operating alone), and a complex operation was required to secure the aircraft and safely remove the passengers and crew (see Fosher 2008: 168).
6. Because information is scarce, the views of key commentators can be misleading. For example, Paul Ekman (2006: n.p.), father of lie detection, gives this account of the Transport Security Agency's (TSA's) SPOT programme:

> SPOT's officers, working in pairs, stand off to the side, scanning passengers at a security checkpoint for signs of any behaviours on the officers' checklist, such as repeated patting of the chest -- which might mean that a bomb is strapped too tightly under a person's jacket – or a micro-expression.

Ekman's narrative naturally prefaces micro-expressions, but actual screening, especially in Europe, is far more elaborate, hence the distorted view in the critical social sciences.

7. Willis reported on the results of an extensive survey of TSA's behavioural screening SPOT programme carried out by the American Institutes for Research. The report compared the SPOT Referral Report process with a random screening process. Two data sets were used, one for 71,589 randomly selected travellers subject to SPOT referrals in 43 airports, and the other for 23,265 Operational SPOT Referrals during the same time period. Perhaps most importantly, referral indicators showed a consistent relationship to outcomes.

8. One clear 'benefit' of the FAST technology and the theory of malintent is the promise of using racially neutral screening methods (for critical evaluation see Maguire 2012).

9. It is worthwhile noting that FAST stands a greater chance of success precisely because it is an assemblage. Take for example the possible use of thermal readings of the face in systems such as FAST. In 2002, Pavlidis et al. reported in *Nature* magazine that they had developed a high-definition thermal-imaging technique that would be suitable for remote and rapid security screening, 'without the need for skilled staff' (2002: 35). They later published an erratum distancing themselves from their own claims. The key problem was the false-positive rate; however, if used in conjunction with other technologies and with the more modest ambition of screening within ranges in order to choose individuals for further questioning, suddenly the assemblages offer great assurance by nesting imperfect technologies together.

References

Adey, P. (2009) 'Facing airport security: affect, biopolitics, and the pre-emptive securitisation of the mobile body', *Environment and Planning D: Society and Space*, Vol. 27, No. 2, pp. 274–295.

Ahmed, A.S. (2010). *Journey into America: The Challenge of Islam* (Washington, DC: Brookings Institution Press).

Anderson, D. (2011) *Report on the Operation in 2010 of the Terrorism Act, 2000 and of Part 1 of the Terrorism Act, 2006* (London: The Stationary Office).

Bentham, J. (1838 [1792]) 'Indirect legislation', in *Works of Jeremy Bentham*, Bowring, J. (ed.) (Edinburgh: William Tait).

Bigo, D. and Tsoukala, A. (eds) (2008) *Terror, Insecurity and Liberty: Illiberal Practices of Liberal Regimes after 9/11* (London: Routledge).

Carlile, L. (2010) *Report on the Operation in 2009 of the Terrorism Act, 2000 and of Part 1 of the Terrorism Act, 2006* (London: The Stationary Office).

Chaliand, G. and Blin, A. (2007) *The History of Terrorism: From Antiquity to Al Qaeda* (Berkeley: University of California Press).

Choudhury T. and Fenwick, H. (2011) *The Impact of Counter-terrorism Measures on Muslim Communities*. London: EHRC.

CNN (2002) Bush's 'axis of evil' (fact sheet). http://archives.cnn.com/2002/US/01/30/ret.axis.facts/index.html (accessed May 2012).

Collier, S.J. and Lakoff, A. (2008a) 'Distributed preparedness: the spatial logic of domestic security in the United States', *Environment and Planning D: Society and Space*, Vol. 26, No. 1, pp. 7–28.

—— (2008b) 'The vulnerability of vital systems: how critical infrastructure became a security problem', in Dunn, M.A. and Kristensen, K.S. (eds) *The Politics of Securing the Homeland: Critical Infrastructure, Risk and Securitisation*, pp. 17–39 (New York: Routledge).

Comaroff, J. and Comaroff J. (2006) *An Excursion into the Criminal Anthropology of the Brave New South Africa* (Berlin: Verlag, Zentrum für Afrikastudien Basel).

Conrad, J. (2001 [1911]) *Under Western Eyes* (New York: Modern Library).

ECJ (European Court of Justice) (2010) Judgment of 12 January 2010 in Gillan and Quinton v. United Kingdom, paragraphs 83–84.

Ekman, P. (2006) 'How to spot a terrorist on the fly', *Washington Post*, 29 October. www.washingtonpost.com/wpdyn/content/article/2006/10/27/AR2006102701478.html (accessed 11 May 2012).

Ekman, P. and O'Sullivan M. (1991) 'Who can catch a liar?' *American Psychologist*, Vol. 46, pp. 913–920.

Feldman, G. (2005) 'Estranged states: diplomacy and the containment of national minorities in Europe', *Anthropological Theory*, Vol. 5, No. 3, pp. 219–245.

Fosher, K.B. (2008) *Under Construction: Making Homeland Security at the Local Level* (Chicago: University of Chicago Press).

Foucault, M. (2007) *Security, Territory, Population* (London: Palgrave Macmillan).

Frank, M.G., Menasco, M.A. and O'Sullivan, M. (2010) 'Human social and behavioural research', in Voeller, J.G. (ed.) *Wiley Handbook of Science and Technology for Homeland Security*, pp. 39–54 (London: Wiley-Blackwell).

Freud, S. (1965) *The Psychopathology of Everyday Life* (New York: Norton).

GAO – United States Government Accountability Office (2010) *Aviation Security: Report to the Ranking Member, Committee on Transportation and Infrastructure, House of Representatives*, GAO-10-763 (Washington, DC: GAO).

Goldstein, D.M. (2010) 'Toward a critical anthropology of security', *Current Anthropology*, Vol. 51, No. 4, pp. 487–517.

Grasseni, C. (2009) 'Introduction', in Grasseni, C. (ed.), *Skilled Visions: Between Apprenticeship and Standards*, pp. 1–23 (Oxford: Berghahn).

Hertzfeld, M. (2009) 'Envisioning skills', Grasseni, C. (ed.) *Skilled Visions: Between Apprenticeship and Standards*, pp. 207–219 (Oxford: Berghahn).

ICAO (2010) *Security Manual for Safeguarding Civil Aviation against Acts of Unlawful Interference*, Doc. 8973/6 2002 (Québec, Canada: ICAO).

Kitchin, R. and Dodge, M. (2011) *Code/Space: Software and Everyday Life* (Cambridge, MA: MIT Press).

Leach, E. (1977) *Custom, Law and Terrorist Violence* (Edinburgh: Edinburgh University Press).

Maguire, M. (2010) 'Vanishing borders and biometric citizens', in Laziardis, G. (ed.) *Security/Insecurity in Europe*, pp. 31–51 (London: Ashgate).

—— (2012) 'Race, biopolitics and new security technology', *Social Identities*, Vol. 18, No. 3, pp. 593–607.

Markarian, G., Kölle, R. and Tarter, A. (2011) *Aviation Security Engineering* (Norwood, MA: Artech House).

Masco, J.P. (2010) 'Sensitive but unclassified: secrecy and the counter-terrorist state', *Public Culture*, Vol. 22, No. 3, pp. 433–63.

Nietzsche, F. (1997 [1881]) *Daybreak: Thoughts on the Prejudices of Morality* (Cambridge: Cambridge University Press).

Pavlidis, I., Eberhardt, N.L. and Levine, J.A. (2002) 'Human behaviour: seeing through the face of deception', *Nature*, No. 415, p. 35.

Pratt, A. (2010) 'Between a hunch and a hard place: making suspicion reasonable at the Canadian border', *Social & Legal Studies*, Vol. 19, No. 4, pp. 461–480.

Rabinow, P. (1996) *Essays on the Anthropology of Reason* (Princeton, NJ: Princeton University Press).

Simcox, R., Stuart, H. and Ahmed, H. (2011) *Islamist Terrorism – The British Connections* (London: Henry Jackson Society).

Slack, J. (2009) 'Police search more whites "just to balance the books", watchdog claims', *Daily Mail*, 17 June, p. 2.

Sluka, J. (2008) 'Terrorism and taboo: an anthropological perspective on political violence against civilians', *Critical Studies on Terrorism*, Vol. 1, No. 2, pp. 167–183.

Strathern, A., Stewart, P.J. and Whitehead, N.L. (eds) (2006) *Terror and Violence* (London: Pluto).

Weinberger, S. (2011) 'Terrorist "pre-crime" detector field tested in United States', *Nature*, Vol. 465, pp. 412–415.

Willis, L. 2011. 'Testimony of Mr. Larry Willis', www.dhs.gov/ynews/testimony/testimony_1302031116813.shtm (accessed May 2012).

Wright, A. (2009) 'Machine that predicts terrorists' intent showing progress', *National Defence Magazine*, November, NDIA.org (accessed May 2012).

Zulaika, J. and Douglass, W.A. (1996) *Terror and Taboo* (New York: Routledge).

7

Whose Security? The Deportation of Foreign-national Offenders from the UK

Ines Hasselberg

During the past decades, immigration policies have been refined to broaden eligibility for deportation and allow easier removal of unwanted foreign nationals. Deportation is today a normalised and distinct form of state power. It is a practice that is imbricated by anxiety, uncertainty and unrest that elicits different perceptions of justice, injustice and entitlements. Public authorities often justify deportation policies as measures to respond to anxieties over security and migration, but such policies also create uncertainty and anxiety among 'deportable' migrants and their families. When calling for a critical anthropology of security, Daniel Goldstein emphasises the importance of recognising 'the significance of security discourses and practices to the global and local contexts in which cultural anthropology operates' (2010: 487). Indeed, as migration is tied ever more tightly to security concerns (Inda 2006; Guild 2009; Feldman 2011 and in this volume), it is of particular importance to look at how such security concerns are operationalised in migrants' daily lives and the effects on their sense of self.

   In this chapter I seek to show that exactly whose security is being threatened in the context of deportation is far from clear. I discuss experiences of deportability alongside their policy imperatives, and call for further discussion of the rationale behind deportation and related practices of state control over migrants. Drawing on ethnographic fieldwork conducted in London among foreign-national offenders facing deportation (following a criminal conviction), I take deportation not as an event but as a process that begins long before a migrant comes to be forcibly removed from one country to another (for methodological notes see Meissner and Hasselberg 2012; Hasselberg 2013). The chapter begins with an outline of the major developments that have led to the categorisation of foreign-national offenders as a threat to public security (see Guild 2009), and how this has translated into operational practices that affect all foreign-national offenders, independent of the risk they ostensibly pose to society. I will then present foreign-national offenders' narratives of deportation, revealing the intrusion of deportability into their daily lives, social relations and sense of self. Finally, I examine the rationale for deportation of foreign-national offenders in the UK, which rests on three imperatives: to protect the public, deter crime and demonstrate societal values.

Excluding the Unwanted

British immigration legislation distinguishes between administrative removal and deportation, both of which entail the expulsion of foreign nationals from the UK. Similarly, in the USA, according to Daniel Kanstroom (2000), deportation laws may be divided into those aiming at border control and those aiming at social control. Border control deportation laws are essentially contractual and expulsion emerges as 'a consequence of a violation by a non-citizen of a condition imposed at the time of entry' (Kanstroom 2000: 1898). These laws cover foreign nationals who enter the country illegally or under false pretences, who are not complying with a condition of entry (e.g. a migrant on a student visa is expected to be enrolled in a school, college or university), or who breach a prohibition (for instance, if the visa stipulates that the migrant is not to be on benefits for a certain amount of time). US border control deportation laws are similar to administrative removals in the UK. Social control deportation laws, on the other hand, concern long-term lawful permanent residents. These are not tied to borders or to admissions, according to Kanstroom, but 'follow what might best be termed an "eternal probation" or perhaps, an "eternal guest" model' (2000: 1907). Here deportation is used 'as a method of continual control of the behaviour of non-citizens'; it is closer to criminal law and 'more punitive than regulatory' (2000: 1898). It resonates with what British immigration law terms as deportation – the tactic of social control discussed here. Of course, Kanstroom acknowledges that this division is analytical, and the increasing criminalisation of immigration offences, such as the use of false documents, is leading to a blending of the two.

In the UK, provisions for automatic deportation mean, broadly speaking, that all foreign nationals convicted and handed down a 12-month sentence (or longer), regardless of the offence committed, will be issued with a deportation order whether or not they were legal residents in the UK.[1] Upon serving their sentence, foreign-national offenders may be detained in an Immigration Removal Centre while their deportation files are processed. Deportation may be appealed at the Immigration Tribunal on human rights grounds. The migrant, if detained, may also apply at the Immigration Tribunal for bail, which may be granted under certain conditions. Reporting to the Home Office at designated reporting centres monthly or weekly is usually part of the terms of bail, which remain in place until the migrant is either detained again for removal or their deportation appeal is granted.[2] Immigration detention and reporting are techniques of social control that in the UK, as elsewhere, are conceived legally as administrative practices necessary for the enforcement of the removal process. This means that they are not enacted through a judicial process, even though these same practices are used within the context of punishment in penal supervision and incarceration.

International law generally holds that sovereign states have the right to regulate and control foreign nationals' entrance and residence status in their territories, and their expulsion. Immigration legislation therefore includes clauses allowing for the deportation of foreigners on national security grounds. Such clauses have been in British legislation throughout the twentieth century, though they tended to be used to exclude people at particular times of crises, such as the world wars or in the odd case of espionage (Bloch and Schuster 2005; Schuster 2005; Cohen 1997). With the Commonwealth Immigrants Act, 1962, deportation was decoupled from war and emergency scenarios and it became available as a broader migration control tool (Bailkin 2008: 880). Subsequent legislation has worked to expand deportation eligibility, yet it was not until the end of the twentieth century that deportation, along with detention and dispersal, became normalised tools, deemed necessary to control and manage immigration (Bloch and Schuster 2005; Schuster 2005; Gibney and Hansen 2003; Fekete 2006) – a trend that has been amplified since the events of 11 September 2001. This is not particular to the UK: the US and Canada, for instance, have been deporting foreign citizens *en masse* since the mid 1990s, with devastating effects both for the receiving countries and for the families left behind (De Genova 2002; Zilberg 2004; Peutz 2006).

In the UK the 'deportation turn' (Gibney 2008) was brought about by a change of government and increasing public concern over rising numbers of asylum seekers. Detention and deportation came to be seen as the 'solution'. Although at first glance these practices seem incompatible with liberal democratic rule, Matthew Gibney (2008) argues that it was actually through a discourse of human rights protection that the Labour Party managed to enforce such polices. By advocating the need to protect the asylum system from 'bogus' refugees, the government was able to enact harsh measures with little opposition. Since 2000, the British government has increasingly used removal as a strategy to deal with rejected asylum seekers and other unwanted foreign nationals.[3]

It was in a climate of a politicised suspicion of asylum seekers, exacerbated by the 2005 London bombings and fear of future terrorist attacks, that in 2006 the public confronted the news that during the previous seven years 1023 foreign-national prisoners had been released after completing their sentences without being considered for deportation (BBC News 2006; Macdonald and Toal 2006; Bhui 2007). The 'scandal' amplified public anxieties over crime and immigration – two areas of great political sensitivity – and ultimately led to the resignation of then British home secretary, Charles Clarke. Thereafter, deportation policies and enforcement came to be seen as necessary elements in any public debates on crime trends (see Bhui 2007: 370), despite the absence of evidence that foreign-national prisoners present greater risks to society than British prisoners when released after completing their custodial sentences. Embedded in the discussions were both an underlying prejudice against foreign nationals and a concern on the part of politicians to re-instantiate public confidence in migration management (Bhui 2007: 378). Foreign-national offenders thus appeared on the political agenda 'as a virtual combined threat (immigrant/criminal) presenting a series of political hazards and operational headaches' (Bhui 2007: 378). As the editors argue in the Introduction to this volume, potential threats are blended and transformed by a 'calculus' of risks and precautions. The deportation of foreign-national offenders is a priority for the Home Office. The scandal also prompted a series of changes in immigration law and policy that culminated in automatic deportation for foreign nationals convicted of criminal offences. Broadly speaking, this now means that any foreign national sentenced to 12 months or more of imprisonment is now automatically served with a deportation order, whereas before consideration was given to the seriousness of the offence, the likelihood of re-offending, and the extent of any deterrent effect. Provisions for automatic deportation under the UK Borders Act, 2007 'created a statutory obligation to make a deportation order in many criminal cases, and deem these to be conducive to the public good' (Clayton 2008: 572) – meaning that there is a presumption in favour of deportation. New Labour thus created legal intersections between criminal justice and migration control, and spoke of crime and immigration in political discourse as inseparable phenomena (Bosworth 2011: 587).

The process of criminalisation of immigration in the UK resonates with the transformation of immigration management and control in many liberal democracies (Bosworth 2011; Bosworth and Guild 2008; Gibney 2008; Ellermann 2009). The deportation of foreign-national offenders has become a symbol of both border control and governance in the UK, visible in the adoption and promotion of annual targets for deportations (Bosworth 2011). An official post, dated 1 July 2008, on the Home Office webpage proudly announced the following in big, bold letters: 'Since January, more than 2,400 convicted criminals have been deported, putting the government on track to improve on its record-breaking level of removals in 2007' (HOCD 2008). This represented a 22 per cent increase on 2007 figures. The Home Office was also proud to claim that removals of failed asylum seekers had risen by 127 percent between 1997 and 2006, with 18,235 individuals removed in 2006 alone (HOCD 2007). By 2009, three years later, the targets were no longer numerical but rather expressed as headline-like targets, for example, 'a record number of foreign prisoners' (Smith in Bosworth 2011: 587).

In 2007 Hindpal Bhui challenged the supposed dangers posed by foreign-national offenders, arguing that the dangers had been 'overstated and that a move towards risk aversion in both the political and operational arenas has effectively resulted in group sanctions against all foreign-national prisoners' (2007: 369). This is particularly clear in the detention of foreign-national offenders on immigration grounds. Current policy states that there is a presumption in favour of temporary admission or release for foreign-national prisoners, which may only be outweighed when the individual circumstances of the migrant reveal a high risk of absconding or re-offending (UKBA [UK Borders Agency] n.d.). Yet, a recent report by the Independent Chief Inspector of the Borders and Immigration (ICIBI) noted a culture of detention where 'a decision to deport equals a decision to detain' (2011: 22). Moreover:

> In interviews with staff and managers, we encountered genuine fear and reluctance to release foreign national prisoners from detention in case they committed a further crime. This, together with the potential media and political scrutiny, is fuelling a culture where the default position is to identify factors that justify detention rather than considering each case in accordance with the published policy. (2011: 22)

The reluctance to release foreign-national offenders, despite what is prescribed in policy, is translated into operational procedures in which the level of authorisation required to release a foreign-national offender is much higher than that required for detention (ICIBI 2011).

Another result of the 2006 media scandal has been an increasing inter-dependence between the UKBA and Her Majesty's Prison Service (HMPS) in the management of foreign-national prisoners (Bosworth 2011). The latter is responsible for providing the former with the details of any foreign national serving a custodial sentence so that deportation can be considered. Since 2006, the government has made efforts to re-structure the penal estate in order to facilitate the deportation of foreign-national prisoners. In line with this, a 'hubs and spokes' system was devised to concentrate foreign-national prisoners in designated prison estates to facilitate their removal. Hub prisons are exclusive to foreign-national prisoners and have UKBA staff on-site. Prisons acting as spokes house a significant proportion of foreign-national prisoners who are to be directed to the hub prison.

Included in the rationale for such segregation is the realisation that this particular section of the prison population has its own needs and challenges. They all face immigration issues, some might have only recently arrived in the UK and hence face language barriers and isolation. In this sense, these prison facilities may provide better cultural support to foreign-national prisoners – many provide English as a second language classes, for instance. However, concerns have been raised over this segregation, especially regarding the quality of care and support provided to the foreign-national prisoner population and the need to ensure that rehabilitation and reintegration initiatives are equally accessible to them as to the British prisoners (Webber 2009; Clinks 2010; ILPA 2011). Transfer to open prisons, home detention curfews and other parole arrangements are not made available to foreign-national prisoners, thus hindering their rehabilitation. Other key issues relate to contact with family and friends, maintaining access to legal advice and gaining access to other support services that may not be part of the hub prison facility. Mary Bosworth (2011: 586) argues that the 'hub and spokes' system focuses on deportation at the expense of addressing the rehabilitation of prisoners and preparation for their lives upon release. The development of policies regarding foreign-national offenders has thus resulted in the portrayal of foreign-national offenders as a risk to (British) society: a risk to be (1) controlled through operational procedures that impact on all foreign-national offenders independent of the risk they are assessed as posing to society, and (2) a risk ultimately dealt with by deportation.

Everyday Experiences of Deportation

When migrants are confronted with the Home Office's intent to deport them they are usually confused and surprised, some are even shocked. They don't fully understand why this is happening to them, how they can prevent deportation and what the full consequences of deportation are. As these questions are gradually answered in one way or another, migrants grasp the circumstances they are in and uncertainty prevails as to whether or not they will remain in the UK and the degree of damage to their present and future life. When filing the notice of appeal against the Home Office intent to deport them, migrants become appellants at the Immigration Tribunal and new routines emerge within their daily lives.[4] Some might lose their right to work. Most will be subjected to some form of state surveillance, be that immigration detention or the requirement of weekly reporting appointments as conditions of bail from immigration detention. All will experience long-term uncertainty. Furthermore, if penal incarceration is the expected outcome of being convicted of an offence, deportation and related practices of state control, such as detention and reporting, are taken as unfair consecutive punishments. These seem unreasonable and discriminating, and deportees carry with them a sense of injustice. Having already served their time in prison, they feel they are doubly punished – rather than moving on with their lives as a British national would, they find themselves facing expulsion from their country of residence which, in the meantime, subjects them to constant restrictions and surveillance. Migrants' lives are affected greatly by detention and reporting (Hasselberg 2013). Being under such surveillance also has an impact on migrants' sense of self: many describe feeling untrustworthy, infantilised and dehumanised. Research participants had instilled in them an overwhelming sense of vulnerability, powerlessness and injustice that is clearly shown in the narratives presented below. In line with emerging scholarship (see De Genova 2002; Willen 2007), I describe the everyday effects of deportation in the still relatively under-explored realms of embodied and sensory experiences, in terms of the weight of the present and of the near future, and from within existing social relations and subjecthood. Herein, I show that deportability is an embodied experience expressed not in relation to 'being caught' but in appealing at the Immigration Tribunal and presenting a good case, in complying with state orders, and enduring uncertainty.

This embodiment of deportability is informed by migrants' own experiences and memories of arrest, detention and the appeals process; by stories read in the media or heard from other detainees and appellants; and by migrants' own sensory fields: spotting white vans, hearing airplanes or the sound of keys, for instance, eliciting memories of arrest and detention and feelings of insecurity, anxiety and outright fear. Hamid, for example, originally from northern Africa, is married to a British citizen. His wife has two children from a previous marriage, and together they have a daughter. By the time I met him, Hamid had been appealing against his deportation for two years:

I can't, I can't be like this. I can't. Is hard, is like when you go to sleep, you're thinking, when you're having a shower you're thinking, when you eat you're thinking, when get up and go. You're thinking all the time about this. What's going on? Sometimes when I look to my daughter, happy ... I'm not happy. I have to show her I'm happy. I have to play with her. 'Cause you know children they have that feeling. If you're not, they can find out. So what I have to do? In my home, I don't know what I have to do, but I cannot do nothing. For a man to sit every day without a job, it is very difficult for me. It is very difficult to wait for my wife to spend money for me. It is very difficult for me, especially in my country. It's not woman spending money for man. [...] In my country if a woman spends money for me, he is not a man. He has to spend money for her. He has to get it, even if she is working, he has to spend money for her. Has to buy her clothes, gifts, you know, car, he has to do that. If he's got good money he has to do that. If he hasn't got good money he has to do that. He has to look after the woman. Not the woman look after the man. It is not possible. So I'm feeling like, I'm nothing. So that's the problem. I feel like I'm nothing. I wanna do something, I wanna … you know? One year without working is…. I'm gonna be sick. I'm sick already.

Hamid's description echoes in the narratives of many other research participants. Hamid hides his concerns from the children in order to protect them. Appearing well to others, especially to close relatives, was important to most research participants. Constant efforts were made to conceal visible bodily expressions of worry. This is no easy task. Like Hamid, many research participants spoke of feelings of constant tension, of being consumed by persistent worry. Their lives are intruded upon by feelings of anxiety, and even the most basic daily chores must be performed while thinking about their predicament. This is exacerbated when appellants are unable to work, thus having few distractions from their worries.[5]

For Hamid, being financially dependent on his wife undermined his masculine identity; research participants often described feeling emasculated (see also McGregor 2009, 2011). Like Hamid, others constantly felt idle, useless and a financial burden to their families. Facing deportation can be a significant financial strain on the household. Some appellants have lost their permission to work; others cannot be employed as a consequence of conditions of bail. Some are self-employed, but their income is uncertain. The household income may thus be significantly reduced or lost altogether. There are also the added expenses of facing deportation, such as solicitor's fees and the costs associated with reporting or being in detention. Being able to work and provide for one's family is something appellants long for. George, from Latin America, had been living in the UK for 19 years at the time of the interview. He has four children, three of whom were born in the UK. We always met at the hospital where his premature son was in recovery at the time:

I am just a normal person, I just want to work and be with my wife and my kids. They depend on me and I want to feel able to work and do my things. Before, we did well, we were not rich but we had enough. Yesterday I did something I never thought I would, I gathered all my stuff and I sold it. They gave me £730. If I want to get the things back I have to give them back £1000 in six months. I want to be relaxed, to work for my kids, I don't care if I have criminal record, I have people who know me and who will give me work.

Feeling useless is compounded by an additional sense of worthlessness due to awareness that their presence in the UK is not desired. Maria came to the UK as a child over 40 years ago:

> It's breaking me down spiritually, it's this feeling that I am worthless, that the government is so disgusted by me, that I'm not even worth being listened to. That I'm just.... A cockroach, you know, has more status than I have, more respect than I have. [...] And I know that I am not a bad person. But that I am looked at as a monster and as an unwanted and as an undesirable. Like a leper, like when they used to walk around with bells on and it's inhuman and it's degrading and it's demoralising. It's heartbreaking. Sorry [cries].

This identity as one who is rejected, undesirable and unwanted is experienced as an assault on one's sense of self (Burman 2006; Willen 2007). Forms of state control such as detention and reporting hinder migrants' sense of self by instilling feelings of untrustworthiness, infantilisation and dehumanisation (Hasselberg 2013). What is at stake here is chronic stress arising from long-term uncertainty embodied somatically as appetite loss, binge eating, sleep loss, nightmares, headaches, migraines, exhaustion, depression, inability to concentrate, sadness, crying, loss of energy or drive. Many research participants, appellants and relatives experienced some or all of these 'symptoms'. Most gained or lost visible amounts of weight, and all described feeling aged through loss of hair or growth of white hair, and the appearance or intensification of wrinkles. Hamid had this to say: 'I was 78 kilos, I'm going down, I'm going down. My age is nearly 33. I feel like I'm 75. Can you imagine that? Because of this.'

Research participants were well aware of how much deportation was affecting their bodies like a corrupting agent, and many health problems experienced by appellants and their relatives were directly attributed to their deportability, as described by George:

> And now I have a premature baby, born at six months. And the question is why was he born at six months? Because the day the lawyer told me that the determination [which denied his appeal against deportation] was not appealable, there were no grounds for further appeal, I returned

home, I told my wife that. That was at 7 p.m., we went out to the park with the kids. I saw she was very pensive. At 3 a.m. she is feeling unwell, her water breaks and she is ready to give birth. My first reaction was to apologise to her for putting her in this situation. I called the ambulance and we came here to the hospital. And this was the biggest consequence of the stress. I kept asking her to forgive me. Because now it was not just about her life but the life of my son as well. The two were in danger. Because of an unfair determination.

This was not an isolated incident. Jen also had a premature baby, and Rashid's wife had a late miscarriage, both when appealing their husbands' deportation. In all three cases, and as exemplified by George's words above, a direct link is established by research participants between stress derived from deportation and the early births and miscarriage. It is not my place to verify these claims. The point is that appellants and families do believe that one was the consequence of the other, and this belief has consequences: it reasserts their vulnerability, and influences their perception of justice as once again they feel wrong is being done to them.

Those who were employed, such as appellants' immediate relatives, frequently reported missing work and spending whole days in bed. Hamid, like other research participants, also repeatedly described feeling on the verge of a breakdown:

If they deport me I'm not gonna fight again. I'm not going to do that. 'Cause it's finished. No more. [...] If I have to go back, I will go back. I'm not gonna die. I'm still strong, I still have energy. But if stay here like this, I will be destroyed like this. That's the problem here. I will be destroyed.

For Hamid, as for most others, the deportation appeal process has been long and intense: he is reaching the point of giving up, which is exactly what migrants believe to be the objective of the system. Hamid met with me a few days after his last appeal at the Immigration Tribunal. At the time, he was still waiting for the determination, but his mind was set that this was it for him. He hoped for a good outcome, but should the appeal be denied he would fight no more and would return to northern Africa. He felt nothing any more: he couldn't work, and it hurt him to see his wife's pain. He felt he had reached his limit and could not take his family through another round of appeals. Although not all were this ready to give up, many research participants described similar feelings of hopelessness, abandonment and isolation.

Hamid described how he feels responsible for the circumstances his family finds itself in:

> I haven't got any feeling any more. I don't feel nothing. I've been without work one year. I've been in prison one year, so I've been trying to have my proper future legally and properly I didn't have it. And my wife she's … now she's not ok. She's not like before. My wife, she's been changing a lot. She is tired. She been tired before, a lot of problems from when she was married, violence, and now she … it's more than that. She got a depression, she's very … I … I cannot see that. I cannot stay like this and watching her destroying. … I don't like it, it's because of me. Because us just trying to have a good, a proper family, that's what we're trying to do. But now it doesn't make any difference for me.

Again, this is not particular to Hamid. For George, the early birth of his son added to his guilt, as his narrative above illustrates. Randall (1987: 466) calls this the 'imposition of false guilt' – feeling responsible for what family and other close ones go through on account of one's imminent deportation. This is a feeling echoed by most research participants. As David says, 'Because of my mistakes the family pays the price.' David had been appealing his deportation for two years by the time I interviewed him. He arrived in the UK with his wife and his oldest son in the 1990s, escaping the civil war that devastated their country. His two younger children were born in the UK:

> It is a frustrating process, stressful, depressing, because your life stops there. And in these two years, believe me Ines; I was not able to do anything. […] It is also a bit shameful, embarrassing to be living like this after 14 years [in the UK]. It really gets frustrating, stressful and also for my wife, this is very difficult for her, difficult for us, very, very difficult. Because I always say that I rather have trouble with the police, with the police I know when my troubles will end. But immigration problems with the Home Office … with the Home Office you never know, at any time they can come and say, 'No, it's time to go.' […] So this is something that really affects the family you know? Because the family is not settled, is not grounded, is not safe. So this is bad, especially for me and for my wife. The children don't really know what is happening

because I hide it from them. But imagine that when they came to take me last March and said my flight was booked for April; imagine if my kids would hear that Dad is in Africa, that Dad was deported and that Dad won't be able to see them in the next ten years. What is that? It's absurd! It doesn't make sense.

Underlying the narratives presented above is a constant feeling of uncertainty. Migrants' plans for their future lives were devised based on their staying in the UK. The threat of deportation has left their future plans and present lives pending. The long-term waiting, marked by acute uncertainty, is internalised and embodied by appellants and their close relatives. The feeling research participants had that wrong was being done to them, and that there was little to protect them from it, should not be underestimated. Unwanted in their country of residence, prevented from working and supporting their families, and feeling responsible for the impact of their own deportability on their relatives, migrants' everyday lives become marked with extreme nervousness, anxiety, irritation, guilt, fear, anger and suspicion. Deportation thus translates into an overwhelming sense of vulnerability, powerlessness and injustice.

Whose Security?

The rationale for deportation of foreign-national offenders from the UK lies in three imperatives: (1) the protection of the public from possible future offences by the deportees, (2) deterrence of crime and (3) demonstration of society's revulsion (e.g. in cases of incest and paedophilia). As a protection measure, deportation appears as a successful strategy only if the deportee is likely to reoffend. There are, however, no definitive indicators of recidivism – the fact that one has committed a crime before does not guarantee that one will offend again. Furthermore, 'risk is framed in relative terms [...] with terms such as "possible" and "probable" necessarily being imprecise and subjective' (Grewcock 2011: 62).

As a tool to control crime, deportation is successful only locally, as the deportee is sent elsewhere, and in the short-term, as it does not address the roots of criminal behaviour (Kanstroom 2000; Clayton 2008). But, as Kanstroom adds, 'efficiency is not justice' (2000: 1898). What of those who have been 'rehabilitated', present a low risk of re-offending, have long been in the UK and have established family and social links?

Citizenship is often a technicality as it can be granted after three years of residency in the UK (Clayton 2008), which means that many long-term migrants being deported would have been eligible for British citizenship prior to conviction had they applied for it. Thus, Clayton argues that the deportation of foreign nationals and the harm it inflicts on their families and social networks, as illustrated in the narratives above, 'is a greater fracturing of the social fabric than the continued presence of someone who has committed a criminal offence' (2008: 573). This is crucial considering that, for citizens and non-citizens alike, the risk of re-offending does not prevent release once the custodial sentence has been served (Grewcock 2011: 62). As a tool of crime deterrence, deportation's effectiveness is untested and far from established. What is clear is that a particular practice can only serve to deter certain actions if people are aware that that is the consequence of those actions. My own findings reveal that migrants were usually not aware that they were liable to deportation. Field research took place just three years after the 2006 scandal and the consequent systematic enforcement of deportation policies. This meant that prior to conviction, research participants did not know of anyone (with leave to remain) within their circles who had been deported. Furthermore, while the deportation of foreign offenders features increasingly in the British media, the migrants participating in this research assumed that it applied to those who did not possess leave to remain. Being legal residents in the UK for years prior to their convictions, it had never occurred to them that they might be deported. In any case, it remains unclear whether such knowledge would have prevented them from committing their offences. The prospect of imprisonment certainly has not.

Deterrence and protection are closely interrelated. The idea is that if deportation is successful in deterring criminal activity then the public will be safer (Macdonald and Toal 2009: 373). However, the validity of these imperatives can be contested. First, one may ask, whose public good is being protected? The deportation of foreign-national prisoners can only be conducive to the *British* public good. Deportees are sent elsewhere. As Grewcock asks in the Australian context, 'If they are considered a risk, how does banishing them reduce the risk either to themselves or others?' (2011: 61). If one believes that the public needs protection from the individuals who are being deported, then deportation becomes but a means of 'exporting and circulating crime – "not in my back yard – you can have them"' (Macdonald and Toal 2009: 374).

Indeed, many have argued that there is a general 'lack of post-deportation accountability' (Grewcock 2011: 64), which is particularly relevant in the case of second-generation migrants (Bhabha 1998). Pertinent here is whether crime prevention should be an aim of immigration control in the first place. Clayton argues that 'punishment as meted out by the court is already intended to deter others and prevent re-offending and if it fails to do so that is a matter for criminal policy, not immigration control' (2008: 573). The author goes further stating, 'If deportation is not a punishment, the philosophical basis for it is hard to find' (2008: 573). It cannot be seen as a breach of hospitality when often the deportees have spent most of their adult lives as 'contributing' citizens. Ironically, deportation can hinder the efforts of rehabilitation developed by both HMPS and the foreign-national offenders themselves, as they are prevented from moving on with their lives (furthering their education, obtaining employment, etc.) after serving their sentences. An idle rehabilitated convict is hardly in the best interests of the public good.

Grewcock argues that deportation and the 'routine imposition of multiple punishments' inherent to the system – detention, reporting, etc. – 'undermines the principles of rehabilitation and reintegration and enforces permanent separation from social and family networks beyond any measure contemplated by the sentencing court' (2011: 69). In this sense, the author suggests that the deportation of foreign-national offenders operates as a kind of 'social death', as they are no longer given the opportunity to reintegrate in society and their communities. This is, in fact, a perception reflected throughout the narratives presented above. Foreign-national offenders are not just imprisoned and deported. Between one and the other they are often stripped of their right to work (and support their families), to travel and even of their freedom of movement, when placed under detention. Between imprisonment and deportation, migrants and their families live in limbo. Their lives are unsettled, uncertain and insecure.

Whose security is then being served by deportation policies? In this chapter I have sought not so much to answer this question as to formulate why we need to ask it and why it is important to reflect more on it. Despite its dubious effectiveness both in managing migration and protecting national security, deportation has come to be regarded as the unavoidable way to deal with those foreign nationals who are deemed unwanted. This is so not just in the UK but also in an ever-growing number of countries across the globe (see De Genova and Peutz 2010). Yet, how people respond to a given set of policies cannot be fully anticipated. Studying the ways people understand, interpret and experience policies allows for a better understanding of how they work in practice. Following Goldstein's (2010) call for anthropological engagements with security discourses and practices, and in line with the objectives of this volume, I have examined here how security concerns within the state's control of migration translate into migrants' everyday life, affecting their sense of self and instilling an overriding sense of vulnerability. The deportation narratives here presented are well illustrative of how those who are deemed a threat to security and hence are subjected to surveillance and banishment constantly feel vulnerable and in need of protection. Their sense of security is surely being affected by such policies.

In her study of cultures of immigration detention in the UK, Hall (2012: 7) argues that detention is not operationalised as the answer to a problem of border control, such as illegality. Rather, through detention the government has an effective tool 'through which individuals and mobile populations become managed as illegal, undesirable or threatening'. In much the same way, this chapter suggests that discourses of security in the context of deportation policies in the UK, have been successful not in addressing a threat to security but in producing and managing foreign-national offenders as dangerous to the public. This segment of the population has thus come to be understood as a threat to security and governed accordingly (see Bigo 2008). The policy imperatives for deportation are far from tested and require further discussion, if not questioning.

Notes

1. There are no available statistics on the offences committed by those deported from the UK. Offenders participating in this study had been convicted of drug-related offences (50 per cent), immigration offences (25 per cent), assault (20 per cent) and other offences such as fraud and robbery (5 per cent).
2. Reporting means that every week (or month) during a given time-slot migrants must go to the designated reporting centre and present their papers.
3. Statistics on deportations from the UK (i.e. excluding administrative removals) are not readily available. A Freedom of Information request revealed that between 2007 and 2010 the UKBA deported over 20,000 people, averaging 5000 per annum. This number does not include all those who have been issued with deportation orders but have not yet been deported either because

they are appealing their deportation or simply because the state cannot deport them (see Paoletti 2010).

4. There have been multiple reforms to the immigration tribunal system. At the time of research, in 2009, immigration appeals were heard at the single-tier Asylum and Immigration Tribunal, which subsequently reverted to being a two-tier system in February 2010. To avoid confusion over terminology I chose here to refer to it only as the Immigration Tribunal.

5. It may be more than coincidental that the one appellant interviewed who was not consumed by thoughts about his deportation was Basem, a very busy businessman.

References

Bailkin, J. (2008) 'Leaving home: the politics of deportation in postwar Britain', *Journal of British Studies*, Vol. 47, pp. 852–882.

BBC News (2006) 'How the deportation story emerged', 9 October. http://news.bbc.co.uk/1/hi/uk_politics/4945922.stm (accessed 1 August 2008).

Bhabha, J. (1998) '"Get back to where you once belonged": identity, citizenship and exclusion in Europe', *Human Rights Quarterly*, Vol. 20, pp. 592–627.

Bhui, H.S. (2007) 'Alien experience: foreign national prisoners after the deportation crisis', *Probation Journal*, Vol. 54, pp. 368–382.

Bigo, D. (2008) 'Globalised (in)security: the field and the ban-opticon', in Bigo, D. and Tsoukala, A. (eds) *Terror, Insecurity and Liberty: Illiberal Practices of Liberal Regimes after 9/11*, pp. 10–49 (London: Routledge).

Bloch, A. and Schuster, L. (2005) 'At the extremes of exclusion: deportation, detention and dispersal', *Ethnic and Racial Studies*, Vol. 28, No. 3, pp. 491–512.

Bosworth, M. (2011) 'Deportation, detention and foreign-national prisoners in England and Wales', *Citizenship Studies*, Vol. 15, No. 5, pp. 583–595.

Bosworth, M. and Guild, M. (2008) 'Governing through migration control: security and citizenship in Britain', *British Journal of Criminology*, Vol. 48, No. 6, pp. 703–719.

Burman, J. (2006) 'Absence, "removal" and everyday life in the diasporic city', *Space and Culture*, Vol. 9, pp. 279–293.

Clayton, G. (2008) *Textbook on Immigration and Asylum Law* (Oxford: Oxford University Press).

Clinks (2010) *NOMS' Hub and Spoke Arrangements for Foreign National Prisoners*. www.clinks.org

Cohen, R. (1997) 'Shaping the nation, excluding the other: the deportation of migrants from Britain', in Lucassen, L. and Lucassen, J. (eds) *Migration, Migration Theory, History: Old Paradigms and New Perspectives*, pp. 351–373 (Bern: Peter Lang).

De Genova, N. (2002) 'Migrant "illegality" and deportability in everyday life', *Annual Review of Anthropology*, Vol. 31, pp. 419–447.

De Genova, N. and Peutz, N. (eds) (2010) *The Deportation Regime: Sovereignty, Space, and the Freedom of Movement* (Durham, NC: Duke University Press).

Ellermann, A. (2009) *States against Migrants: Deportation in Germany and the United States* (New York: Cambridge University Press).

Fekete, L. (2006) 'Europe: "speech crime' and deportation', *Race & Class*, Vol. 47, No. 3, pp. 82–92.

Feldman, G. (2011) *The Migration Apparatus: Security, Labor and Policymaking in the European Union* (Stanford, CA: Stanford University Press).

Gibney, M.J. (2008) 'Asylum and the expansion of deportation in the United Kingdom', *Government and Opposition*, Vol. 43, No. 2, pp. 146–167.

Gibney, M.J. and Hansen, H. (2003) 'Deportation and the liberal state: the forcible return of asylum seekers and unlawful migrants in Canada, Germany and the United Kingdom', *New Issues in Refugee Research*, Working Paper No. 77 (Geneva: UNHCR).

Goldstein, D.M. (2010) 'Toward a critical anthropology of security', *Current Anthropology*, Vol. 51, No. 4, pp. 487–517.

Grewcock, M. (2011) 'Punishment, deportation and parole: the detention and removal of foreign prisoners under section 501 Migration Act 1958', *Australian & New Zealand Journal of Criminology*, Vol. 44, No. 1, pp. 56–73.

Guild, E. (2009) *Security and Migration in the 21st Century* (Cambridge: Polity Press).

Hall, A. (2012) *Border Watch: Cultures of Immigration, Detention and Control* (London: Pluto Press).

Hasselberg, I. (2013) *An Ethnography of Deportation from Britain*. Doctoral thesis, University of Sussex. http://sro.sussex.ac.uk/43788 (accessed February 2014).

HOCD (Home Office Communications Directorate) (2007) 'Asylum figures lowest since 1993', briefing note, 27 February. www.homeoffice.gov.uk/about-us/news/asylum-quarter-report (accessed 25 August 2008).

—— (2008) 'Record numbers of foreign criminals deported', briefing note, 1 July. www.homeoffice.gov.uk/about-us/news/record-numbers-foreign-criminals (accessed 25 August 2008).

ICIBI (Independent Chief Inspector of Borders and Immigration) (2011) *A Thematic Inspection of How the UK Border Agency Manages Foreign National Prisoners. February–May 2001.* http://icinspector.independent.gov.uk/inspections/inspection-reports/2011-inspection-reports-2/ (accessed February 2014).

ILPA (Immigration Law Practitioners' Association) (2011) *Breaking the Cycle: Effective Punishment, Rehabilitation and Sentencing of Offenders.* ILPA response to the Ministry of Justice consultation. www.ilpa.org.uk (accessed February 2014).

Inda, J.X. (2006) *Targeting Immigrants: Government, Technology and Ethics* (Oxford: Blackwell).

Kanstroom, D. (2000) 'Deportation, social control and punishment: some thoughts about why hard laws make bad cases', *Harvard Law Review*, Vol. 113, pp. 1890–1935.

Macdonald, I.A. and Toal, R. (2006) *Macdonald's Immigration Law and Practice: First Supplement to Sixth Edition* (London: Butterworths).

—— (2009) *Macdonald's Immigration Law and Practice: First Supplement to Seventh Edition* (London: Butterworths).

McGregor, J. (2009) *Narratives and Legacies of Detention: Zimbabwean Asylum Seekers' Experiences in Britain*. London: UCL Migration Research Unit and Zimbabwean Association. http: //zimassoc.files.wordpress.com/2010/09/final-report3.pdf (accessed February 2014).

—— (2011) 'Contestations and consequences of deportability: hunger strikes and the political agency of non-citizens', *Citizenship Studies*, Vol. 15, No. 5, pp. 597–611.

Meissner, F. and Hasselberg, I. (2012) 'Forever malleable: the field as a reflexive encounter', in Snellman, H. and Hirvi, L. (eds) *Where Is the Field? Exploring Migration through the Lenses of Fieldwork*, pp. 87–106 (Helsinki: Finnish Literature Society).

Paoletti, E. (2010) 'Deportation, non-deportability and ideas of membership', Working Paper Series No. 65 (Refugee Studies Centre, University of Oxford).

Peutz, N. (2006) 'Embarking on an anthropology of removal', *Current Anthropology*, Vol. 47, No. 2, pp. 217–241.

Randall, M. (1987) 'Threatened with deportation', *Latin American Perspectives*, Vol. 14, pp. 465–480.

Schuster, L. (2005) 'A sledgehammer to crack a nut: deportation, detention and dispersal in Europe', *Social Policy & Administration*, Vol. 39, No. 6, pp. 606–621.

UKBA (UK Border Agency) (n.d.) *Enforcement Instructions and Guidance*. https:// www.gov.uk/government/collections/enforcement-instructions-and-guidance ww.ukba.homeoffice.gov.uk/policyandlaw/guidance/enforcement/ (accessed February 2014).

Webber, F. (2009) 'Segregating foreign national prisoners', News post, 16 July, Institute of Race Relations. www.irr.org.uk/news/segregating-foreign-national-prisoners/ (accessed February 2014).

Willen, S.S. (2007) 'Towards a critical phenomenology of "illegality": state power, criminalization, and abjectivity among undocumented migrant workers in Tel Aviv, Israel', *International Migration*, Vol. 45, No. 3, pp. 8–38.

Zilberg, E. (2004) 'Fools banished from the kingdom: remapping geographies of gang violence between the Americas', *American Quarterly*, Vol. 56, No. 3, pp. 759–779.

8

Grey Zones of Illegality: Inhuman Conditions in Receiving Irregular Migrants in Greece

Jutta Lauth Bacas

This chapter focuses on the securitisation of migration on the Greek island of Lesbos, which is situated on the border between Greece and Turkey in the eastern Mediterranean Sea.[1] Today, Lesbos is becoming more and more integrated into transnational migration processes and flows, and on the island migrants are increasingly perceived not as persons in need of support and humanitarian aid but rather as potentially threatening and illegal presences in the country. The aim of the chapter is to analyse irregular border crossing and its consequences where the blue waters of the Mediterranean Sea divide not only two countries, but also the Schengen Area from the non-Schengen world.

The Schengen Agreement is of special importance for understanding the particular situation in Lesbos. In 1985, France, Germany and the Benelux Economic Union signed the Schengen border control agreement, which led to the removal of systematic border controls between the participating countries and the enhancement of border controls at the entry points to the Schengen Area. Greece joined the Schengen Area in 2000, and by 2010 the Schengen Area had expanded to include 25 European Union (EU) Member States.[2] Several commentators have pointed to the Schengen Agreement as the genesis moment of 'Fortress Europe' and the progressive securitisation of migration (see Bigo 1994; Huysmans 2006; see also Goldstein 2010). When undocumented migrants cross EU borders and enter the Schengen Area without authorisation they are not only completing dangerous journeys over difficult routes but also entering into the EU migration apparatus, with its *acquis*, or body of law, its policies and systems of policing and controlling migration (see Feldman 2011 and in this volume).

The Schengen borders between Greece and Turkey are complex in the sense that they are both maritime and land borders. With an overall length of about 13,670 km (Greece has the most extended borderline of all EU Member States) they provide various opportunities for undocumented migrants to enter Europe.[3] In 2010, the large majority of the mixed migratory flows entered the EU through the Greek-Turkish border. In 2010, 47,079 undocumented migrants used the land border between northern Greece and Turkey as a 'gateway to Europe', and 54,795 irregular migrants used it in 2011.[4] In reaction to this migratory pressure, the Greek authorities decided to further securitise the Greek-Turkish border and completed a 4-metre tall barbed-wire fence 12.5 km in length in northern Greece in December 2012.[5] As a consequence of this action, the numbers of irregular land border crossings dropped, and a shift in the pattern of clandestine arrivals could be observed from the Greek-Turkish land borders to the sea borders. Data from 2013 show that an increasing number of irregular migrants and refugees are attempting to enter Greece by sea because of strengthened security in Greece.[6]

This chapter places particular emphasis on the local reception structure that has been established for so-called 'boat people' on the Greek border island of Lesbos. I will investigate the trajectories of desperate men, women and children who manage to cross the maritime border and enter Greece clandestinely. The argument presented here is based on an anthropological research project where quantitative and qualitative data have been collected concerning the means and forms of irregular border crossing and the local reception structure caring for those strangers who have left home and country to flee war and social injustice. The term used here to refer to this group is undocumented or irregular boat migrants.[7] I track the routes of their clandestine border crossing and the practical consequences for those following such routes. First, border regulations and the bi-national framework for legal border crossing between Greece and Turkey will be analysed in order to provide a better understanding of the patterns of irregular border crossing occurring in the North Aegean Sea. Second, I attend to the social framework and the consequences of receiving undocumented migrants on the island of Lesbos. The procedure of arrest and detention in Mytilini, the island's capital, will be described, with special emphasis on securitisation within the reception process for persons arriving in Greece in an irregular manner. The final remarks will draw more general conclusions on the phases of administrative reception and the experiences boat migrants have to go through after their arrival on a European border island, together with the process of Othering and making them strangers in a 'grey zone of illegality'.

Border Crossing Between Greece and Turkey

When one begins to discuss Lesbos Island, one has to remember that until 1912 the Greek islands lying off the coast of Asia Minor were still under the rule of the Ottoman Empire (Tzimis 1996: 196fn). The maritime border between Greece and Turkey in its present form was defined and agreed upon by both countries as recently as 1923 subsequent to the Treaty of Lausanne (Clogg 1992: 101). The borderline between Greece and Turkey lies exactly in the middle of the maritime strait that separates the island from the mainland opposite.

Today, traffic of persons and goods between Greece and Turkey is governed not only by bi-national legislation but also by EU regulations on the Greek side. Mytilini is a port of exit providing customs services where people can leave Greece and enter Turkey as tourists without further complications. Since 2000, when Greece first implemented the Schengen Agreement, its land and sea borders with Turkey also became external borders of the Schengen Area, where strict checks on people exiting or entering the area are obligatory. The result is that the visa requirements for EU nationals entering Turkey are radically different from the requirements placed on Turkish nationals entering Greece, and thus the Schengen Area. Today, the legal entry of Greeks and other European tourists into Turkey is a relatively smooth process as long as one possesses the requisite valid identification documents, and there are no further visa requirements. Mytilini, then, has become a port of exit for increasing numbers of tourists. Indeed, Greek and Turkish national statistics show that Greek tourism to Turkey has been increasing steadily since 2000 (see Lauth Bacas 2003: 249).

In contrast to Greece–Turkey movement, traffic and legal border crossing from Turkey to Greece is more tightly regulated, and nation-state border control has been 'uploaded' to the EU and Schengen Agreement (see Baldwin-Edwards 2006: 117). Since Greece implemented the agreement in the year 2000, legal entry of Turkish nationals to Greece requires a visa, which can only be obtained at the Greek embassy in Ankara and the Greek consulates in Istanbul and Izmir. As a consequence of this visa regime, Turkish residents of Ayvalik or Dikkili (the provincial towns opposite Lesbos) have to travel 100 km to Izmir to queue for a Schengen visa at the Greek consulate in order to be able to travel 10 km to Mytilini for a temporary visit. The result of this costly and time-consuming procedure is that only a very few inhabitants of Turkish coastal towns do so.

Unauthorised entry from Turkey to the Greek border islands is relatively easy because the maritime frontier is difficult if not impossible to guard, especially at night. In the case of Lesbos, the water channel of 5–10 nautical miles serves as a bridge often used by boats and inflatable dinghies carrying undocumented migrants. Departure points for clandestine exits from Turkey are usually tiny fishing harbours, where the Turkish coastguard does not have a strong presence, or remote beaches on the mainland of Asia Minor, where small groups of undocumented migrants from Asian and African countries employ various types of vessel to cross the maritime border and slip into Europe clandestinely. Visitors to the remote beaches of Lesbos can come upon dozens of abandoned boats and dinghies, which have been used for unauthorised entry, with belongings such as wet blankets, plastic water bottles and plastic boots left by the migrants.

Considerable numbers of undocumented migrants manage to arrive on Lesbos every year. Figures from the Lesbos Police Department show that the number of arrests after clandestine arrival was growing constantly in the last decade, with 13,252 irregular boat migrants apprehended in 2008 and 8893 boat people apprehended in Mytilini in 2009. The total number of undocumented migrants arriving on the island every year is, in all probability, even higher, since it will include those who have not been detected and arrested by the authorities. In 2012 the number of clandestine arrivals on Lesbos dropped to a total of 1417 persons, but new data for the period January to August 2013 released by the Ministry of Public Order clearly reveal a new trend. In the first eight months of 2013, the island experienced an unforeseen increase of irregular arrivals of 2834 persons (an increase of over 100 per cent) due to the ongoing military conflicts in Syria, which added to the already large number of refugees present in Turkey.

In spite of efforts made to prevent undocumented entry of migrants into Greece through an elaborate system of border controls, the sea channel inevitably provides plenty of opportunities for unauthorised border crossing. The majority of boat migrants apprehended on the island don't originate from neighbouring Turkey, and even the Kurds form a minority of less than 1 per cent of the arriving boat people on Lesbos. Most of the refugees complete long journeys to get to Europe and mainly come from West Africa and the Far and Middle East, especially Palestine, Iraq, Syria and Afghanistan (Lauth Bacas 2012). As official data show, those boat migrants who declared Afghanistan as their country of origin clearly represent a majority of about two-thirds of the undocumented migrants arriving.

Today the island functions, for many irregular migrants from countries involved in armed conflicts, as a main 'port of irregular entry' to Greece and the West in general. This is likely to be closely related to military conflicts in their home countries and to ethnic networks involved in organising the journey of young people from Turkey to Western Europe.[8] In the years 2008–2009, next to Afghan refugees another group of desperate boat people arrived in increasing numbers on the island: refugees from Somalia. In comparison to boat migrants from Afghanistan, undocumented migrants declaring Somalia as their home country form the second largest group of arrivals in 2008 and in 2009. And, in the first eight months of 2013, seemingly all of a sudden, the number of Syrians arriving on Lesbos rose rapidly.

The influx of undocumented migrants from Syria started at the beginning of a year that seemed to promise smaller number of arrivals. Pressure on the regional administration increased rapidly as it adjusted to deal with constantly growing numbers of desperate, frozen and hungry foreigners arriving on the island's beaches. The reception of these boat migrants is organised and managed by the local authorities in a framework constrained, on the one hand, by national budget possibilities and national asylum and migration law and, on the other, by European-level policies and approaches towards irregular immigration. Several contributions to this volume note the complex entanglements of the EU-level migration apparatus with Member State and 'local' circumstances, from Demossier's work on Sarkozy and the Roma to Schwell's discussion of compensatory measures. What really happens in the process of receiving undocumented migrants in the local context is the question in focus in the following anthropological analysis. Though my analysis draws on extended fieldwork in this region, here I mainly refer to the situation as I observed it in Lesbos in the period from July to September 2013, a constantly changing period during which changes regarding the reception of undocumented boat migrants had already been implemented and could be observed in operation.

Entering the System of Administrative Detention

Hereafter my analysis tracks the process of administrative detention. First, I describe the process of detaining boat migrants on Lesbos before, second, analysing the legal procedures through which undocumented migrants are permitted to leave the island. I draw on participant observation in Mytilini in an effort to elicit the effects of this process within transit migrants' lived experiences. My aim is to use ethnographic research to provide an outline of how the detention of unauthorised migrants at the Greek-Turkish maritime border works at present in a way that shows the texture of actual experiences of security.

After arrest by members of the Hellenic Coast Guard or Greek police, undocumented migrants are taken to the local port where an improvised centre has been established. The term 'centre' denotes a mobile barracks in the fenced section of the port, where the first registration and a screening process takes place. In this screening process police officers assigned by FRONTEX are directly involved. FRONTEX is the European Agency for the Management of Operational Cooperation at the External Borders of the Member States of the EU. It was established pursuant to Council Regulation (EC) No. 2007/2004 and is active especially in the Schengen Area. FRONTEX is primarily a coordination agency that aims to assist Member States in 'managing' their borders but also facilitates 'the return of third-country nationals illegally present' – deportation, in other words. FRONTEX is also a training, research and intelligence agency with a budget of approximately €90 million in 2013 and access to significant military and surveillance resources. As the introduction to this volume argues, agencies such as FRONTEX are increasingly important features in the contemporary *security-scape*. The role played by FRONTEX concerning the Greco-Turkish border is controversial, especially in Lesbos. In 2009, Turkish authorities alleged that an Estonian aircraft on a FRONTEX mission violated their airspace.[9] More broadly, concerns have been raised about the role of the agency in indiscriminate deterrence of border crossing by third-country nationals with legitimate asylum claims. My recent ethnographic research showed the central role played by FRONTEX officers in initial screening interviews with newly arrived irregular migrants. This is a process sometimes completed with the help of translators that aims to elicit and register basic data such as a person's name, country of origin and age. Photographs and fingerprints are taken and a file is opened for every undocumented person who has arrived on European soil. After this first screening detainees were transferred to the Central Police Station.

It is important to note that all boat migrants arriving on Lesbos in an irregular manner are subjects of administrative detention, regardless of their age, health (serious health conditions or pregnancy) or vulnerability (as victims of torture). In Mytilini, babies, toddlers and small children are detained together with their mothers, as well as unaccompanied minors or other vulnerable persons with special needs. This systematic practice has been criticised by the Athens-based branch of the United Nations High Commissioner for Refugees (UNHCR) many times, who stated in a press release in July 2013 (yet again) that 'the administrative detention of persons seeking international protection, arriving or staying in Greece in an irregular manner, should constitute an exceptional measure of last resort and not a systematic practice'.

Improvised Reception Structures and Their Consequences

Due to the unprecedented numbers of irregular migrants and asylum seekers arriving, and the overcrowded conditions in holding premises in the Central Police Station of Mytilini (and in other local police stations in the villages of Mandamados, Kalloni, Plomari, Agia Paraskevi, Gera), the reception procedure changed during the spring of 2013. In March 2013, an improvised detention camp was opened in the fenced section of Mytilini port to detain newly arrived boat migrants for a limited period under the authority of Hellenic Coast Guard.[10] Participant observation in Mytilini during the summer of 2013 allowed me to document the insufficient and degrading conditions in which people were being detained. The 'camp' I was able to visit and to photograph consists of four tarpaulins ostensibly providing shelter and shade for about 100 undocumented migrants. A couple of mattresses and filthy blankets are thrown on the concrete floor completing the 'infrastructure' of the 'holding centre'. Two chemical toilets placed next to the tarpaulins are presumed to be sufficient to serve the needs of dozens of men, women, small children, and unaccompanied minors.

Figure 1   Mytilini Port Camp, Greece, 2013 (Photograph by Jutta Lauth Bacas)

A medical practitioner from 'Doctors of the World' argued that the most pressing problem that detainees encounter during their stay in the 'port camp' is the 'gap' in food supply.[11] Although the legal responsibility for the Mytilini port camp was assigned to the Hellenic Coast Guard by a district attorney of Lesbos, the authorities did not meet their obligations and failed to provide food to all detained boat migrants in the port. During my first visit to the port camp in July 2013, a friendly coast guard officer on duty informed me, 'Donations in all forms are warmly welcome.' Shortly after this encounter, I witnessed the arrival of a private vehicle. After entering the guarded and fenced port area, volunteers started to unpack bottled water, loaves of bread, packed cheese, fresh tomatoes and a few watermelons. The local press later reported that on that one day some 105 people, including pregnant women and 20 small children, were supported by local volunteers and non-governmental organisations (NGOs).[12] The donation I observed was a part of a regular, daily pattern of NGO-provided care: the arrested boat migrants were left without their basic needs being met (including medical and psychological support) by the Mytilini port authorities, and everything – including food and drinking water – was provided by volunteers to the detainees. This observation was not an isolated case: on 25 June 2013 a local network supporting refugees in the port of Mytilini had reported that 'about 100 refugees are currently detained in the port without any protection from the sun. Meanwhile temperatures have reached more than 35 degrees Celsius. A baby had to be transferred to hospital due to dehydration today.'[13] The 'gap' lingered on; it was only through donations of local volunteers and non-profit organisations like Odysseas and The Village of All-together that basic food supply was provided to newcomers who were in need of immediate support.[14] In other words, it was not the national authorities responsible but, rather, civilians' initiatives that prevented a humanitarian crisis from unfolding in the fenced port area of Mytilini.

Although the number of clandestine arrivals had doubled (in comparison with the previous year) to 2834 persons by end of August 2013, the local reception structure for desperate boat people remained ill prepared.[15] Another feature of the degrading conditions for detainees was the insufficient supply of drinking water. The only tap providing fresh water was intended for the operational needs of the Hellenic Coast Guard and the FRONTEX patrol boat. It was only after the coast guard vessels had been served that detainees were allowed to provide fresh water for their personal needs. Figure 2 shows a number of boat migrants from Afghanistan using the water tap the same day (27 July 2013) that an Italian patrol boat – operating in Greece during a FRONTEX mission – is mooring in Mytilini port.

An important question presents itself: why do European funds dedicated to Greece under the EU External Borders Fund for improving migration management – in 2013, for example, Greece has been allocated €44,745,804 – not lead to sufficient provisions of food supply and drinking water for refugees and boat migrants in Mytilini port?[16] While the aim of the External Borders Fund is to assist EU Member States in the implementation of common standards for border control and the management of migration flows, the ways and forms of receiving desperate boat migrants at a south-eastern border of Europe can clearly be

Figure 2   A FRONTEX patrol boat and Afghan refugees, Greece, 2013 (Photograph by Jutta Lauth Bacas)

characterised as sub-standard, despite the millions that have been provided and spent (other than on humanitarian aid to boat people in Mytilini).

As mentioned above, the Hellenic Coast Guard and FRONTEX border guards systematically screen newly arrived boat migrants. FRONTEX officers perform systematic interrogations and take photographs and fingerprints of all detainees older than 14 years, which are then entered into the Eurodac database. The security system seems to function, but it does so in the face of the fact that intercepted persons have not been supplied with food and drinking water by the local authorities. The European Commission allocated approximately €231 million to Greece under the

European Return Fund and the External Borders Fund during the period from 2011 until end of 2013.[17] My anthropological research quickly revealed 'bad practices', unlawful treatment and clear human rights abuses, all of which seem to be occluded in the gaze of the migration apparatus.

Degrading Detention in the Police Stations of Lesbos

The second phase of administrative detention takes place at the Central Police Station in Mytilini, where most boat migrants are transferred after the initial screening by FRONTEX. This transfer takes place without providing new arrivals with information on the future steps of the reception procedure, or their legal rights and obligations, in a language they understand. It is not difficult to imagine that the fact of being transferred in police vans from the port to an unknown police station, guarded by officers with machine guns, causes considerable stress to refugees who have fled armed conflicts in their home countries.

Permission to enter the holding premises inside the Central Police Station in Mytilini is not granted to citizens. According to information provided by local lawyers, the holding premises for undocumented migrants are situated on the first floor of the building. They consist of two holding compounds, which are often overcrowded and not suitable for long-term detention. The room for detained male migrants (on the right side) has the capacity to hold 27 people – but levels of overcrowding are often appalling, and up to 100 men have been detained in that room together. The room for detained female migrants (on the left side) has the capacity to hold up to between 4–5 persons, but is sometimes used to detain up to 20 migrant women (including pregnant women). Sanitary conditions are poor (only a few toilets used by both sexes on the floor) and have been the object of critical intervention by human rights lawyers, though without any results. Local volunteers also describe the premises as 'filthy police cells'.[18] Food for detained migrants is not provided in an organised way by the administration, but money is handed over by the local police (€5.80 per person per day). According to information provided by human rights organisations, detained migrants are allowed to order food at local fast food companies (using their mobile phones).[19] They order, for example, one pizza or two souvlaki sticks with a slice of bread as their daily provision. A conclusion can be drawn that, together with the ongoing practice of administrative detention for irregular entry, basic needs of newly arrived refugees and undocumented migrants are not addressed in an appropriate manner in the police holding premises.

Due to the absence of competent interpreters or social workers, any form of communication with the foreigners behind bars is extremely limited, and the needs of specifically vulnerable groups are difficult to communicate, and it is hard for them to be met. The social setting in the holding premises of the Central Police Station is clearly hierarchical and treats the foreign boat people not as people in need but as 'illegals', giving rise to a hostile reinventing of the 'other'. Instead of finding support and humanitarian aid, the boat people who arrive on Lesbos find themselves the subjects of administrative detention and their expectations for a secure life in Europe badly disappointed. The administrative detention is clearly a cause of psychological stress. A medical doctor from Doctors of the World, a key NGO that delivers medical aid to the newcomers at Mytilini port, underlined this in an interview carried out in August 2013.[20]

On the other hand, the young police officers on duty at the Central Police Station perceive the undocumented migrants as suspects, not as asylum seekers or potential refugees. They approach the growing numbers of detainees with institutionalised disinterest, seeing it as a part of their professional roles to remain emotionally detached (see also Feldman in this volume). Thus personal contacts and interaction between detainees and the police personnel are kept to a minimum. Due to the absence of interpreters they can communicate with the detainees only through gestures.[21] The general picture is that the newcomers are segregated and kept in custody in a transitional zone where they are made to wait for things to happen under particularly worrying conditions.

The degrading and inhuman conditions in Greek police stations and holding facilities for irregular migrants have been the subject of severe criticism by human rights organisations and rulings of the European Court of Human Rights. Many of the criticisms of Greek detention sites are highlighted by a report by Amnesty International in 2010 with the telling title, *Greece: Irregular Migrants and Asylum Seekers Routinely Detained in Substandard Conditions*. Apart from visits to detention centres and interviews with undocumented migrants and asylum seekers detained there, this report is based on judgements by the European Court of Human Rights (ECHR), in which third-country nationals challenged the legality of their detention after unauthorised entry to Greece. A well-documented case is that of Eivas Rahimi (*Rahimi vs Greece 2011*), a young Afghan boy who arrived on Lesbos in July 2007. Regardless of his status as a minor and poor health condition, Rahimi was arrested after his clandestine arrival and transferred to a detention centre where he was held along with adult males. He had to sleep on a dirty mattress, eat sitting on the floor, and was not allowed any contact with the outside world – in practice he was unable to contact a lawyer.

Upon his release, the 15-year-old boy was left without any means of transport or support by the Greek authorities and travelled to Athens by his own means. With the support of Greek NGO Arsis, the young Afghan launched an asylum application and also lodged a complaint with the ECHR in January 2008 over the degrading treatment and the lack of support in the Mytilini detention centre. In April 2011, the Court ruled that Rahimi was held in *degrading conditions* of inadequate care and *unlawful detention* and, therefore, his treatment by the Greek authorities violated the European Convention on Human Rights.[22]

In several other cases, the ECHR found Greece to be in violation of the right to freedom from inhuman or degrading treatment. In the case of *S.D. v. Grèce* (2009), the ECHR found that the conditions of a Turkish national's detention amounted to degrading treatment, citing the lack of facilities for outdoor exercise, the inability to establish contact with the outside world, the lack of medical attention, and an excessively long detention period of over two months given those poor conditions.[23] The conditions in Greek police stations and holding facilities are still the subject of criticism to this day. One telling comment was made by a member of the UN Working Group on Arbitrary Detention, stating after a visit to Greece:

> The imprisonment of a migrant or an asylum seeker for up to 18 months, in conditions that are sometimes found to be even worse than in the regular prisons, could be considered as a punishment imposed on a person who has not committed any crime.[24]

Leaving the Local System of Administrative Detention

The legal framework for regulating administrative detention of undocumented migrants in Greece changed several times during the past decade, mainly prolonging migrants' and asylum seekers' detention. During the early 2000s, the maximum duration of detention was limited to six months (see Spathana 2003). After a revision of this ruling in 2005, the law allowed for up to 12 months of detention of undocumented migrants and asylum seekers. In July 2009, with a new Presidential Decree, the legally permitted detention period was extended once more to up to 18 months.[25] While this ruling was still in effect in 2013, in practice, many boat migrants detained on Lesbos are *de facto* released earlier. According to information provided by a medic from Doctors of the World in August 2013, especially those families with small children are released and allowed to leave the island of Lesbos within two or three days.[26]

Most of the detainees on Lesbos expect to be released sooner or later. Indeed, after a couple of days, a Greek document is handed over to every detainee and he/she is informed about their future fate: the document is an official expulsion order.[27] Signed by the Head of the Police Department, the expulsion document orders the irregular immigrant to leave the country *within four weeks* at his or her own expense and go *to a country of his or her own choice*. Usually the undocumented migrants from various Asian and African countries are unable to read that Greek document or to appeal against the decision taken. But this is secondary to the side-effect of the deportation order. According to Greek law, the authorities may permit a provisional stay, whenever the immediate expulsion of an alien is not feasible (Kanellopoulos 2005: 37). As a practical consequence, the expulsion order handed down to the undocumented migrant is accompanied by a provisional 'residence permit', which is granted by the Greek authorities. This provisional stay is limited – as stated above – ordering the undocumented migrant to leave the country within 30 days. But for four weeks he/she has been officially granted a moratorium and is allowed to move freely and to leave Lesbos.

During the years 2003–2011, undocumented boat migrants from Afghanistan and East Africa formed a majority of clandestine arrivals. The situation in 2013 is instead characterised by the arrival of a large number of refugees from Syria. The report on Lawand Deek, a 21-year-old refugee from the Ar-Raqqah province in Syria, who arrived on Lesbos in spring 2013, is illustrative:

> Lawand and his travelling companions spent one night in Lesvos port in the custody of the coastguard, and another night in a police station. The police issued them with documents allowing them to stay in Greece for six months. After this period they must either apply for the documents to be renewed or leave the country. Having received his papers, Lawand bought a ferry ticket to the Greek capital, Athens. 'I have no words to

explain this feeling. I feel free and happy to be out of Syria', he says. The ferry arrived in the port of Piraeus, near Athens, at first light.[28]

Greek authorities treat undocumented migrants from Syria differently because of the ongoing war there. Syrians in detention receive an expulsion order with a time limit of six months (instead of one month). In contrast to other crisis refugees, Syrians are thus granted a 'special moratorium' of 180 days during which they are allowed to stay in Greece (due to the intervention of the Greek branch of UNHCR). In addition to this administrative practice, a renewal of the 'moratorium' granted to Syrian refugees is possible for another six months, which prevents their detention or forced return.

Also irregular migrants from countries like Somalia or Afghanistan without a passport are not forcibly returned to Ayvalik or Dikkili (the opposite ports of entry in Turkey) in spite of a valid expulsion order. To implement deportation in these cases is not feasible since, in most cases, the Turkish authorities do not accept their re-entry. As a result, in 2012 a lawyer in Mytilini could only record nine cases of forced returns of Iranian citizens from Lesbos to the opposite Turkish port of Dikkili (out of a total of 1417 arrivals in 2012).[29]

Apart from exceptional cases, the present situation is that, after a certain period in administrative detention, nearly all undocumented newcomers in Mytilini are *de jure* expelled and *de facto* released. The provisionally 'regularised' migrants usually walk away from the Central Police Station on foot and turn (again) towards the harbour.[30] At the harbour they prove their identity (with the expulsion order) and are able to buy a third-class ferry ticket to Athens from offices of NEL, the Lesbos Maritime Company. Rumour has it that in some cases the Lesbos Maritime Company provides free transport for those foreigners who are not able to pay for their trip to Athens. The aim of this procedure can be clearly understood as a way to export a possible social problem from the island to mainland Greece. After their release the irregular migrants legally embark on the afternoon ferry to Athens – under the gaze of the Hellenic Coast Guards – and disembark at Piraeus the next morning. Although they move freely to the mainland and the national capital, their stay in Greece is not 'legal' in a strict sense. They are not holders of a regular residence permit allowing them to stay and work in the country. The expulsion order with its time limitation has a side-effect: due to the special Greek administrative practice of 'squaring the circle' (that is ordering undocumented migrants to leave the country *and* allowing them to stay to prepare their departure), irregular migrants with an expulsion order have entered a 'grey zone of semi-illegality' (Lauth Bacas 2006) to manoeuvre inside the national territory for 30 days. As soon as this 'moratorium' expires, the newcomers' stay on the national territory is defined as 'illegal' by the Greek authorities and they could become subjects of administrative detention once more. This happened during the so-called 'sweeping operations' that began in Athens in August 2013. Since then, more than 6000 migrants without a valid residence permit have been detained in various detention centres (see Lauth Bacas 2012: 432).

The Hellenic Coast Guard and the Reception of Boat People

In the process of receiving clandestine boat migrants on Greek border islands, the officers of the Hellenic Coast Guard have a distinct function (see also Lauth Bacas, 2005, 2012). Like other national coast guards, the Hellenic Coast Guard is a paramilitary organisation that can support the Hellenic Navy in wartime, but is under separate civilian control in times of peace. The main tasks of the Hellenic Coast Guard are defined (on its official website) as law enforcement at sea, search and rescue operations, fishery patrolling and prevention of illegal immigration.[31]

The latter was also the topic of an executive meeting between the Greek minister of maritime affairs, Miltiadis Barbitziotis and the German ambassador to Greece, Wolfgang Dold, on 27 September 2013. In this meeting, a new role of the Hellenic Coast Guard was announced by the Greek minister: 'Among others, the officers of the Hellenic Coast Guard have taken over a very important task, which is providing humanitarian aid, the provision and care for illegal [sic] migrants during the first 24 or 48 hours [after their arrival].'[32] The key terms 'humanitarian aid, provision and care' (in Greek: ανθρωπιστική βοήθεια, η φροντίδα δηλαδή και η περίθαλψη των παράνομων μεταναστών) sound good in an air-conditioned minister's office in urban Piraeus. The experiences of boat people on a remote border island are different, as participant observation shows.

The main tasks of the Hellenic Coast Guard are sea patrols along an 'open' maritime border which cannot be guarded by fences and chicken wire netting.[33] Since 2011, joint maritime patrols with the European border agency FRONTEX are conducted on the Greek-Turkish sea border in the framework of Joint Operation Poseidon.[34] The borderline to be monitored lies precisely in the middle of the sea channel between Lesbos and Turkey, which gives a chance for small plastic boats (less visible on radar screens) to cross this line clandestinely. Therefore, patrol boats cover the Greek part of border night after night, aiming to find foreign boats close to the national territory. In such cases, foreign boats in the middle of the strait which try to navigate into Greek national waters are systematically threatened and discouraged by coast guard actions. These efforts to prevent undocumented entry are officially called 'preventions' (in Greek: αποτροπή) as part of the mechanisms of maritime surveillance. In discussions, coast guard officers stress their duty to guard the national waters and their right to prevent the entry of clandestine boats before they can reach the Greek national territory.

These 'preventions' of entry happen far away from the eyes of the public, but they are no secret. The local newspapers report on various cases where small boats were rejected and forced to return into the Turkish part of the water channel. One night, 26 immigrants managed to reach the island's shores, but two other boats with nine persons on board were discovered by Greek patrol boats and forced to return to the Turkish waters.[35] The Hellenic Coast Guard also publishes data under the category 'entry deterrence' (in Greek: Αποτροπή Εισόδου Λαθρομεταναστών) on its web site: reporting 1566 cases in 2006 and 3108 cases in 2007.[36] In all these preventions of entrance, Greek patrol vessels approach the tiny dinghies at high speed with the aim of threatening the foreigners and discouraging them from entering the Greek part of the strait. But increased border controls in the context of these operations have not been without criticism. The critical question is whether foreign boats already within national territorial waters have been scared off and pushed back. These push-back practices might result in asylum seekers being returned to Turkey without being given an opportunity to make their asylum claims in a European country.

In contrast to Greek coast guard officials who stress the effective and legal ways their staff monitor the maritime border in line with the Schengen Treaty, other voices are more critical towards the patrol operations in the strait between Lesbos and Turkey. The NGO PRO ASYL was particularly decisive in its criticism, arguing that boat migrants have been threatened by Greek patrol boats and obliged by force to return to Turkish waters in order to prevent their entry to Greek territory (PRO ASYL 2007, 2010). The Greek Ombudsman, as an independent institution, investigated the accusations and found no legally valid evidence for these allegations, but did hint at a 'grey zone' outside public control where it is difficult to estimate and to prove what is really happening on international sea borders at night.[37]

A conclusion can be drawn that the present structure of receiving boat migrants on Lesbos is not only a complex one, but also an ambiguous procedure where the state is not carrying out its responsibilities and humanitarian obligations. These ambiguities became obvious once more during the final stage of my fieldwork in September 2013. On 25 September, local press announced the opening of a new holding centre for undocumented migrants outside of the island's capital – close to a village called Moria. The first 13 detainees, refugees from Palestine and Afghanistan including unaccompanied minors, had been transferred to Moria the day before.[38] The Moria holding centre, operating under the authority of the national police, has the capacity to hold 196 persons (in 14 containers).[39] Although the new detention centre started to operate on 25 September 2013, the Hellenic Coast Guard still has responsibility for the basic needs of boat migrants in the first 24 or 48 hours after their arrival, according to a public statement of the Greek Minister of Maritime Affairs on 29 September 2013. At the time this statement was made, the appropriate infrastructure to carry out the task of first reception had been *de facto* missing in Mytilini harbour for six months (since March 2013) and a new detention centre close to the capital had been opened a few days before.

Not only critical observers, but all the actors involved in the process of migrants' reception (local police and coast guard forces as well as arriving boat migrants and local volunteers) are a bit puzzled: who is officially responsible for the basic needs of growing numbers of hungry, wet, frightened and suffering newcomers? Even the FRONTEX Operational Office in Piraeus, established in October 2010 to strengthen its regional presence, cannot provide an answer to this question.[40] Unfortunately, lack of coordination and cooperation, and the sub-standard level of the local reception infrastructure make a bad basis for any effective 'management of migration flows'.

Securitisation and Managing the Arrival of Undocumented Migrants

On Lesbos, all detected boat migrants are immediately arrested and kept in detention for several days or weeks, thus few islanders actually come into direct contact with the undocumented newcomers. Efforts are made to keep them as strangers in a transit zone outside the island's everyday social life. It has to be stressed that this social and legal construction and positioning of 'the Other' can be observed not only locally but also on the national and European level as well.

In the framework of the European Pact on Immigration and Asylum, EU Member States jointly decided in 2008 to tackle illegal immigration, with the result that state employees on Europe's periphery have little room for manoeuvre in their everyday interactions with irregular migrants. As fieldwork data show, the institutionalised and hierarchical form of reception of undocumented boat migrants on a Greek border island is governed not by the well-known hospitality of the Greeks, but by locking the newcomers off in a segregated space. With hundreds of irregular migrants arriving every year, the stranger is no longer conceptualised as a 'guest' (with whom face-to-face interaction takes place according to culturally elaborated rules), but as a 'stranger', who has to be kept away from the personal sphere to minimise encounters and possible threats.

The situation has become much more tense in 2013, which is also the fifth year of the financial crisis is Greece and the associated austerity measures. As participant observation in summer 2013 has clearly shown, the local reception structure is generally insufficient to meet the basic needs of newly arrived boat migrants. The material needed to provide shelter and medical aid to newcomers is certainly insufficient, but even basic needs such as water and food are not provided by the local or national authorities. On one hand, then, one sees superficial technical support provided by the European border agency FRONTEX, and enhanced patrolling and safeguarding of the maritime Greek-Turkish border is apparent from Lesbos. However, on the other hand, the basic human rights of undocumented boat migrants arrested by FRONTEX and the Hellenic Coast Guard are violated and the whole system lacks integrity.

As has been stressed in the chapter, the structure of immigrant and refugee reception in Greece is focused on securitisation and reinforcing border control. To the public, FRONTEX officially defines itself as an agency that 'promotes, coordinates and develops European border management in line with the EU fundamental rights charter'. In doing so, the European border agency wants its missions to ensure 'that respect for fundamental rights and the human dignity … is maintained at every stage'.[41] To achieve the agency's core tasks FRONTEX was granted a budget of approximately €90 million in 2013.[42] Some of these funds are allocated to the FRONTEX Operational Office (FOO) in Piraeus, Greece. Launching the office on

1 October 2010, FRONTEX Executive Director, Ilkka Laitinen stressed, 'the need to develop a more rapid response capacity to unforeseeable events'[43] (for example serving the needs of growing numbers of irregular boat migrants?). But in contrast to what is officially stated, empirical data collected in summer 2013 on a remote south-east European border island reveal not a rapid response, but unlawful treatment of newly arrived boat migrants and clear human rights abuses – including the missing supply of food and drinking water – in the presence of FRONTEX officers.

In this chapter I have attempted to portray actually existing securitisation of irregular migration to Greece and how it is performed. By carefully investigating the procedures and processes of securitisation at the local level, a conclusion can be drawn regarding irregular migration as a complex process of unauthorised entry and reception management which, in the Greek case, is characterised by unacceptable conditions in the local reception facilities and a series of legal omissions and violations of EU regulations as well as fundamental human rights as defined by the European Charter of Human Rights. By doing so, the Greek state and an EU agency in charge of ensuring 'a high level of control' at EU external borders add to the complex mix of unlawful acts involved in irregular transit migration a national and European component, ignoring the individual needs and best interests of undocumented migrants and their children.

Notes

1. Fieldwork on the Greek border island of Lesbos was conducted from July to September 2013 (following on from previous fieldwork projects on Lesbos starting in 2004 until 2010), investigating the principle routes of clandestine entry from Turkey across the Aegean Sea to Lesbos island.

2. A Treaty of Amsterdam, 1997, protocol brought the Schengen Agreement into the EU framework, and the Schengen *acquis*, or body of law, is now in the legal and institutional framework of the EU. This provides for, *inter alia*, police, surveillance, judicial cooperation and the Schengen Information System (SIS).

3. Coastline length from: http://world.bymap.org/Coastlines.html (accessed 10 October 2013).

4. Data released by the Minister of Public Order and Citizen Protection. www.astynomia.gr/index.php?option=ozo_content&perform=view&id=5071&Itemid=429&lang=EN (accessed 10 October 2013).

5. See the Greek newspaper *ekathermini* of 7 December 2012 (in English): 'Greece completes anti-migrant fence at Turkish border'. www.ekathimerini. com/4dcgi/_w_articles_wsite1_1_17/12/2012_474782 (accessed 10 October 2013).

6. Data released by the Minister of Public Order and Citizen Protection, see: www.astynomia.gr/index.php?option=0z0_content&perform=view&id=247 27&Itemid=73&lang=EN (accessed 10 October 2013).

7. In this essay, the terms 'irregular migrant' and 'undocumented migrant' are used as synonyms. For further information on categories of migrants in Greece see Lauth Bacas (2012: 411–413).

8. Ethnic networks are reported to play a major role in organising irregular entry of Kurdish refugees into Greece by the land route in the Epiros area of northern Greece (see Papadopoulou 2004).

9. According to findings made by the Hellenic authorities and the airplane crew there was no violation of Turkish airspace. See www.balkanalysis. com/greece/2011/09/23/safeguarding-europe%E2%80%99s-southern-bor-ders-interview-with-klaus-roesler-director-of-operations-division-frontex/ (accessed 10 October 2013).

10. The date of the operational opening of the improvised detention center (March 2013) was confirmed in interviews on 31 August 2013 with a medical practitioner from the Greek NGO Doctors of the World and a lawyer appointed by the Ecumenical Refugee Programme (KSPM) of the Church of Greece.

11. The Greek NGO Doctors of the World started a project 'Supporting Vulnerable Groups in Need of International Protection on the Island of Lesvos' in August 2013. See www.mdmgreece.gr (accessed 10 October 2013).

12. See *Empros*, 27 July 2013 (in Greek): www.emprosnet.gr/article/48107-105-metanastes-sto-limani (accessed 10 October 2013).

13. See Welcome 2 Lesvos, a blog run by a network of civil rights activists on Lesbos Island and beyond: http: //lesvos.w2eu.net/page/2/ (accessed 10 October 2013).

14. Odysseas is a non-profit organization providing educational courses to young asylum seekers living in the 'Villa Azari' in Agiassos on Lesbos Island: www. odysseas.at/ (accessed 10 October 2013). The Village of All-together is a network of local volunteers who support irregular boat migrants by cooking food, bringing warm clothes and other things they might lack: http://lesvos. w2eu.net/2012/12/08/civilians-initiative-the-village-of-all-together-opening-of-pikpa/ (accessed 10 October 2013).

15. In comparison with a total of 1417 persons arriving clandestinely on Lesbos in 2012, data for the period 2012 and 2013 released by the Greek Ministry of Public Order and Citizens Protection. See: www.astynomia.gr/index.

php?option=0zo_content&perform=view&id=24727&Itemid=73&lang=EN. (accessed 10 October 2013).

16. See http://europa.eu/rapid/press-release_IP-11-953_en.htm?locale=en (accessed 10 October 2013).

17. From 2011 to 2013, Greece received €98.6 million under the Return Fund and €132.8 million under the External Border Fund. See Committee on Migration, Refugees and Displaced Persons (2013).

18. See 'Welcome 2 Lesvos' blog: http://lesvos.w2eu.net/ (accessed 10 October 2013).

19. Information provided by a lawyer appointed by the Ecumenical Refugee Program (KSPM) of the Church of Greece, during an interview in Mytilini on 31 August 2013.

20. Interview conducted on 31 August 2013 in Mytilini with P.S., medical practitioner, employed on the project 'Supporting Vulnerable Groups in Need of International Protection on the Island of Lesvos' by the Greek NGO Doctors of the World.

21. Information provided by DS, a lawyer appointed by the Ecumenical Refugee Program (KSPM) of the Church of Greece, during an interview conducted on 31 August 2013 in Mytilini.

22. Vgl. European Court of Human Rights, Press Release No. 297 of 05 April 2011: *Rahimi vs. Greece* (Appl. No. 8687/08): http://cmiskp.echr.coe.int/ tkp197/search.asp? sessionId=69375377&skin=hudoc-pr-en&action=request (accessed 10 October 2013).

23. See: *S.D. v Grèce* 2009: http://echr.ketse.com/doc/53541.07-en-20090611/ (accessed 10 October 2013).

24. Quote from Vladimir Tochilovsky, member of UN Working Group on Arbitrary Detention, at the end of his visit to Greece on 31 January 2013. http://www. ohchr.org/en/NewsEvents/Pages/DisplayNews.aspx?NewsID=12963&LangID=E. (accessed 10 October 2013).

25. See: http://www.msf-seasia.org/news/14913

26. Information provided by PS, a medical practitioner from the Greek NGO Doctors of the World, during an interview in Mytilini on 31 August 2013.

27. Foreign smugglers arrested by the Mytilini coastguard undergo a different procedure. They are accused of illegal trafficking in immigrants and a court case is opened. For example, the Mytilini court sentenced a Turkish human-smuggler to seven years in prison and a fine of €14,600, as the *Aeolian News* (in Greek Αιολικά Νέα) reported on 17 April 2004.

28. The report is presented by the Greek NGO Doctors without Borders, who were providing medical support to irregular boat migrants and refugees on Lesbos during the summer of 2013: www.msf-seasia.org/news/14913 (accessed 10 October 2013).

29. Information provided by DS, a lawyer appointed by the Ecumenical Refugee Program (KSPM) of the Church of Greece, during an interview in Mytilini on 31 August 2013.

30. It is important to note that this type of provisional 'regularisation' of migrants without documents crossing the Aegean differs from the regularisation offered to undocumented economic migrants in Greece in 2001 and in 2005. For the regularisation of the latter see Fakiolas (2003) and Cavounidis (2006).

31. See the section 'History and Present Tasks of the Hellenic Coast Guard' on the official web site of the Hellenic Coast Guard (in Greek). www.hcg.gr/node/95 (accessed 10 October 2013).

32. See Press Report of the Greek Coast Guard of 27 September 2013 (in Greek): Όπως υπογράμμισε ο Υπουργός Ναυτιλίας και Αιγαίου, «εκτός των άλλων έχει επωμιστεί ένα ιδιαίτερα σημαντικό για εμάς έργο, που είναι η ανθρωπιστική βοήθεια, η φροντίδα δηλαδή και η περίθαλψη των παράνομων μεταναστών για τις πρώτες 24 ή 48 ώρες». www.hcg.gr/node/5920 (accessed 10 October 2013).

33. In the growing literature on the anthropology of borders, the Mexican-US border, with its sophisticated surveillance installations, has become a paradigm of border control against irregular migration (see Alvarez 1995). The sea route for irregular entry, increasingly chosen on Europe's southern borders, has also recently been investigated (see Lauth Bacas 2013).

34. FRONTEX announcement on the Joint Operation Poseidon Sea 2011 of 2 March 2011, see www.frontex.europa.eu/news/rabit-operation-2010-ends-replaced-by-jo-poseidon-2011-iA6Kaq. (accessed 10 October 2013).

35. Press report in the local *Aeolian News* (in Greek Αιολικά Νέα), 22 July 2002.

36. See Greek Ministry of Maritime Affairs, see www.yen.gr/wide/yen. chtm?prnbr=32028. (accessed 10 October 2013).

37. Public letter by the Greek Ombudsman to the Greek Ministry of the Merchant Marine on 22 November 2007 (in Greek). URL: www.synigoros.gr (accessed 10 October 2013).

38. See: Welcome 2 Lesvos blog, http://lesvos.w2eu.net/ (accessed 10 October 2013).

39. See: Welcome 2 Lesvos blog, http://lesvos.w2eu.net/ (accessed 10 October 2013).

40. See: www.frontex.europa.eu/news/frontex-operational-office-opens-in-piraeus-hk4q3Z (accessed 10 October 2013).

41. See: www.frontex.europa.eu/about-frontex/mission-and-tasks (accessed 10 October 2013).

42. Another €118,187,000 has been spent by FRONTEX in 2012. Budget information for 2012 and 2013 given on the FRONTEX web site, see: www. frontex.europa.eu/assets/About_Frontex/Governance_documents/Budget/ Budget_2012.pdf. (accessed 10 October 2013).

43. Quote given on the FRONTEX web site, www.frontex.europa.eu/news/fron-tex-operational-office-opens-in-piraeus-hk4q3Z. (accessed 10 October 2013).

References

Alvarez, R.R. (1995) 'The Mexican–US border: the making of an anthropology of borderlands', *Annual Review of Anthropology*, No. 24, pp. 447–470.

Amnesty International (2010) *Greece: Irregular Migrants and Asylum Seekers Routinely Detained in Substandard Conditions.* www.amnesty.org/en/library/asset/EUR25/002/2010/en/07291fb2-dcb8-4393-9f13-2d2487368310/eur250022010en.pdf (accessed 10 October 2013).

Baldwin-Edwards, M. (2006) 'Migration between Greece and Turkey: from the "exchange of population" to the non-recognition of borders', *South-East Europe Review*, No.3, pp. 115–122.

Bigo, D. (1994) 'The European internal security field' in Anderson, M. and den Boer, M. (eds) *Policing across National Boundaries*, pp. 161–173 (London: Pinter).

Cavounidis, J. (2006) 'Labour market impact of migration: employment structures and the case of Greece', *International Migration Review*, Vol. 40, No. 3, pp. 635–660.

Clogg, R. (1992) *A Concise History of Modern Greece* (Cambridge: Cambridge University Press).

Fakiolas, R. (2003) 'Regularising undocumented immigrants in Greece: procedures and effects', *Journal of Ethnic and Migration Studies*, Vol. 29, No. 3, pp. 535–561.

Committee on Migration, Refugees and Displaced Persons (2013) *Report to the Council of Europe: Migration and Asylum: Mounting Tensions in the Eastern Mediterranean*, Doc. 13106, 23 January. http://assembly.coe.int/ASP/XRef/X2H-DW-XSL.asp?fileid=19349&lang=en (accessed 10 October 2013).

Feldman, G. (2011) *The Migration Apparatus: Security, Labour, and Policymaking in the European Union* (Stanford, CA: Stanford University Press).

Goldstein, D.M. (2010) 'Toward a critical anthropology of security', *Current Anthropology*, Vol. 51, No. 4, pp. 487–517.

Huysmans, J. (2006) *The Politics of Insecurity: Fear, Migration and Asylum in the EU* (London: Routledge).

Kanellopoulos, C. (2005) *Illegally Resident Third-country Nationals in Greece: State Approaches Towards them, their Profile and Social Situation* (Brussels: European Migration Network and KEPE).

Lauth Bacas, J. (2003) 'Greek tourists in Turkey: an anthropological case study', *Journal of Mediterranean Studies*, Vol. 15, pp. 239–258.

—— (2005) 'Marble monuments and symbolic boundaries on Lesbos: a case study from the Greek-Turkish border', in Wilson, T.M. and Donnan, H. (eds) *Culture and Power at the Edges of the State: National Support and Subversion in European Border Regions*, pp. 55–80 (Berlin: LIT).

—— (2006) Θαλάσσια σύνορα και μη νόμιμη μετανάστευση: ο θαλάσσιος δρόμος προς την Ελλάδα ('Maritime borders and undocumented migration: the maritime road to Greece), in Stylianoudi, L. (ed.) Ελληνική Κοινωνία. Επετηρίδα 2006 του Κέντρου Ερεύνης της Ελληνικής Κοινωνίας [Greek Society: Yearbook 2006 of the Research Centre for Greek Society], pp. 95–139 (Athens: Ακαδημία Αθηνώ).

—— (2012) 'Griechenland und seine Ausländer: Integration und Exklusion in Zeiten der Krise', in Südosteuropa. Zeitschrift für Politik und Gesellschaft, Vol. 60, No. 3, pp. 410–432.

—— (2013) 'Managing proximity and asymmetry in border encounters: the reception of undocumented migrants on a Greek border island', in Lauth Bacas, J. and Kavanagh, W. (eds) Border Encounters: Proximity and Asymmetry at Europe's Frontiers, pp. 256–280 (New York: Berghahn).

Papadopoulou, A. (2004) 'Smuggling into Europe: transit migrants in Greece', Journal of Refugee Studies, Vol. 17, No. 2, pp. 167–184.

PRO ASYL (2007) The Truth may be Bitter, But it Must be Told: The Situation of Refugees in the Aegean and the Practices of the Greek Coast Guard (Frankfurt: PRO ASYL). Griechenlandbericht_Engl.pdf (accessed February 2014).

PRO ASYL (2010) Flüchtlinge in Griechenland. Gestrandet, entrechtet und ohne Schutz. Frankfurt: PRO ASYL. GR_BroschuereFluechtlinge2010.pdf (accessed February 2014).

Spathana, E. (2003) Legal Aid for Refugees and Asylum Seekers in Greece (Athens: Greek Council for Refugees).

Tzimis, S. (1996) History of Lesbos, 2nd edn (Mytilini: Association of Philologists).

UNHCR Greece (2013) 'Current issues of refugee protection in Greece', Press release, Athens, July. www.asylumineurope.org/files/resources/greece_positions_july_2013_en.pdf? (accessed 10 October 2013).

Conclusions

Mark Maguire, Catarina Frois and Nils Zurawski

In *Precarious Life*, Judith Butler asks readers to consider the following question: 'Under what conditions is critique itself censored, as if any reflexive criticism can only and always be construed as weakness and fallibility?' (2004: 42). The present volume represents an effort to further develop a critical anthropology of security by drawing together anthropological work on different domains, aspects and experiences of security and insecurity today. Therefore, *critical* anthropological perspectives and critique itself are central concerns. To engage in critique is not, we believe, to show weakness, even if it turns reflexively on anthropology's conceptual work and research practices, and even if it is voiced from outside dominant institutions and articulated in unofficial ways. On the contrary, many of the chapters in this volume pay particular attention to the everyday lives of people who experience the thin end of the security wedge. Moreover, the experiences and stories that emerge from everyday life, as Michael Jackson reminds us: 'testify to the very diversity, ambiguity, and interconnectedness of experiences that abstract thought seeks to reduce, tease apart, regulate, and contain in the name of administrative order and control' (2002: 53).

One of our goals, then, is to challenge the calculus of security. To speak of experiences of security is also to speak of experts, technocrats, professionals, police, policy-makers and politicians. We must not censor critique when researching these domains. In a moment during which there is great demand for anthropological insights and ethnographic research in security circles – the same moment during which there is also an emphasis on 'culture' – it behoves us to find orientations for a critical anthropology of security. These orientations include attention to the styles of reasoning that subsist in policing or counter-terrorism interventions; these orientations also include attention to the gaps, blind-spots and fissures in security knowledge and in its norms and practices (see Marcus 2012). But much more also needs to be achieved. The critical anthropology of security must strengthen its own sense of what criticism is, turning to questions of activism, ethics, secrecy and forms of expertise that operate in the near future. For now, however, we offer a summary of some of the preliminary steps taken in this volume.

In contrast to approaches adopted in Security Studies, security in this volume appears to be far more than uniformed officials or speech-acts by powerful and authorised voices. At first glance, authorised speakers appear to ventriloquise the security apparatus. But, as Joseph P. Masco (2010) argues, such speakers rarely feel the need to define security. Instead, security is evoked either a self-evident good or, we would add, it acts like a linguistic 'shifter' (Silverstein 1976), acquiring content in opposition to ill-defined threats, fears and risks. As the work of Marion Demossier and Catarina Frois in this volume has shown, security manifests itself in complex and sometimes contradictory relations. Attending to complexity and contradictions is not an unimportant matter, because anthropological perspectives are rooted in actual experiences. Therefore, one must sift, compare and contrast in principled ways.

If one compares the contributions of Didier Fassin and Alexandra Schwell in this volume one may see coherences emerging. Fassin describes policing in the form of reactions to phone calls from citizens, but serious crime is declining – how often do the police catch a criminal 'red-handed'? The alternative uses of police 'resources' take the form of proactive policing, characterised by interventions and the 'numbers'. Similarly, one of Schwell's key research participants explains to her that in Compensatory Measures the police 'have to find their work by themselves'. These anthropological perspectives indicate the important roles played by the force of boredom and the desire to perform policing to the public, to political influencers and to the media. Policing, then, is a key site of transformations that refuses any handy institutional boundaries. Instead, we must attend anthropologically to the continuum that connects seemingly distinct areas such as security theatre played out publicly, bureaucratic norms, policing practices, and the security and insecurity experienced by human beings, even those within security apparatuses.

Performativity emerges in this volume as a key area of research. From Marion Demossier's efforts to situate Nicolas Sarkozy's *discours de Grenoble* amid multi-level and contested politics to Fassin's and Schwell's discussions of policy and policing, we see an underscored need to attend to performativity. Standards, statistics (the 'numbers') and various governmental calculations seem to emanate fully formed from state and non-state domains. However, there is no clear route, dotted with the speech-acts of authorised speakers, that links the imagined inside of security apparatuses with their intended targets. Rather, as Gregory Feldman eloquently expresses it: 'Performativity, then, is not simply about the social construction of subjects, but rather it is about the discursively-regulated practices that inscribe boundaries between subjects and reify them in that very process' (2005: 222). Security performances are emergent within norms and practices, the interplay between order and chaos, and the specific interventions that one may observe on the streets of Parisian *banlieues* or in the corridors of an airport. That said, one must also note that in regions like Europe today particular formations of security are becoming normalised, from Didier Fassin's description of the 'petty state of exception' in the intensive policing of the urban poor to Catarina Frois's analysis of the relentless, deaf-to-criticism rollout of public CCTV in Portugal. One might conclude from the chapters in this volume that security is normalised and even naturalised through performance, from the selective displays of evidence (or numbers) to the theatricals surrounding the management of migration. But the normalisation of (in) securitisation deserves further consideration.

In an often-cited passage in Gilles Deleuze's essay on 'societies of control' he suggests:

> We don't have to stray into science fiction to find a control mechanism that can fix the position of any element at any given moment ... a town where anyone can leave their flat, their street, their neighbourhood, using their (dividual) electronic card that opens this or that barrier; but the card may also be rejected on a particular day, or between certain times of day; it doesn't depend on the barrier but on the computer that is making sure that everyone is in a permissible place, and effecting a universal modulation. (1997: 182)

The image of normalised, computer protocol-led security is provocative, but is such securitisation too heavy, too obvious and too utopian to exist for long? Are we, in other words, in an era of permanent insecurity crises and exceptional security measures?

Michel Foucault, as is well known, rooted his meditations on panopticism in a discussion of plague measures, the interplay of order and chaos, and the temporary appearance through discipline, security and surveillance of 'the utopia of a perfectly governed city' (1991: 198). But Foucault eschewed narrow-gauge readings of security 'technology'. Instead, he attended to the possible lightness, rapidity and amplifying capacities of security situated in governmentality and biopolitics (see also 2007: 5–22, 42–45, 64–65). Though this volume pays especial attention to Europe, around the world security is an enormous growth area in many domains of societies, transforming relations and connections as it grows. Just as nineteenth-century developments such as biometric security travelled through routes of Empire and found congenial environments in which to flourish as a means to identify and control the urban poor and the colonial Other, so in the contemporary moment one may see the uneven amplification of security in differing contexts. Considering examples such as universal identification in India to biometric securitisation in the Middle East, today we must consider the broad temporal and geographic dimensions of normalisation and naturalisation in the specific contexts studied by anthropologists (see Rao 2013; Maguire 2012).

In recent years, several venturesome scholars have pointed to the deep connections that are emerging between the security laboratories represented by conflict zones in Iraq and Afghanistan, the neoliberal spaces of exception such as securitised expert zones in the Global South, and the emphasis placed on security in the Western world. Terms such as 'borderworld' are now becoming popular as a way to describe a coherent and fortified landscape of targets, techno-science, policy, norms and practices (see Graham 2010; Muller 2013). In contrast, anthropologists have preferred the term 'security-scape' to help frame the multiple and diffuse security locations that often refuse conventional notions of 'locality'.

In this volume the local looms large; the perspectives here are of the specifics – experiences and contestations in areas such as policing, counter-terrorism, border-control and public surveillance. But there is a tension in this, spoken to eloquently by Gregory Feldman: within security apparatuses the local may not exist as traditionally conceived by anthropologists. For Ulf Hannerz, 'locality' denotes the connections between friends and family, collegial and business relations, ethnic and other identities that produce and reproduce 'habitats of meaning' (1996: 22–25 passim). Other anthropologists have criticised the disciplinary emphasis on locality. Arjun Appadurai goes as far as to argue that the ethnographic project is curiously isomorphic with the local knowledge of locality it seeks to discover and document (1996: 179, 182). What, he wonders, is the fate of traditional anthropological notions of locality when scale, spatiality and social interaction are not isomorphic? What, we wonder, is the anthropological response to research on and in security apparatuses, where standards and norms prevail, but isolation, alienation and a sense of futility are also experienced.

Counter-terrorist officers valorise their professional 'culture' and eye warily the growing deployments of techno-science. One may catch glimpses of their world briefly, but they themselves have limited perspectives on it and on one another. Security policy-makers on the European Union (EU) border wrestle with the effects of their work but are isolated and endure empty rituals that thinly disguise the nature of the apparatus. The critical anthropology of security, then, must retain much of its focus on experience and the depth of knowledge that comes from ethnography, but we must also continue to interrogate security apparatuses themselves, following knowledge, technologies, policies and practices through non-local worlds. This collection is especially valuable because it allows one to see like a security apparatus but also to see security apparatuses and their ramifications in everyday life.

We write the conclusions to this volume (October 2013) in the wake of a human tragedy in the Mediterranean Sea. Divers are still attempting to remove the bodies of the 300 migrants who drowned when an overloaded fishing vessel capsized *en route* to the Italian island of Lampedusa. There are loud calls for a strengthening of Member State cooperation and for additional resources for the EU border agency FRONTEX. The Italian government is considering granting the dead migrants full citizenship, while pursuing the survivors as illegal clandestine migrants – the deportable. In places such as Lampedusa one sees worlds coming together and being forced apart. Lampedusa is a holiday resort-island for the wealthy. It is a reachable point for migrants journeying to what they hope will be a better life. The island is thus a nodal point in the i-Map of illegal routes produced by the EU's migration management apparatus. This tragedy reminds us that when one considers security apparatuses, techno-science and professional expertise, which are all so often at a distance from the world, one is also considering matters of rights, ethics, and even empathy and its limits.

In this volume, Gregory Feldman attends to the abstract, rationalised procedures of the migration apparatus, which denies migrants subjecthood. He notes the biopolitical dimensions of how the apparatus operates while fixing his gaze on the always-present potential for violence. Indeed, the relationships between violence and security merit sustained attention going forward. It is the violence of security that we see in Hasselberg's contribution to this volume on the deportation regime in the UK and, of course, in Jutta Lauth Bacas's descriptions of border security in Greece. The critical anthropology of security has important perspectives to bring precisely because it enables discussions of Greek 'camps' for the poor with 'gaps' in the food supply in the same scholarly space as discussions of high-tech counter-terrorism, policing, politics and instrumentalised policy workers.

References

Appadurai, A. (1996) *Modernity at Large: Cultural Dimensions of Globalization* (Minneapolis: University of Minnesota Press).
Butler, J. (2004) *Precarious Life: The Powers of Mourning and Violence* (London: Verso).
Deleuze, G. (1997) *Negotiations, 1972–1990* (New York: Columbia University Press).
Feldman, G. (2005) 'Essential crisis: a performative approach to migrants, minorities, and the European nation-state', *Anthropological Quarterly*, Vol. 78, No. 1, pp. 213–246.
Foucault, M. (1991) *Discipline and Punish: The Birth of the Prison* (London: Penguin).
—— (2007) *Security, Territory, Population* (London: Palgrave Macmillan).
Graham, S. (2010) *Cities under Siege: The New Military Urbanism* (London: Verso).
Hannerz, U. (1996) *Transnational Connections: Culture, People, Places* (London: Routledge).
Jackson, M. (2002) *The Politics of Storytelling: Violence, Transgression, and Inter-subjectivity* (Copenhagen: Museum Tusculanum Press).
Maguire, M. (2012) 'Biopower, racialization and new security technology', *Social Identities*, Vol. 18, No. 5, pp. 36–52.
Masco, J.P. (2010) 'Comment on "Toward a critical anthropology of security" by Daniel Goldstein', *Current Anthropology*, Vol. 51, No. 4, pp. 509–510.
Marcus, G.E. (2012) '"Be all that you can be:" the anthropological vocation in the securityscape', in Albro, R., Marcus, G.E., McNamara, L.A. and Schoch-Spana, M. (eds) *Anthropologists in the Securityscape: Ethics, Practice, and Professional Identity*, pp. 245–259 (Walnut Creek, CA: Left Coast Press).
Muller, B. (2013) 'Borderworld: biometrics, AVATAR and global criminalization', in Pakes, F. (ed.) *Globalisation and the Challenge to Criminology*, pp. 129–146 (London: Routledge).
Rao, U. (2013) 'Biometric marginality', *Economic and Political Weekly*, Vol. 47, No. 13, pp. 71–77.
Silverstein, M. (1976) 'Shifters, verbal categories and cultural description', in Basso, K. and Selby, H. (eds) *Meaning in Anthropology*, pp. 11–57 (Albuquerque: School of American Research).

Afterword
Security: Encounters, Misunderstanding and Possible Collaborations

Didier Bigo

How might the disciplines of anthropology and International Relations enter into a dialogue concerning the analysis of security? Do they speak the same language? Do they understand security practices and meanings the same way? Do they have contradictory or complementary framing in terms of episteme, arts of writing and methods? These questions are central for the development of common research agenda between critical scholars coming initially from different disciplinary backgrounds. This book is among the first to pave the way for such a critical commitment concerning Security Studies by bringing scholars of anthropology to the heart of the discussion. It brings well-known names in anthropology together with younger researchers, all of whom have chosen specific topics where an anthropological stance challenges traditional Security Studies and also part of the methods of critical International Relations (IR) Security Studies. Importantly, it succeeds in tracing the paths by which it is possible to connect the different bodies of knowledge and to enrich considerably the literature on Critical Security Studies. Clearly different channels are possible; clearly also the connections pass through some minority positions in both anthropological studies and IR research, because they are the ones to be sceptical of the doxa of each discipline which are based on reverse assumptions, and it is in this common criticism that they might well have more in common than the two orthodoxies.

A Traditional Opposition in Terms of Narrative and Episteme: The IR Interpretation of Security and Securitisation

At first glance, the traditional disciplines of anthropology and IR are mainly opposed to or ignorant of each other. IR claims to have a specific object and a specific method that creates its originality and implies a capacity to subsume or even reverse most of the assumptions of political theory, sociology and also anthropology. In the IR 'canon' security is defined on the basis of an international state of anarchy between nation-states and a balance of power where only the most powerful can secure their position. There are certainly many and varied debates opposing offensive and defensive realism as well as different variants of realisms and liberalism, but for most of them, security is about the survival of a nation-state, about the capacity to impose an international order profitable to the major actors, about the possibility of acquiring wealth, money and information, according to national interests. The underpinning assumptions about human nature draw from a simplified reading of eighteenth-century philosophies of contracts and their universalisation. Anthropology and ethnographic methods are seen as an approach with too much attention to detail, lacking the great synthesis that is necessary to speak of 'the world'. Even if the postcolonial debate has recently enriched discussions about stateness and the question of the status of the international, most of the literature considers anthropology only in terms of eliciting local or national cultural differences, variations around the invariants that they have 'discovered' – human beings always struggle for more power; the balance of power supposes alliances to stabilise the world; the global horizon is still filled with anarchy as no one global sovereign has emerged. It is not at all rare for some authors who claim to be US realists to argue about a 'human nature' in ways that speak for all human beings and not only for US citizens. They refuse the idea that the author is a prisoner of his or her temporal or spatial location and is thus positioned. Security is a 'universal' question that all human beings living in a collective group have to deal with – otherwise they disappear. This is *survival*, and in a contemporary world it is survival of states that matters. The books on security are for this reason on 'international' security, the only 'serious' security question. They deal with war, conflicts as 'scientific matters' that have correlates and patterns. The authors want to find laws, or at least tendencies. They want to inform policies in terms of war avoidance and risk reduction. They want to be abstract, to have a general reasoning, and offer simple but elegant ways of describing pure problems, which have to be disengaged from the 'gauge' of descriptions (Guzzini 2002). They do not like details, local events, or precise and complex life stories. They also do not like to spend time on fieldwork, as they assume that the international is better understood by means of a form of reasoning at the office rather than on a specific terrain that may bias the overall perspective. Their art of writing and its excellence is represented by a thin book, with one or two general hypotheses, which have a potential to explain a large group of phenomena, formulated as a theoretical point that has to be tested against case studies and thus falsifiable in a Karl Popper's sense. Kenneth Waltz still looms large in the field (Waltz and Fearon 2012). Physics and mathematics are the ideal.

This way of thinking and writing has also permeated some aspects of the Critical Security Studies emanating from IR, and especially those labelled as the Copenhagen school. Buzan and Hansen (2009) have clearly marked their terrain by tracing the boundaries of what counts as international security, its evolution and 'enlargement', and what has to be relegated to law and order, internal politics, everyday practices. Ole Waever (2010) has criticised the lack of sociology, the lack of flesh on this skeletal history of international security, but when he recently came to synthesise the core of securitisation theory he made a U-turn and formulated a series of claims criticising its critics for their lack of understanding of what was a theory and what was a scientific attitude in IR, quoting Kenneth Waltz at length (Waever 2011). Certainly the attention to the linguistic framing of the speech act presupposes a precise description of an event and its context, but the writing needs to be 'clinical' and explain step-by-step some pre-identified moves: who is the locutor, what does he or she say, who are the audience, and what are the conditions of success? It works as a blank model-sheet to be filled in with a specific case study. The thickness of history and anthropology is often limited to a varnish. A synthesis, to be great and elegant, needs to be short. The model is a 'physics' of the social and not lived experiences. Securitisation theory is still attached to a mode of reasoning that prevails in political science.

This is why in most IR Critical Security Studies, authors could not care less about anthropology, except perhaps a very structuralist and abstract one that has divorced itself from history and sociology and which mimics linguistics. They may read with pleasure ethnographic descriptions in order to get one or two examples that are significant in their eyes, but they refuse to take into account the basic principles of anthropological studies. Their way of writing opposes them to anthropology, and this includes part of the critical security approach.

Anthropology and Its Ethnographic Approach: A Different Security?

Canonical anthropology relying on ethnographic methods, in some ways, can be described as the most adversarial episteme of this abstract art of writing in IR. For the anthropologists, what looks like a simple village is already a complex work of art. All the details are significant. Everyday life is a 'miracle': the extraordinary reproduction and transformation of social life. The 'local' is never 'simple'. The 'details' are always ambiguous. Foreigners interested in nothing more than tourist snap-shots see nothing special or mysterious in the details; ethnographers seek out the meaning in all the little cultural differences (Augé 1995, 2009). The '*fait social total*' of Marcel Mauss is not a theory that applies to case studies in a top-down logic, it is a reconstruction of the complexity and heterogeneity that a group bears, and which can never be fully resolved logically (Karsenti 1994). The empathy needed to get the description as right as possible in terms of translation between two different sets of codes is therefore a bottom-up approach, an approach that is fascinated by the relational practices of mimesis and distinction, and by the heterogeneity of human lives. No one description is more or less important than another. Each intimate estrangement puts at risk the certainties of one's doxa in confronting it with other practices and values. The miracle of life is embedded into this effort of 'translation' that the ethnographer will have to build in order to de-assemble his or her own certainty and to re-assemble by his or her writings a process of simil-otherness that may be a fragile but solidified expression of the total social of the others. Marcel Mauss was keen on this image of the tapestry of the social and the process of weaving. Malinowski and Margaret Mead have shown the transformative work of the 'field' in the relation between ethnographers and their 'subjects'. Reflexivity is at the very heart of anthropological reasoning (Turner 1979; Leach 1985; Welz 1997; Lindemann 1999). As an anthropologist, one is always obliged to be aware that one speaks from somewhere, positioned in a certain time frame. As explained in the Introduction to this volume, anthropologists of various stripes have long engaged with security, crime, violence, war, insecurity, fear, but they have often done so separately instead of conceiving of a process of (in) securitisation at work. Nevertheless, they have been key to translating the lived experiences and the embodiments of the effects of (in)security into a specific narrative born out of this reflexivity that is so often lacking in IR.

More recently and in a more critical vein, Marc Augé has given a reinvented perspective on this anthropology in the societies of speed and mobility; Arjun Apadurai has also presented the different 'scapes' that globalisation produces and the effects they create in terms of the fear held by the majority that they might become minorities (Appadurai 2006, 2013). They have insisted on the diversity of the processes and the heterogeneity of their effects in different social universes. This interest by anthropologists in diversity and heterogeneities, or radical differences, has created a split between the structuralist approaches of Claude Lévi-Strauss, closely connected with Saussure and linguistics on one side, and the post-structuralist approaches that reinvent ethnography of the everyday and the art of distinction of little differences as the central form of knowledge. Post-structuralist anthropologists historicise ethnography, they refuse the division between primitive and complex societies, as well as the division between sociology and anthropology. Anthropology and sociology work together as moments of reflexivity.

Michel Foucault, Paul Veyne, Gilles Deleuze, Marcel Détienne and Jean Pierre Vernant insisted as one on the 'metis' of social sciences (Detienne and Vernant 1974; Fuglsang and Sørensen 2006; Martin 2007, Veyne 1984). They opposed the 'Popperian' agenda, as well as the 'Kuhnian' one, the subordination of social sciences to a 'hard' science model. Social sciences are part of 'humanities'. Because of this they permit an alternative art of writing, which refuses the great synthesis and its explanatory-predictive way of thinking. Social sciences are not a physics of human beings who can be predicted, they are an Aboriginal sand painting, colourful and evanescent. Michel de Certeau is certainly one of the main voices of this different philosophy that considers ethnography as a form of sublime union of differences (During 1999; Chartier 1997; de Certeau 1974, 1969).

Passerelles: Multiple Possibilities and Limitations

Anthropology, gender studies and security

Gender studies were the first to be inspired by this anthropological way of thinking and take it seriously under the influence of Luce Giard. Ann Tickner (1992) connected this feminist anthropological perspective and 'gendered' IR Critical Security Studies by showing the masculine part of these universal myths taken as forms of universal truth. Passerelles are now constructed between a certain ethnographic way of thinking, gender and Critical Security Studies, and they have been strongly influential

(Brown 2010; Scott and Brown 2008; Wibben 2011). Vivienne Jabri (2007) has analysed the transformation of global politics. Roxanne Doty (2010) discusses the production of insecurities. In this book, different authors are inspired directly or indirectly by this line of thought.

Ethnographic methods, everyday politics and security

Distancing themselves from the linguistic approach of IR Security Studies, and more in line with the approach represented by the sociological Paris school, Jef Huysmans and Xavier Guillaume have recently developed a discussion on everyday security following the work of Michel de Certeau, where the description of the details of the everyday are central to understand the 'acts' of security and their 'enactments' (Guillaume and Huysmans 2013). These are not 'speech acts' only, they are 'acts' (Isin and Nielsen 2008). These important works on Critical Security Studies have been crucial for creating passerelles with ethnographical methods. Nevertheless, they sometimes struggle to make sense of their own ethnographies (of security and insecurity). The tactics of the everyday are described well but they are not so much understood in their genetic structurations. In some books that attempt a *rapprochement* between ethnography and IR, ethnographic methods are imported into IR as a technique to complement research that is without an in-depth discussion of the episteme. It comes into a palette of colourful methods that have to be blended in the name of diversity (Salter and Mutlu 2012). The problem of this consociationalist approach by critical IR is that it reproduces the errors of an ethnographic romanticism wherein the history of others is transformed into anecdotes and novels – a critique that anthropological studies have often posed to those with a vague understanding of ethnography.

Methodologies cannot be in a pick-and-choose list where a combination is a sign of openness and consensus. Interdisciplinary research is not a supermarket; methodologies are not an intermediary step between a research design and a case study. Claudia Aradau and Jef Huysmans have recently argued against this vision of combined methods by trying to rethink methodologies as 'acts' in order to avoid the reduction of other epistemes to technicalities (Aradau and Huysmans 2013 forthcoming).

Since its inception in the 1990s, the journal *Cultures et Conflits* has shown that the interdisciplinary connections between sociology, anthropology and IR supposes a coherence with an episteme, with a problematisa-tion that frames the question, and with an art of writing which promises explicitly to avoid combinations that lead to irreconcilable bifurcations in terms of reasoning.[1] A socio-anthropology of conflicts and security offers to break down the political science narrative of IR constructed around the 'scientific project of expert knowledge of the prince counsellors' that have been incorporated by Hans Morgenthau and others at the heart of the IR subdiscipline; no conciliation is possible (Bigo 1992a, 1992b; Guilhot 2008). Modernity has been built on the division of knowledge in disciplines with profound differences in terms of the art of writing and projects undertaken (Walker 1993). Anthropology and sociology contradict IR approaches and cannot be reduced to fungible methods, to add-ons to an untouched IR project. These are the fundamentals of what has been developed in the journal *International Political Sociology* that has brought to the forefront of IR studies the critical sociological school of French origin and its relations with a specific attention to the contradictions under which the modern episteme and political theories have been built, and especially the lack of reflexivity of IR specialists (Bigo and Walker 2007a, 2007b).

In that sense, the encounter between Critical Security Studies and anthropology may be misleading if anthropology is reduced to ethnographical methods, on one side, and if Critical Security Studies are reduced to the linguistic approach of Critical Security Studies, on the other side. On both sides, an anthropology of security which wants to be critical will emerge as a central productive crossroads if, and only if, the anthropologists are aware of the debates and formulations of controversies in Critical Security Studies, and look at the little differences between the approaches with attention, and if the critical security IR researcher takes the time to learn what a critical anthropological perspective does to a research project and means in terms of the art of writing. They must understand the variety of anthropological styles of research, and the powerful controversies that exist.

The Key Notions of Relations and Process, an Approach by the Practices

As shown in this volume, the debates in anthropology and sociology may inform the knowledge of Critical Security Studies if ethnographic descriptions are not confused with anthropological reasoning. Insisting on heterogeneity and diversity is important as a bulwark against some forms of imperialism of a unique reasoning, the one of the *commerçant* and its cost-benefit approach, which calls itself rational choice theory. Louis Dumont in *Homo Aequalis* (1977, 1991) provides us with a lesson on the pluralisation of reason(s) necessary to understand the world with different eyes than the Western idea of reason. But he has also addressed warnings against the 'cult' of diversity and its infinite description of 'beauty', insisting on an understanding of the relations generating the little differences, the little nothings. For him, anthropology has to struggle against the false universalisation of the dominants but also against the aestheticisation of the singularities and the Deleuzian dispersions that lead one to think of differences as radical differences that potentially reconstruct some arguments for Apartheid if these differences are displayed and reconstructed as essential. This is also the position held by James Scott. The ethnographic description of the hidden transcripts and their details is necessary, but what is even more important is the understanding of the reciprocal positioning of the official and hidden transcripts. One can never make sense of its relation to the other. Anthropology is relational (Scott 1990). The diversities of practices are not a randomisation of history: they are connected in and by processes, 'assembled'. Structural approaches without the history of heterogeneities are works of 'dead knowledge', but political tendencies emerge: seeing like a state is imposing a certain vision of reality. Despite differences in content, one may recognise a parallel in Pierre Bourdieu's efforts to develop the notion of practical sense with Abdelmalek Sayad: he proposed an approach composed not simply of agencies and structures but rather in terms of fields and *habitus* (Bourdieu 1979). Correlated with a Spinozist approach to practices and with a relational and processual understanding of how they are generated, different from the idea of a will to act, it is by their distinctive deviations that each practice can be understood. No one practice exists in itself, in an 'absolute' (theological) moment of the 'act' (of creation); it is only in relation to other practices that differences can be observed. The notions of field and *habitus* developed by Pierre Bourdieu are born out of the anthropological and sociological perspective that he calls 'genetic structuralism'. These notions are at the heart of the development of a sociological school of Critical Security Studies (Bigo 2011).

An International Political Anthropo-Sociology

For the sociological school of Critical Security Studies, practices, relations, processes, translations and complexity are not resolvable as simple elements; theorisation of human lives in order to interpret them and not to govern them are evident in the potentialities and expressions that anthropology may bring. Anthropology can do so by looking especially to some configurations of social agents or 'actants' in such a way as to embed materiality into the analysis of the relations between agents.

The perspective from a very small remote village may illuminate more about international life than a synthesis of the dominant perspective and its stereotypisation of all others as 'the Other', or the enemy, or the suspect. Politicisation and its multiple transcripts (public, hidden, translucent, shadowy) is not a subject of a 'science' that will discover patterns but is a topical site for developing an art of humanity – an art that is open to being surprised by the inventiveness and capacities of human beings when they are in actual relations, whatever the length of the cascades of interdepend-ences that traverse their universes, be they short, that is, 'local', middle range, that is, national, or long range, that is, the so-called global.

This applies to how one conceptualises states, boundaries, sovereignty, security, risk, freedom, justice, privacy and democracy – these need to be discussed relationally in order to understand their genesis and transforma-tions, and these relations cannot be segmented by disciplines. So-called Security Studies are by themselves an intellectual joke if they naively cut the relations of security off from freedom, democracy or justice, and if they do so consciously they may have a conservative hidden agenda that should be attended to (see, for example, Balibar 2003; Bartelson 1995, 2010; Bourdieu et al. 1993; Rancière 2006; Ashley and Walker 1991). No single discipline or subdiscipline can claim to have a monopoly on knowledge about any of the notions listed above. These notions make sense only by the way they relate to other notions, as they are mutually interdependent inside a specific episteme (or discursive frame) (Foucault 1971). Consequently, in contrast to traditional political science, the task of a critical researcher is not to substitute his or her reasoning for that of the actors in order to anticipate what they will do but, rather, to understand their practical reason and the historicity of their actions. This should help to eliminate the false distinctions between levels (man, state and war) as well as the privileging of the state and the interstate over human action (Walker 2009; cf. Waltz 1954). The discursive frame itself makes sense only in *relation* to the practices that such notions encompass, ignore or exclude. The process by which a specific label of 'security' and/or 'insecurity' is connected with other terminologies in terms of proximity or opposition will therefore be more important than the isolation of a 'true' meaning through the space and time of security in order to build a concept and a theory of security or securitisation. This process is not one of knowledge construction or expertise; rather it is the result of struggles and hierarchies inside these discursive activities and their competition for a truth that offers certainty. Indeed, the search for a definition of security that will capture its essential meaning is beginning to resemble passages from Lewis Carroll's *The Hunting of the Snark* (1898).

The term 'security' has been used to describe very different practices inside the disciplines of IR, sociology, history, criminology and anthropology. It cannot be subsumed under one main category – for example, survival and 'human needs' in IR; personal safety, fear of crime, but also urban policing and computer hacking in criminology; self-identity and group-think in psychology; social security and flexi-security in welfare states in economics; risk management and catastrophic risk in sociology; privacy, personal guarantees and human rights for those working in law. The works of Eric Fassin and Mariela Pandolfi demonstrate the limits of the forms of essentialism that try to 'discipline' security under a specific form of knowledge. This is also the case in the work of Alexandra Schwell in this volume. The multiple practices of the actors cannot be subsumed by a linguistic approach in terms of locutors, speech acts and audience, even with an attention to the multiplicity of audience, they have to be understood in terms of frames, of process, of 'spectacle', and each social universe has its own configuration, its own practical regime of justification, its rhetorical argumentation about the delimitation between security and insecurity. One of the preliminary tasks of the researcher is therefore to uncover the tensions and aporia that are revealed when putting these connotations and their related bodies of knowledge all together. The study of the primary metaphors delineating these forms of knowledge is a key element as they built the boundaries of what each discipline labels 'security' and 'insecurity' and describes as the 'object' of security (Kubálková et al. 1998).

As noted in the Introduction to this volume, which refers to the work of Frédéric Gros, research on security metaphors and the 'hotbeds of meanings' they produce, explains why it makes no sense to try to analyse security as 'something', as an object belonging to a specific discipline studying an 'external reality' (for example, military or strategic studies, or even IR) as they are both – that is, the something and its external reality – the product of a 'world of our making'. To put it another way, in order to maintain its realness the world has to be constructed with meanings that are constantly reproduced and translated to cope with change, but these meanings do not converge into one natural social world called society bounded by a state, rather, they are always objects of transactions, conversions between multiple professional and cultural worlds (Ashley and Walker 1991; Rancière 1987). The label of security often reveals its political origin, or, more precisely, the process of politicisation, through its justificatory claims, and it may be a site of contestation about the legitimacy of an action.

Security is, then, never absolute, integral, total or global: it always reaches a limit, and appears as a reversal, a tipping point, against other qualifications. Security presupposes political judgements about freedom, property, mobility, privacy and democracy, and security presupposes recognising the practices associated with these other concepts. So, contrary to many contemporary discourses affirming that 'more security is always the solution' and that 'security is for all and needs to be global', a sociological and anthropological approach examines Security Studies in relation to 'liberty' studies, 'human rights' studies, 'criminology and risk' studies and will investigate the nexus where disciplines may converge or reveal fundamental contradictions. Therefore, a very diverse array of practices of justification of ambiguous acts of governing others (often involving violence), coming from diverse professional worlds and heterogeneous bodies of knowledge, are both enabled and hidden by the terminology of security. Security is, finally, no more than a label, which sets the limits to other labels like freedom, mobility and privacy. It has no autonomy and does not describe a class of specific objects or facts.

What is needed first and foremost is an anthropology of knowledge de-essentialising what security means and analysing what (in)securitisation does in terms of setting the boundaries of the 'acceptable' (Neumann and Sending 2010). A sociological approach rooted in the work of critical theorists will share with critical anthropology the idea that what matters is the process by which (in)securitisation takes place and its effects in different social universes and social contexts. The journal *Cultures et Conflits* has analysed the conditions of production of the notions of danger, of the diverse contexts in which threats are constructed, and the key roles played by governmental and non-governmental agencies that claim to act to secure and protect people. This research programme has received insufficient attention in the Anglo-American world, with the exception of Weldes et al.'s (1999) *Cultures of Insecurity: States, Communities, and the Production of Danger*. Instead of analysing security professionals under the labels of epistemic communities or experts, legitimising *de facto* what these actors say as truth claims, the Paris school has always insisted on the accumulation of symbolic capital by institutions that have routine access to the different mechanisms of coercion, but also to the public production of the discourses prioritising the struggles against specific threats. They have insisted that this definition of the boundaries of danger and insecurity is a central political mechanism carried out via the political spectacle of the politicians, but also, and mainly, by the various public and private bureaucracies in charge of organising the missions, budgets and priorities targeting the different 'threats'. And this is why a terminology suitable for describing a transnational field of (in)security professionals has been developed. In this framework, the naming of security is a political act, and so too is the naming and framing of insecurity. Both are the visible part of a larger political process of (in)securitisation, which implies sacrifice, decisions and symbolic domination bound up with the legitimacy of the measures taken. This is not at all an exceptional moment, it is the routines of the everyday work and competition over priorities that generate a process of (in)securitisation. Depending on power relations, the measures and routinised practices that will be called for, either violence and insecurity, or security and safety might be the outcome – perhaps, even, the dynamic is between the elimination of change and the re-emergence of fate. These power relations affect certainly the field of the political professional, but they do not affect them alone. They are at play in each bureaucratic or technical fields as soon as the actors try to manage (in)security by using coercion, surveillance or pastoral techniques of integration, prevention and prediction. The process of politicisation is in each professional universe driven by the permanent struggles among the actors concerning these claims to define the domains of insecurity and of security, the refusal to accept them, and the competitions they engage in to determine in their own universes what is security, what is insecurity and what is fate. Centrally, the analysis of these practices goes against the idea of an empirical securitisation theory, implying a 'beyond of the political realm', a mega-securitisation that renders the solutions exceptional and transforms everyday politics into a security scene.

The Key Notion of a Process of (In)Securitisation

The web of significations coming from these contradictory bodies of knowledge shows quite immediately that, in a certain body of knowledge, 'security' is the name given to certain practices that might otherwise be called insecurity, violence, coercion, fear, freedom, mobility or opportunity. This is why I have proposed using the notion of a process of (in)securitisation in order to describe the unavoidable consubstantiality of insecurity inside security and of security inside insecurity, a little bit like a yin-yang or a Möbius strip. It is central to break with the dialectical opposition of security/insecurity, which presents the rise of security as the diminution of insecurity, and to understand the relationships between (in)security and violence as a sphere, a bubble. According to Mick Dillon:

> Because we can never think security without insecurity, and vice versa, there is an essential conflict, which the word itself bears within itself. This conflict is a conflict of unequal opposites, which are rooted and routed together. We are dealing here, then, with a unified agonal relationship of mutual definition rather than a dialectical relationship in which one term overcomes the other. It is evident, if we pause to think about security for a moment, that any discourse of security must always already, simultaneously and in a plurality of ways, be a discourse of danger too. (Dillon 1996: 120–121)

But perhaps we do not have a chiasm inside the word security, and instead we have only one side of a non-orientable surface (as in a Möbius strip) that we have to call (in)security, or an (in)securitisation process. We have a unique phenomenon of (in)security, even if it appears – depending on the point of view that actors have – as security for some, while for others it appears as its opposite, insecurity. The Möbius strip is constituted as one band, and looks as if it has opposite sides, but when one is asked to precisely identify where the opposite side begins, one realises that if he or she can see a border and name the two sides, other actors will not contest that a border exists but will contest the choice made in naming the inside and the outside – and, in our case, the choice is between what is security and what is insecurity (Bigo 1997, 2001). It is this intersubjectivity and the impossibility of a common agreement about where is the inside and where is the outside that blocks the phenomenon of closure and exclusion that a circle creates. It is not possible to assert with any assurance the territory of the security enclosure (circle or domain) and to exclude, to purify it from insecurity, because in a Möbius strip someone will just affirm the exact contrary concerning the place of the inside and the outside, the content of what is security and what is insecurity. And it seems to me central to understand the logic at work. Actors are disagreeing about what is security and what is insecurity. They may have inverse positions, but at the same moment they agree about the places of the boundaries and they are surprised if they are obliged to trace them to realise that where they have seen an opposition, they can only find continuity. They look for the distinction between security and insecurity and they find only (in) security.

I have used the notion of a process of constitution of an (in)security continuum in order to show how the different institutions have tried to enlarge their scope concerning the threats they were dealing with, especially after the end of the Cold War, and how they have connected different threats and prioritised them in order to justify their role (Bigo 2002: 63). It has been central to justify the transposition of techniques and special laws or regulations coming from drug trafficking and terrorism to the domain of border controls and for immigration purposes. But the key question is found in the relationship between (in)security and experiences of violence or peacemaking. What is the process of 'veridiction' of the (in) security process, and who are the players? How is this process connected with a regime of justification by justice or secrecy? How is it possible to be critical about the positions of some actors while accepting the positions of others without entering directly into the game and their 'bets'? By answering these questions, the encounter between a critical anthropology of security and international political sociology, which is grounded in a sociological-historical episteme and art of writing, offers the most promising way to build a companionship between the two perspectives that share the same general episteme and respect for each other.

Note

1. See: http://conflits.revues.org/28

References

Appadurai, A. (2006) *Fear of Small Numbers: An Essay on the Geography of Anger* (Durham, NC: Duke University Press).
—— (2013) *Condition de l'homme global* (Paris: Payot).

Aradau, C. and Huysmans, J. (2013) 'Critical methods in international relations: the politics of techniques, devices and acts', *European Journal of International Relations*, online 30 May, doi: 10.1177/1354066112474479.

Ashley, R.K. and Walker, R.B.J. (1991) 'Reading dissidence/writing the discipline: crisis and the question of sovereignty in international studies', *International Studies Quarterly*, Vol. 34, No. 3, pp. 367–416.

Augé, M. (1995) *Non-places: Introduction to an Anthropology of Supermodernity* (London: Verso).

——(2009) *Pour une anthropologie de la mobilité* (Paris: Payot).

Balibar, E. (2003) *We, the People of Europe? Reflections on Transnational Citizenship* (Princeton, NJ: Princeton University Press).

Bartelson, J. (1995) *A Genealogy of Sovereignty*, Cambridge Studies in International Relations Vol. 39 (Cambridge: Cambridge University Press).

—— (2010) 'The social construction of globality', *International Political Sociology*, Vol. 4, No. 3, pp. 219–235.

Bigo, D. (1992a) 'Les conflits post bipolaires: dynamiques et caractéristiques', *Cultures & Conflits*, Vol. 8, pp. 3–14.

—— (1992b) 'Les jeux du politique et de la transnationalité', *Cultures & Conflits*, Vol. 5, pp. 3–22.

—— (1997) 'Sécurité(s): intérieure et extérieure: le ruban de Möbius', version française et anglaise présentées à la 38th ISA conference.

—— (2001) *The Möbius Ribbon of Internal and External Security(ies), Identities, Borders, Orders: Rethinking International Relations Theory* (Minneapolis: University of Minnesota Press).

—— (2002) 'Security and immigration: towards a governmentality of unease', *Alternatives*, Vol. 27, pp. 63–92.

—— (2011) 'Pierre Bourdieu and international relations: power of practices, practices of power', *International Political Sociology*, Vol. 5, No. 3, pp. 225–258.

Bigo, D. and Walker, R.B.J. (2007a) 'Editorial', *International Political Sociology*, Vol. 1, pp. 1–5.

Bigo, D. and Walker, R.B.J. (2007b) 'Political sociology and the problem of the international', *Millennium: Journal of International Studies*, Vol. 35, No. 3, pp. 725–739.

Bourdieu, P. (1979) *Algeria 1960: The Disenchantment of the World, the Sense of Honour, the Kabyle House or the World Reversed – Essays, Studies in Modern Capitalism* (Cambridge: Cambridge University Press).

Bourdieu, P., Calhoun, C.J., LiPuma, E. and Postone, M. (1993) *Bourdieu: Critical Perspectives* (Chicago: University of Chicago Press).

Brown, W. (2010) *Walled States, Waning Sovereignty* (Cambridge, MA: Zone Books).

Buzan, B. and Hansen, L. (2009) *The Evolution of International Security Studies* (Cambridge: Cambridge University Press).

Carroll, L. (1898) *The Hunting of the Snark* (London: The Macmillan Company).

Chartier, R. (1997) *On the Edge of the Cliff: History, Language, and Practices, Parallax* (Baltimore, MD: Johns Hopkins University Press).

de Certeau, M. (1969) *L'Étranger: ou, l'union dans la différence, foi vivante* (Paris: Desclée de Brouwer).

—— (1974) *La Culture au pluriel, 10/18* (Paris: Union générale d'éditions).

Detienne, M. and Vernant, J.-P. (1974) *Les Ruses de l'intelligence: la mètis des Grecs, champ philosophique* (Paris: Flammarion).

Dillon, M. (1996) *Politics of Security: Towards a Political Philosophy of Continental Thought* (London: Routledge).

Doty, R.L. (2010) 'Do you know if your borders are secure?', *International Political Sociology*, Vol. 4, No. 1, pp. 92–95.

Dumont, L. (1977) *Homo Aequalis: Genèse et épanouissement de l'idéologie économique*, Bibliothèque des sciences humaines (Paris: Gallimard).

—— (1991) *Homo aequalis, II: L'Idéologie allemande: France-Allemagne et retour*, Bibliothèque des sciences humaines (Paris: Gallimard).

During, S. (1999) *The Cultural Studies Reader*, 2nd edn (New York: Routledge).

Foucault, M. (1971) *The Order of Things: An Archaeology of the Human Sciences* (New York: Pantheon).

Fuglsang, M. and Sørensen, B.M. (2006) *Deleuze and the Social, Deleuze Connections* (Edinburgh: Edinburgh University Press).

Guilhot, N. (2008) 'The realist gambit: postwar American political science and the birth of IR theory', *International Political Sociology*, Vol. 2, No. 3, pp. 281–304.

Guillaume, X. and Huysmans, J. (2013) *Citizenship and Security: The Constitution of Political Being*, PRIO New Security Studies (London: Routledge).

Guzzini, S. (2002) 'The different words of realism in international relations', *Millennium*, Vol. 30, No. 1, pp. 111–121.

Isin, E.F. and Nielsen, G.M. (2008) *Acts of Citizenship* (London: Zed Books).

Jabri, V. (2007) *War and the Transformation of Global Politics: Rethinking Peace and Conflict Studies* (Basingstoke: Palgrave Macmillan).

Karsenti, B. (1994) *Marcel Mauss: le fait social total* (Paris: Presses Universitaires de France).

Kubálková, V., Onuf, N.G. and Kowert, P. (1998) *International Relations in a Constructed World* (Armonk, NY: M.E. Sharpe).

Leach, E. (1985) 'A crack in the mirror – reflexive perspectives in anthropology', *Semiotica*, Vol. 53, No. 1–3, pp. 169–173.

Lindemann, G. (1999) 'Double contingency and reflexive anthropology', *Zeitschrift Fur Soziologie*, Vol. 28, No. 3, pp. 165–181.

Martin, J.-C. (2007) *Constellation de la Philosophie* (Paris: Kimé).

Rancière, J. (1987) *Le Maître ignorant: cinq leçons sur l'émancipation intellectuelle* (Paris: Fayard).

—— (2006) *On the Shores of Politics* (London: Verso Books).

Neumann, I.B. and Sending, O.J. (2010) *Governing the Global Polity: Practice, Mentality, Rationality* (Ann Arbor: University of Michigan Press).

Salter, M.B. and Mutlu, C.E. (2012) *Research Methods in Critical Security Studies: An Introduction* (New York: Routledge).

Scott, J.C. (1990) *Domination and the Arts of Resistance: Hidden Transcripts* (New Haven, CT: Yale University Press).

Scott, J.W. and Brown, W. (2008) *Women's Studies on the Edge* (Durham, NC: Duke University Press).

Tickner, J.A. (1992) *Gender in International Relations: Feminist Perspectives on Achieving Global Security* (New York: Columbia University Press).

Turner, V. (1979) 'Dramatic ritual – ritual drama – performative and reflexive anthropology', *Kenyan Review*, Vol. 1, No. 3, pp. 80–93.

Veyne, P. (1984) *Writing History: Essay on Epistemology* (Middletown, CT: Wesleyan University Press).

Waever, O. (2011) 'Politics, security, theory', *Security Dialogue*, Vol. 42, No. 4–5, pp. 465–480.

—— (2010) 'Beyond the evolution of international security studies?' *Security Dialogue*, Vol. 1, No. 41, pp. 659–667.

Walker, R.B.J. (1993) *Inside/Outside: International Relations as Political Theory* (Cambridge: Cambridge University Press).

Walker, R.B.J. (2009) *After the Globe, Before the World*, Global Horizons (London: Routledge).

Waltz, K. and Fearon, J. (2012) 'A conversation with Kenneth Waltz', *Annual Review of Political Science*, Vol. 15, No. 15, pp. 1–12.

Waltz, K.N. (1954) *Man, the State and War: A Theoretical Analysis* (New York: Columbia University Press).

Weldes, J., Laffey, M., Gusterson, H. and Duvall, R. (eds) (1999) *Cultures of Insecurity: States, Communities, and the Production of Danger* (Minneapolis: University of Minnesota Press).

Welz, F. (1997) 'Review of Bourdieu, P. and Wacquant, L.J.D. (1996) *Reflexive Anthropology* (Frankfurt a M: Suhrkamp)', *Kolner Zeitschrift für Soziologie und Sozialpsychologie*, Vol. 49, No. 2, pp. 342–344.

Wibben, A.T.R. (2011) 'Feminist politics in feminist security studies', *Politics & Gender*, Vol. 7, No. 4, pp. 590–595.

Contributors

Didier Bigo is Professor at the King's College London, Department of War Studies.

Marion Demossier is Professor of Modern Languages at the University of Southampton.

Didier Fassin is James D. Wolfensohn Professor at the School of Social Science, Institute for Advanced Study, Princeton University.

Gregory Feldman is Professor at the School for International Studies, Simon Fraser University.

Catarina Frois is Assistant Professor at the Department of Anthropology, Lisbon University Institute.

Ines Hasselberg is a Postdoctoral Research Fellow at the Centre for Criminology, University of Oxford.

Jutta Lauth Bacas is Professor at the Academy of Athens, Greece.

Mark Maguire is Head of the Department of Anthropology, National University of Ireland Maynooth.

Alexandra Schwell is Assistant Professor at the Department of European Ethnology at the University of Vienna.

Nils Zurawski is a Senior Researcher at the Institute for Cultural Anthropology and Applied Professor at the Institute for Criminological Social Research at the University of Hamburg.

Index